PRAISE FOR JAN STOCKLASSA

"An absolutely thrilling story."

—*Més 324* (Spain)

"Stocklassa's research evolves into a true Stieg Larsson thriller."
—*Stern* magazine (Germany)

"A hybrid between essay, investigative journalism, and espionage that moves through the path opened by the author of Millennium and approaches the definitive solution."

—*El País* (Spain)

"A book that includes the works of Larsson and Stocklassa, written as a crime novel. With conspiracies, characters, and situations that seem to come from one of Larsson's stories, but real."

—Catalunya Ràdio

"[Stocklassa] handles the legacy of Stieg Larsson, staying true to the author, and gives it a dramatic and action-packed dimension that holds all the way through . . . He comes to the end with a story of a single shot that hit Sweden right in the heart."

—*Politiken* (Denmark)

"The inspiration from Stieg Larsson is clear, [and] the book is written as if it were a novel; Stocklassa . . . succeeds in keeping the excitement up and the skepticism down—and [in] . . . tying all the threads together in this extremely complicated affair."

—*Weekendavisen* (Denmark)

THE MAN
WHO PLAYED
WITH FIRE

THE MAN WHO PLAYED WITH FIRE

Stieg Larsson's Lost Files and the Hunt for an Assassin

JAN STOCKLASSA

TRANSLATED BY TARA F. CHACE

Previously published as *Stieg Larssons arkiv: Nyckeln till Palmemordet* by Bokfabriken in Sweden in 2018. Translated from Swedish by Tara F. Chace. First published in English by Amazon Crossing in 2019.

Published by Amazon Crossing, Seattle

www.apub.com

Amazon, the Amazon logo, and Amazon Crossing are trademarks of Amazon.com, Inc., or its affiliates.

ISBN-13: 9781542092937 (hardcover)
ISBN-10: 1542092930 (hardcover)
ISBN-13: 9781542092944 (paperback)
ISBN-10: 1542092949 (paperback)

Cover design by Rex Bonomelli

Unless otherwise noted, images used by permission of Bokfabriken.

Printed in the United States of America

First edition

Never attribute to malice that which is adequately
explained by stupidity.

—Hanlon's razor

Contents

Foreword

Everything used to be so simple. Pluto was a planet. Milk was good for you. Diesel was cleaner than gasoline. If you swam right after a meal, you might get cramps and drown. The 1986 assassination of Swedish prime minister Olof Palme would never be solved. But old truths are increasingly being turned on their heads. The new truth is: the assassination of Olof Palme is going to be solved.

For me, everything began in 2008 in the most Swedish way possible—judging from the majority of Sweden's murder mysteries anyway. A woman was murdered near a lake in the region of Småland, which gave me an idea for a book about murder locations. A little over a year later, it turned out that the explanation for the death was also very Swedish. The police found new forensic evidence, and the killer turned out to be a moose. But by that point I had already given up on my original idea and was deep into the adventure that created this book.

After five years of research, I found Stieg Larsson's forgotten archives and stepped into a world of people and events that felt like they came right out of one of Stieg's books: access to emails, secret recordings, undercover operations . . . and death, a lot of cruel, sudden death. The characters were as extreme as Lisbeth Salander and Alexander Zalachenko, only real—murderers and their victims, spies who spy on other spies, murdered women and children.

Stieg Larsson's three books—known as the Millennium Trilogy or The Girl with the Dragon Tattoo series—have sold more than eighty million copies, but his greatest achievement wasn't writing thrillers. He devoted his entire adult life to fighting right-wing extremism. By the early 1990s, he was already warning about the threat posed by the newly started Sweden Democrats party, the very party that upended the status quo by garnering over 17 percent of the vote in the recent 2018 parliamentary elections, plunging parliamentary balance and the selection of a new prime minister into a period of months-long chaos.

Stieg's second-biggest project was researching the Olof Palme assassination. This is evident in his archives, where most of the material has to do with right-wing extremism, but that interest segued seamlessly into his research on the Palme assassination and led to concrete theories and tips for the police.

I have carried on the work started by Stieg, analyzing his theories and ideas, digging deeper, and contributing new pieces to the puzzle. The picture emerging explains not only a number of the strange circumstances surrounding the assassination but also accounts for the motive behind it. I believe I have a good picture of what happened during the period leading up to the murder and on the night of the shooting itself, February 28, 1986, as well as who was at the scene. I will lay out a possible solution; you can form your own opinion based on the facts and conclusions I present.

What you are holding in your hands is a work of creative nonfiction. It is written like a thriller, but it's factual. Over thirty pages of this book consist of Stieg's own writing as a journalist—letters and memos—from long before he became a world-famous author. Many of the dialogues are transcribed word for word, while others are dramatized based on documents in Stieg's archives and over a hundred interviews that I conducted with people such as Eva Gabrielsson, Stieg's long-term partner. There's more information in the afterword about background sources and materials and how I used them. If you want to delve deeper into details about the Palme assassination, I recommend the Review Commission's (Granskningskommissionen) one-thousand-page report and any book by Gunnar Wall or Lars Borgnäs—two of Sweden's foremost experts on the Palme assassination—but there are inexhaustible quantities of information to study. One warning is called for if you want to dig deeper: Be careful! The Palme assassination is a nasty virus that many people have caught.

There is some irony to the fact that a prime minister's assassination would go unsolved in Sweden in particular. In a country where everything can be measured and everything can be explained, Palme's assassination remains an open wound, where no truth seems to hold up to scrutiny. But that is going to change.

The mystery will finally be solved. According to Krister Petersson, the chief prosecutor currently leading the Palme investigation, Olof Palme was not shot by Christer Pettersson, the alcoholic who was assumed guilty by many Swedes. And I believe Krister Petersson is right. I am also convinced that Stieg Larsson's research will contribute to the solution. Hopefully this book will as well.

As you read this, the police will have gained access to my materials and will be acting on them. For the first time in many years, a new suspect has been interviewed and the police continue to follow the theory and leads that Stieg laid out thirty years ago.

Within the next year or two, I believe the new truth will be: the Palme assassination has been solved.

Editor's Note

We have made a few editorial alterations while translating this work from Swedish into English, mostly to give context to English-language readers about specifically Swedish context or cultural figures. Occasionally we've made some additional edits to remove repetitive or extraneous information. For example, in Stieg Larsson's letters to Gerry Gable at *Searchlight*, recurring lists of suspects or names of those who were eliminated from involvement have been redacted. We have, however, retained Larsson's original English as he wrote it, while correcting any grammatical or spelling errors.

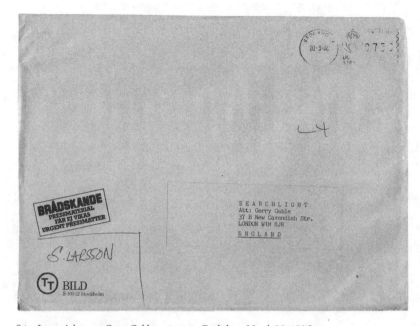

Stieg Larsson's letter to Gerry Gable, written in English on March 20, 1986.

Stockholm, Mar 20, 1986

Dear Gerry & friends,
The assassination of the Swedish Prime
Minister Olof Palme is, to be perfectly
honest, one of the most unbelievable and
amazing cases of homicide I have ever had
the unpleasant job of covering.

Amazing because of the way in which
the story develops by sudden twists and
unexpected turns, continuously resulting
in new, startling discoveries; only to

change again before the next deadline.
Unbelievable because of the sheer magnitude of the political angle, and because
for the first time in history, I believe,
a head of a government has been assassinated without even a clue of whodunnit?
Unpleasant—as murder is always an unpleasant affair—because the victim happened to
be the prime minister; a genuinely loved
and respected person in Sweden no matter
if you happened to be a Social Democrat
or (like myself) not.

As my phone went off in the very early
hours of Saturday, March 1, bringing the
message of the killing and the demand from
my editor in chief to show up at my desk
before I put the phone down, my world
has been in a slight perpetual chaos.
You might imagine what your own situation
would be if you were supposed to cover the
killing of Mrs. Thatcher and the killer
had gotten clean away.

Then the shock of it all. In those
early Saturday hours, as the word spread
through a sleeping Sweden, I met people
spontaneously coming out to the streets
with pale, grim faces. At the news agency
I saw hardened police beat reporters—men
and women who had seen it all many times
over—suddenly stop beating their type-
writers midsentence to bend over crying.

I suddenly found myself crying that morning. It happened when the desperate feeling of déjà vu hit me, making me realize that this was the second time in less than three years I had lost a prime minister, the first being Mr. Maurice Bishop of Grenada—a man I loved, respected, and trusted more than I do most. Not again.

Then, putting grief aside and Mr. Palme below earth, it has come, the moment when reporters suddenly realize what an absolutely splendid murder mystery type of schoolbook drama the entire case is. What a story.

At moments it develops with the speed of a Robert Ludlum novel. Other days it turns out to be more of an Agatha Christie puzzle, only to develop into an Ed McBain police procedural touched off by a Westlake comedy. The name of the victim, the political angle, the vanishing face of the killer, the speculations, the dead-end leads, the comings and goings of presidents and kings, the tracking of cars, the rumors and the crackpots and the knew-it-all-alongers, the phone calls, the anonymous tips, the arrests, and the feeling when you think the story is just about breaking—only to end up in nothing but confusion.

Books are gonna be written about this.

Usually a killer of heads of state is arrested and/or killed within the first seconds or minutes after the act. As murder investigations they usually boil down to open-and-shut cases. Not so in this story.

In this story we have a prime minister taking a midnight stroll in the company of his wife and with no security guard within miles. And we have a killer who simply seems to vanish into thin air.

I mean, where, actually, do you start your investigation with literally thousands of suspects and not one single clue?

Well, sorry about those introductory ramblings of mine. I didn't actually mean to write about all this.

As a matter of fact, I have meant to write you a story on the Palme assassination ever since it took place. I have begun at least eight or nine drafts and finished none. Why? Well, simply because always before I have had a chance to finish the piece, some new and startling discovery is made pushing the story in yet a new direction. So I constantly have to tear it all up and start all over.

So this letter is not an article, but an attempt to brief you on what are the facts and what is the fiction of the murder. Having lived with the assassination for 24 hours a day for the last three weeks, I have a serious problem finding the suitable distance to the subject, and since tonight is the night when all investigation seems to have come to a final big dead end, this briefing will be as much my own way of clearing my mind and summarizing the story. [. . .]

First of all; what happened and what is known about the killing?

A couple of minutes past eleven o'clock on the night of Friday, 28 Feb, Mr. Palme left the <u>Grand</u> Cinema in the company of his wife and eldest son. The visit to the cinema had been decided upon sometime during the day Friday; Mr. Palme mentioned this to a reporter as late as around 2 in the afternoon, but their plans were not common knowledge.

The PM had told the security guards of the SweSecPol, as was his custom, that he would not need them for the evening. This was common practice and everybody knew the PM would happily take strolls on his own at any time of the night, was he not about in an official capacity and was there no call for extra carefulness. At any rate, it is unclear whether the SecPol knew of his plans or not?

Outside the cinema, Mr. Palme and his wife said goodnight to their son and decided—it was a clear night of only ordinary Swedish cold—to walk their way home.

The son happened to look after them a
minute after they had left and noticed
a man following the couple; he later gave
a description of the man corresponding to
the description of the clothes the killer
was wearing, but could see no details of
his face.

A second witness met the PM two minutes later and stopped to watch him pass.
Looking back he noticed the man following and also said his impression was that
in front of the PM another two men were
walking. His impression was that they
all made a group and concluded that the
three unknown persons must be part of Mr.
Palme's security.

The PM and his wife walked down
Sveavägen, crossed the street to do
some window shopping, and continued. At
the corner of Sveavägen and Tunnelgatan
[Tunnel Street] the killer closed in on
the PM and put one 34 mm Magnum bullet in
his back.

According to the police theory, the
killing had all the hallmarks of a professional killing. Journalists–with a bit of
hesitation—tend to agree with this idea.

Item: The killer used only one single
shot, but the weapon was one of the most
powerful handguns in the world; anybody
who has any knowledge about the weapon
knows what a devastating effect the single

bullet would cause. As it turned out, the bullet entered in the center of the prime minister's back, snapped the spinal column, crushed the lungs and ripped the gullet and the windpipe and exited leaving a hole you could throw your hat into. Death was instantaneous or within seconds. The bullet, although it was not meant to disintegrate, was rolling, had a jacket meant to penetrate an eventual bulletproof vest.

The killer fired a second shot aimed at Lisbeth, the wife of Mr. Palme, but apparently not meant to kill. It would have penetrated her shoulder had she not violently twisted away. As it happened the bullet entered her coat at one shoulder and exited at the other, leaving only burns. (And from this fact speculations could be built about the professionalism of the killer, where one school suggests that the bullet was meant to kill but that the shooter was an amateur getting nervous, while another suggests this is proof of it being handled very professionally and that the second bullet was only meant to disable Mrs. Palme as to discourage pursuit.)

Item: Following the murder, the killer made his escape along what appears to have been a QUOTE well-planned route of escape UNQUOTE; up the stairs at the end

of Tunnel Street [Tunnelgatan] which dis-
abled any pursuit by car.

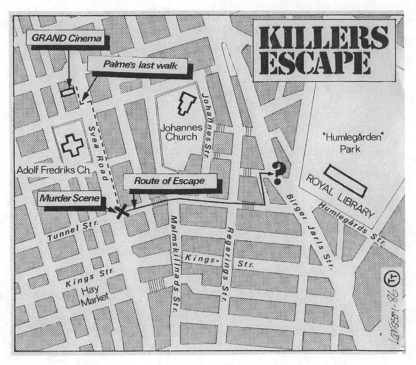

Map of killer's escape route drawn by Stieg Larsson, March 2, 1986. (TT / Expo's archive)

Up to this moment, what I have described
are established facts and in-line with
official police statements.

This is where we run into trouble.

Several witnesses have given vague
descriptions of the killer, statements
that are often conflicting. What is considered to be the most frequent description, therefore presumably the most
accurate, says:

A white male person aged 30-40 years of middle height and broad shoulders. He was dressed in a gray Andy Capp style of headpiece with flaps you can pull down over the ears, a dark sports coat covering the hips and dark trousers. Several witnesses say he was carrying a small bag with a wrist loop; the style you use for money and passports, etc.

The following is established through testimonies of several witnesses:

1) A 25-year-old man, Lars, happened to meet the killer at the end of The Tunnel Street, without being seen by the killer since they passed each other on different sides of a construction hut. Lars hesitated for some precious seconds—not more than a minute—and then decided to take up pursuit by foot. At that stage he did not know it was the PM who was the victim. Following the same route as the killer, Lars quickly ran up the steps (86 of them), but at the top the killer was nowhere to be seen. Acting on instinct, Lars continued straight on along David Bagares Gata where after one block he met . . .

2) A couple strolling towards him. Asking them if they had seen a man running along the street, they both agreed that they indeed had met him only 30 seconds earlier,

and that he passed them continuing down the
street. Lars was mystified, he later said,
that he was unable to get a second sighting
on the killer, believing the man would not
have so much of a lead.

3) A fourth witness—unidentified but known
as "Sarah"—stepped forward the next morning offering new evidence. "Sarah" is a
22-year-old artist specializing in por-
traits, and according to her story he had
passed the <u>Smala Gränd</u> [Thin Alley]—a shot
100 m off road to David Bagares—at the
approximate time of the killing. Midway
along the alley, she met a man corresponding to the general description of the
killer; the man seemed in a hurry but hesitated for a second when meeting her. When
Sarah got home, later on that night, she
put on the radio and caught the news of the
murder. She immediately made the connection to the man she had met and sat down to
do his face on a piece of paper. This is
the same drawing which formed the basis of
the police computer graph of the suspected
killer.

These four witnesses—selected among
the more than 10,000 leads and testimonies, are considered to be reliable people
giving hard-core evidence.

4) A fifth witness—but generally not so
reliable—is a taxi driver who was waiting
in his cab at the Snickarbacken [Carpenters
Hill] when he saw a man run past his car
and hurriedly enter a parked green or dark-
blue Passat, which apparently was waiting
for him. The car took off in a hurry.

The Carpenters Hill is located immediately beyond Thin Alley, and there is
a possibility that the taxi driver's
evidence could have something to do with
the killer's escape, but there are question marks. The cabbie pinpoints the
time of the incident to some 10-15 minutes after the shooting, but it only
takes 3-4 minutes to run the same way.

Also, the cabbie gives the wrong
approach to the Carpenters Hill; not by
the Thin Alley, but by another street.

Nevertheless, the chain of evidence suggests that the killer did pass
the spot of the taxi and police suggest he might have been dozing and made
a mistake in timing. (At any rate, the
cabbie's story gave birth to a nationwide search for a green or dark-blue
Passat, particularly so since he was
able to give some—but not all—of the car
number.)

The police took this chain of evidence to form the theory that the murder
was a well-planned execution, carried

out by a group of people. They have
given no suggestion officially about
what kind of group.

   First question of critique:
   - What would have happened if the
PM hadn't walked home, but instead followed his son down to the subway and
thereby never passed the "perfect" spot
of assassination?
   If this was a well-planned killing,
it would call for either the killer to
postpone the shooting, or for at least a
second getaway car and/or backup team.

   Again witnesses have come forward with
stories that seem to fit into the latter
suggestion. (Mind you, police as well as
reporters have made some very tough questioning of these people, and a few of them
look reliable.)

1) A man passing the Tunnel Street at the
time of the murder, but in the opposite
direction at the other side of Sveavägen,
encountered two middle-age male persons
running away from the scene of the murder.

2) Two second witnesses have confirmed the
story when spotting the men turning around
the corner at Queens Road [Drottninggatan];
splitting up.

3) A fourth witness reports she saw a man running along Queens Road nearby one or two minutes later. The man suddenly stopped, waved for a car which drove up and picked him up; "leaving in a hurry."

At this point, investigation comes to a standstill. Yes, there is uncountable suggestions and reports, but nothing that can immediately be connected to have any-thing to do with the murder.

Dead end. Period.

Most of the above facts were estab-lished over the period of the first one or two days (even first minutes) fol-lowing the murder. After that we have the period of the cranks, the compulsive I-did-it-type to confess, the less or not at all reliable witnesses, and—of course—all those anonymous calls.

In terrorist kills—at least by the "left"—the organizations responsible usually take the credit for the various actions in a convincing manner; usually within the first hour following the kill. In this case no such credit is taken.

Responsibility has been claimed by "Commando" Christian Klar, the Holger Meins Group, the Ustatja, and various right wing and/or neo-Nazi groups. None credible.

Following the assassination, Sweden was under a state of siege for several days; airports were sealed off, border control tight, ferries and harbors scrutinized. (Of course, this means nothing; a planned kill would call for a planned escape.)

Three days after the murder, a police inspector was picked up and heavily questioned for suspected involvement; a right-wing nut known to pack a gun and with a vague alibi. But after two days he was released and the police declared he had nothing to do with the murder.

Then a rough ten days after the assassination, one man was arrested and officially charged with "participation in the murder."

This is the dude identified as Mr. Victor Gunnarsson, age 32, who turned out to be a member of the European Labor Committees.

For almost 24 hours, the story looked really promising, particularly so since the police issued statements to the effect that they indeed had caught the killer. (They changed the charge from "participation" to "killer.") Victor had a lot against him:

- An obvious far-right crackpot, he has a record of obsession with the PM, several times suggesting "he ought to be shot," and known to tag along to wherever Palme went, to public meetings and rallies.

- He was in the general area of the murder at the right time. Sources indicate he was at the cinema together with the PM.

- He could give no account for his movements and obviously lied to the police on several crucial points.

- He owned a gray headpiece and a coat similar to the killer.

- An employee of several private guard firms, he has received arms training and knows how to handle a pistol.

- One witness identified him as trying to stop a car asking for a lift immediately following the murder on a street connected to the steps of the Tunnel Street.

- He was seen entering a cinema roughly 10 or 12 minutes after the shooting and half hour after the movie had actually begun.

- He is known to be associated with a yet unidentified far-right, anti-Semite religious group in California, where he has lived for some time.

For 24 hours the entire nation's interest was focused on the ELC (I wrote several pieces on them) and it finally seemed we had a case.

Then, only hours before he would go to a preliminary court, Gunnarsson was released. Why; the witness suggesting he had tried to hitch a ride with a car following the murder could no longer with one hundred percent accuracy identify Gunnarsson.

Which brings us up to date; today the police cancelled their daily press conference due to the fact that they had nothing new to report. Dead end.

Speculations: It is quite possible that Gunnarsson will be picked up again; the DA's office says they have no case, but that he is still a person of "considerable interest."

Well, that is about all there is to tell; well, I could go on with various speculations for another 200 pages—books are gonna be written about this—(hey, maybe I should write a book on this) but there is nothing of substance.

We have a dead prime minister and a killer who vanished.

Speculations would include the possibility that South African interest was behind the murder; The Palme Commission—of which Palme himself was a crucial

figure—had begun a campaign against arms
dealers selling to RSA.

Speculations also include the Kurdish
PKK which is known to have carried out at
least three political murders in Sweden
over the past two years. So far the dead
ones have been "traitors" within their
own group, but a popular (and pretty racist) suggestion is they were responsible.
Why; their office in Stockholm is located
at the David Bakers Street [David Bagares
Gata] where the killer "disappeared."
(The report avoids asking the question if
a killer would be dumb enough to run and
hide at his political group's headquarters two minutes away from the scene of
the murder.)

At any rate; this is the background.
If the story breaks, I'll phone you a
report of it if you want it, and you can
use information from this as background.
[. . .]

Ok; take care.
        Stieg

Prologue

The windshield wipers struggled against the heavy snow. I hadn't been parked for more than fifteen minutes, but the storm had already covered my dark-red Volvo with a smooth blanket of white flakes. Sound from outside was muffled and the sight of the swirling snow made it hard to get my bearings, even though I knew I was in the parking lot in front of the self-storage facility's metal building.

The faint hum of a motor approaching made me pull my hand across the driver's side window to wipe away the condensation, creating a little trickle that ran down my wrist inside my jacket sleeve. A silver station wagon pulled to a stop on my left. Before I had a chance to turn off my engine, the other car's door opened. The man's face was swathed in a long scarf and his parka hood was up. He gestured over the roof of the car to indicate that we should head to the front door. By the time I joined him there, he had already started entering the code. Apparently it didn't work, because he soon pulled out his cell phone and started dialing. The moments we stood there were tedious; the files I was after had been stored away for ten years, and I couldn't help but think they didn't seem to want to relinquish their quiet existence that easily. Finally a sliding door slipped open and, after walking through an air lock meant to keep the worst of the Swedish winter weather out, we entered a lobby that led to a warm, dry corridor with bright fluorescent lighting and an endless line of metal roll-up doors. Compared with the freezing cold outside, it felt almost cozy.

After I removed my hat, scarf, and hood, I saw that it really was Daniel Poohl from *Expo* magazine who had let me in. We shook hands and walked down the long corridor, took the stairs up one flight, and continued down an identical corridor before Daniel stopped in front of one of the roll-up doors. Nothing aside from a small metal plate with an anonymous number embossed on it showed that we had arrived. Nothing gave away the fact that this specific unit might contain a treasure, a treasure I hoped would point the way to something priceless.

The metal door rolled up with a rattle, and I saw that the small space was filled to the brim. Shelves of moving boxes extended from floor to ceiling. Two narrow aisles were filled in with cardboard boxes, stacked one on top of another, right up to the door. I looked at the end of one of the boxes and the text confirmed that I had found what I had been seeking for so long. In thick felt-tip pen, it said: "Stieg Files."

Together we lifted that box down and set it on the floor. Daniel moved the cardboard lid out of the way, and I grabbed a handful of old-fashioned brown hanging file folders. The top edge of each folder was labeled in fully legible but minuscule handwriting. The ones I held in my hand said "WACL," "the thirty-three-year-old," "Resistance International," "South Africa Clues," and "Christer Pettersson." My fingers began tingling, as if the folders were electrified.

The labels clearly indicated that the documents I was holding related to the murder of Swedish prime minister Olof Palme, the decades-old case that had never been solved and had cast a long shadow across the Swedish psyche for the latter part of the twentieth century and beyond. It had marked the loss of the country's innocence and was sometimes referred to as the European equivalent of the John F. Kennedy assassination, complete with an infinite number of conspiracy theories and shadowy suspects.

There was so much more material in the storage area than I could have hoped for, and I wondered how I would possibly be able to get through it all. Daniel brought me back to reality. Even though he was only thirty-one, he was both the editor in chief and CEO of *Expo* magazine and had dedicated his life to fighting racism and intolerance. He was responsible for these files, and he made it clear that the documents were not to leave the premises without his permission and that I was not allowed to tell anyone where the storage facility was located.

I was going to have to read them on-site, although at the moment there was nowhere in the world I would rather have been than in this storage room in this windowless sheet-metal building, sitting on a moving box with a snowstorm raging outside. But my time was limited; I wouldn't have enough to look at more than a fraction of the material, let alone draw any conclusions about Stieg's thoughts.

The road that led me to this point was long and winding. I had fled from my own private failings and midlife crisis to devote all my free time to the unsolved murder of Olof Palme. From there, I found my way to the forgotten files of one of the world's most legendary writers. This only resulted in more strings to pull and more mysteries to dig into. Stieg seemed to have been pursuing a lead involving the South African security services aided by Swedish right-wing extremists. Personally, I thought the murder had been carried out by an amateur. Our two theories didn't match up.

At the same time, I immediately realized that I could not just walk away from this story. The information in these files was far too interesting not to follow up on. I had no idea at that moment where these towering stacks of files might lead me, that my investigation would soon expose me and many others to great danger as we met with extremists, spies, scapegoats, and murderers.

Part 1

STIEG

The Day of the Assassination

On the day the prime minister of Sweden would die, Stieg arrived late to work, as usual, with a cigarette in his hand. He decided to take the stairs to save at least half a minute over using the new elevator, which was inexplicably slow. The stairs didn't bother him, even if he had to climb all the way to the top floor. The lit cigarette in his right hand somewhat limited his ability to take in oxygen, but he was only thirty-one and still full of unswerving energy. He jogged up, fueled by a mix of caffeine and nicotine, and in his left hand he carried his worn briefcase, empty apart from a couple of pieces of paper.

Just over a year earlier, TT, Sweden's leading news agency, had moved into the newly renovated offices in what used to be Saint Erik's Brewery on Kungsholmstorg. The scale of the staff and equipment was on par with Sveriges Radio, Sweden's national public radio, or *Dagens Nyheter*, the country's biggest morning newspaper. The editorial staff took up the whole sixth floor and Stieg was forced to traverse the entire open office landscape just to get to his desk. The vaguely factory-like feeling was a good match for Stieg's disposition. Just inside the entrance there was a long line of Toshiba fax machines. Everyone knew they had far more than they needed, but in the yuppie 1980s, it was important, particularly for news agencies, to demonstrate that you were willing to go that extra mile to communicate. To the left sat the editorial team, TT's highest-ranking employees, including a few middle managers. Stieg tried to make himself invisible, but his boss, Kenneth Ahlborn, yelled "good morning" a little too loudly for Stieg to be able to get away with not responding.

"You'll get it today," Stieg said. "I promise!"

Stieg had missed his deadline three times already and another boss would have used a sterner tone, but there was a limit to even Kenneth's light touch and Stieg knew he was going to have to hand his piece in today.

Up the stairs from the large editorial department, he came to one of Sweden's largest newspaper archives, with long rows of shelves with wheels on the sides to roll along a rail mounted to the floor, another impressive installation. Stieg walked along the short ends of the archive shelves, turned in behind the last one, and stepped through the doorway into his office. The small room, with an interior window looking out at the archival shelves but no exterior windows, could be described as functional at best. He shared the office with Ulla, the lead archivist, and a few temp workers in need of desk space. Despite the out-of-the-way location, he didn't feel neglected—quite the contrary actually. Everyone he wanted to deal with knew where he sat, and somehow the well-worn armchair he kept for visitors saw more traffic than the flashy sofa out in the actual editorial department one flight down.

Today was special. It was the last Friday of the month and everyone had been summoned for the monthly meeting that was the new CEO's idea—to "get more feedback" from the organization, as he put it. As a matter of fact, the information flow basically went one way only, down, but that suited Stieg just fine. His immediate supervisor's position in the hierarchy was still strong, and he was the one who had placed Stieg so far from the center of the action, where he was often able to work in peace on the stories he was passionate about.

Aside from his regular work as an illustrator, Stieg was sometimes allowed to write longer stories that often pertained to some issue he was highly engaged in, and if there were any hours left over beyond that, he spent them doing what was really important: mapping out Swedish right-wing extremism and its ties abroad. He could hardly remember when it began, but fighting intolerance and injustice had been part of his life even in his early teen years. Growing up with a maternal grandfather who hated anything having to do with Nazism or right-wing extremism was a big part of his motivation, but Stieg was even more committed to the issue than his grandfather had been. He had dedicated his life to it.

Right now, though, he was late to the meeting where his only purpose was to show his face to prove that he shared the company vision so that he could then return to his own work in peace and quiet. It was ten o'clock, which was early for him, so when he walked into the meeting room, his nearest coworkers were surprised to see him. He pulled the door shut behind him and sat down in his chair, winded, just as the CEO switched on his beaming smile and welcomed everyone.

The meeting contained no surprises. The leadership strongly believed in the motto "Repetition is the mother of skill," and Stieg was quite sure that these visuals of the business plan for 1986 had been shown at least three times before, possibly in a slightly different order. Plus, the noise from the fan in the overhead projector was making him very sleepy.

The only surprising thing was that one of the editors got up at the end of the meeting and reminded everyone that the editorial team was invited to the restaurant Tennstopet that night. Unstated but understood was the fact that only colleagues with the job title of reporter, journalist, or editor need bother showing up. Someday, Stieg would become a crime reporter, but before that goal came true, he was excluded from this group.

For Stieg, this Friday was a little unusual since he and Eva had decided that they would eat dinner and spend the evening together. Not that they were going to eat out, just make dinner at home or order pizza, but that still meant that he would need to keep track of the time to make sure he left work by seven or, well, eight at the latest. The city hall subway station was only a block away, and he would be home in suburban Rinkeby in less than half an hour. Otherwise there was nothing much on the docket for the day. He would complete his illustration showing how the entire Swedish economy was controlled by the Wallenberg family, one of the most powerful constellations of business owners in the world's financial markets. True, the relatively recent financial crises of the 1970s had definitely shaken the empire to its core, but their power still permeated Swedish society, extending into anonymous foundations, corporations, and associations, which on paper had no apparent ties to the family, but in which all the key players were close to the Wallenbergs.

After thinking about it for a long time, Stieg created a map with downtown Stockholm as the background. Over that map he had super-imposed a networking diagram that highlighted ties and links back and forth in a way that would have made a conspiracy theorist dizzy if Stieg hadn't made the whole thing easy to read by using dashed lines and gray scale. Four-color printing was out of the question. It had been technically possible for a few years, but only a couple of the evening newspapers were using it, and they weren't among TT's largest clients.

Stieg lit yet another cigarette and set down his coffee cup to the side of the drawing paper and the weights that held it in place. When the ash on his cigarette grew too long, it fell onto the paper and he expertly blew it away, brushed it off into his hand, and put it into one of the empty coffee cups on his desk. Most of his coworkers took an early lunch, but Stieg would work until his mind grew sluggish and he was forced to raise his blood sugar. He had half a cheese-and-cucumber sandwich from the cafeteria, wrapped in plastic, for when he got hungry.

When Stieg next looked at the time, it was already five thirty. Suddenly he really needed to hurry to get the illustration finished. Asking for still more time didn't feel like an option, because then there was an increased risk that he would have to push back his next feature article, which was his chance to discuss important issues in a way that would reach a wide audience.

Stieg tested adding the old Marcus Wallenberg maxim "*Esse non videri*" over part of the map, "to be, rather than to seem." That definitely fit with the image's message of hidden connections, but without including the translation, no one would understand it. And if he added more text, it would be a big mess. He decided he wouldn't leave his seat until he was done. Surely two hours, or three at most, would be enough. Then he could just make it home before Eva gave up hope of ever trying to eat dinner together.

Presumably something magical about the plastic overlay with the lines and symbols made the time fly by. Suddenly it was a little after eight, and he realized that immediate action was required. He picked up the handset of his slightly scratched Ericsson Dialog phone, and with the familiar clicking sound of the rotary dial as backdrop, he wondered how to explain to Eva that he wasn't going to be home until midnight and would thus once again miss their evening together.

The call wasn't actually that hard, because Eva always accepted his explanations, but he felt guilty, which complicated things. It took him ten minutes after he hung up to get back into the flow again, but now at least he would finish his illustration over the course of the evening.

When he finally reached for the on-off switch on the heavy cast-iron base of his desk lamp and turned off his light, it was 11:20 p.m., right about the time that shots were fired on Sveavägen, killing Sweden's prime minister. Stieg, though, was blissfully unaware, wondering instead if he would be able to make the next subway train to Rinkeby.

The Opposition

Few questioned that Olof Palme was one of Sweden's most influential politicians ever, but his ascent had been fraught with many battles, resulting in countless enemies and ever-mounting opposition. In Swedish, the term "Palmehatare" (Palme hater) was used to describe anyone who objected to his leadership—and many did, vehemently.

Palme took over the post of prime minister and party leader in 1969 from Tage Erlander, who resigned after holding the position of prime minister for twenty-three years—a record at that time for the elected head of state in a Western democracy. In Erlander's final election, the Social Democratic Party received more than 50 percent of the vote. There was no way Palme could match his predecessor's enormous popularity. With his obvious upper-class background, Palme was also eyed with suspicion by blue-collar and lower-ranking white-collar workers within his own party. In 1976, Palme lost the first election for the Social Democrats in four decades.

That loss, however, allowed him to dedicate more time to what he cared most about: foreign policy. Olof Palme was a friend to developing nations, and he fought for the rights of the weak and marginalized. He liked to tell the story of his first political act, when he and some friends gave blood to collect money for the struggle against apartheid in South Africa.

But Palme's commitment to those foreign politics often occurred at the expense of the existing superpowers. He annoyed the Soviet Union in April 1975, when he called the regime ruling their satellite state of Czechoslovakia "the beasts of the dictatorship," and again when he criticized the Soviet invasion of Afghanistan in December 1979.

On the other side of the Cold War, he also provoked the United States, which broke off diplomatic ties with Sweden twice due to Palme's actions. The first time was after he marched in a torchlight procession side by side with North Vietnam's ambassador to Moscow in February 1968. The second time was after he criticized the bombing of Hanoi just before Christmas 1972, comparing the United States' actions to the worst massacres of the twentieth century.

Palme's, and therefore Sweden's, political philosophy was referred to as the "third way," a path that negotiated a space between the Capitalist West and the Communist East. Palme spearheaded and became chairperson of what is often called the Palme Commission, where, along with other leading global politicians, he tried to come up with a blueprint for disarmament that would make the world safer. The United States was only moderately interested in this alternative, so the plan died, but because the Soviet Union had shown interest, distrust of Palme increased in Sweden and abroad as he became known as the Russians' tool.

Between 1980 and 1982, Palme was the UN's peace envoy for the Iran-Iraq War. He failed at this impossible task, and when people found out that he had been actively involved in helping Swedish arms manufacturers, primarily Bofors, secure export deals to India, many people considered him hypocritical. One minute he was promoting disarmament and peace, the next he was supporting Swedish arms exports to save jobs.

In Sweden, his critics thought the country didn't have the time or resources to act as the conscience of the world and felt instead that the prime minister should focus on domestic politics, where Palme's standing had also weakened. Through his rhetorical abilities and his deft power plays, he had acquired political enemies on both the left and the right.

But it wasn't primarily his politics that his opponents disliked. Olof Palme's upper-class background left many of his Social Democrat friends suspicious, while the right wing thought he had betrayed his class. There was also something about his personality that irritated people. In debates, Palme was impatient and came off as arrogant whenever he crushed his less adept opponents. With an estimated IQ of 156, which is lower than Swedish movie actor Dolph Lundgren's reported IQ of 160, but higher than any other Swedish politician's, Palme belonged to the fraction of the population who could be called geniuses. And Palme made it very clear that he was aware that he was smarter than his opponents.

He had long been a favorite in cultural circles and was often invited to premieres as a VIP guest, but after world-renowned director Ingmar Bergman was accused of tax evasion in 1976 and arrested in a degrading manner while rehearsing at the Royal Dramatic Theater, Palme's popularity sank. Although the charges against Bergman were ultimately dropped, the Swedish public felt the government had unfairly targeted Bergman due to his fame. Palme received fewer invitations after that.

Palme also had powerful enemies in the media. Aside from the fact that a majority of Swedish newspapers were independent, non-Socialist leaning, he had managed to make Sweden's most influential journalist his enemy. When Jan Guillou, a reporter for the socialist magazine *Folket i Bild Kulturfront*, revealed that the Social Democratic Party, led by Palme, had used the Information Bureau (IB), a military intelligence service, for its own private purposes and, among other things, recorded suspected Communist sympathizers, it was reminiscent of the Watergate scandal. But Olof Palme played his cards better than President Nixon. The result of the revelation over the IB affair was that Olof Palme kept his position, and Guillou and his journalist colleague Peter Bratt were each sentenced to a year in prison for espionage.

Jan Guillou was not an easy enemy to have, and a few years later he went after Olof Palme in conjunction with the Geijer affair, in which Swedish politicians, led by Justice Minister Lennart Geijer, were revealed to have frequented prostitutes. Palme escaped criticism by a hair's breadth because his henchmen, Police Commissioner Hans Holmér and Geijer's press secretary, Ebbe Carlsson, helped write official denials that were based on outright lies.

Guillou's last attempt to attack Palme was called the Harvard case, a case that remained unresolved but was a direct attack on Palme's personal morals. During a live radio interview, Guillou asked Palme if he should have paid tax on the scholarship his son Joakim received from Harvard University in gratitude for the guest lecture Olof Palme had given at Harvard. Olof, who was hardly ever at a loss for words, hesitated a little too long for his denial to come off as honest. Little by little, a media uproar began to brew.

Once the passionate opposition to Palme was well established in various segments of society, there was no stopping it. Then the campaigns began. Newspapers published caricatures of Palme with a hooked nose, bad teeth, and dark rings under his eyes. That said, there were clearly others who didn't think there was anything wrong with his appearance. As women such as actress Shirley MacLaine, among others, came forward and claimed to have had affairs with Olof Palme, rumors of his extramarital infidelities spread, though they were likely exaggerated.

Full-page ads were published in many of Sweden's daily papers directly targeting Olof Palme and his policies. The term "Palmeism" began to be used in a pejorative sense, without it really being clear what the invented ideology supposedly involved. The ads were paid for by actress Gio Petré and her companion, a doctor named Alf Enerström, but it was clear that far more powerful financial forces were behind the publication, people who could pay the millions of kronor that publishing these ads would cost. At the same time, the magazine *Contra*, with a markedly right-leaning profile, was also selling dartboards with a disparaging caricature of Olof Palme's face as the target.

A general election was held in September 1985, which resulted in yet another Social Democratic government coming to power. At one of the Moderate Party's campaign events, a doll depicting Olof Palme was tossed around in the audience for public scorn and derision.

On November 3, 1985, *Svenska Dagbladet* published an op-ed piece by naval commander Hans von Hofsten in which he expressed his and a number of his colleagues' distrust of Prime Minister Palme's policies toward the Soviet Union.

Olof Palme was under pressure. There were rumors that he would step down and retreat to a position at the UN. He was tired, and he was entitled to be. Sweden's most brilliant and influential politician ever was facing opposition from all sides. The path forward was not clear in any direction. Then February 28, 1986, arrived.

The Murder Map

"Palme assassinated."

The words shook Stieg every bit as much as Eva had when waking him up. She had gotten up before him, turned on the radio, and wondered why all three stations were playing funereal music. Then suddenly the music was interrupted by a breaking news bulletin.

Stieg and Eva didn't eat breakfast; they just had a cup of coffee together in their spartan kitchen. Kenneth from TT called and Stieg asked if they had discovered anything more than what was being put out in the news, but the only response he got was that he needed to come in to work immediately. Eva decided to go into the city with him because she felt restless and couldn't imagine staying home by herself.

Rinkeby station was as deserted as it usually was on a Saturday. They paced back and forth along the subway platform for what felt like forever as they waited for the train, but a little less than half an hour later, they had reached T-Centralen, the main hub of Stockholm's subway system. Stieg didn't get off at city hall like he usually did. He wanted to spend a few more minutes with Eva before all hell broke loose at work. They took the Vasagatan exit and turned right onto

Tunnelgatan. After walking five minutes along the narrow street, they spotted a police car near a group of people standing on the corner by the Skandia building. That's when it really hit them: their prime minister had been assassinated on the street right in the middle of Stockholm.

When they reached the spot where the assassination had taken place, they were struck by the silence. A hundred people were gathered around the little blocked-off area. No one was gesturing or moving around much. No one spoke audibly. Those who were crying did so silently. It was a Swedish way of showing grief. People came—some with a rose in their hands—and people went, but it all happened in silence.

Eva and Stieg made their way forward to the plastic police tape that marked the barrier and realized how close they were able to get to the actual spot where Palme had died. His blood had flowed over the icy concrete pavers and frozen into dark-red ice. It was a bigger pool than you would expect the blood from a human being to make. Flowers lay around the edge of the cordoned-off area, mostly roses, and some people had thrown theirs a little farther into the off-limits area. The weather made it too cold to stand still, but Eva and Stieg stayed for a good while. The silence was only broken by the sporadic calls coming over the police car's radio.

From where they stood, they could see down Sveavägen in both directions. About fifty yards down Tunnelgatan, there were a couple of construction trailers that partially blocked their view in that direction. Brunkeberg Ridge (Brunkebergsåsen) towered behind the trailers.

It was only nine and it was going to be a long day in Sweden. Many more people would come to the scene of the assassination and many would place roses there. Maybe, if there was any truth to the old saying that a criminal always returns to the scene of the crime, the murderer would come back as well.

***

On his way up in the elevator to TT, Stieg tried to reset himself mentally from brooding and mournful to energetic. He was counting on it not mattering that he hadn't come straight to work, since it would take a few hours before the editorial staff would be able to form a clear enough picture of the murder to order one or more illustrations from him. It would be a very long day, and he would probably be forced to stay until the wee hours if he was going to manage to finish something.

The mood at the scene of the murder had been reverent and quiet. The intensity that hit Stieg when he stepped into the editorial offices was an extreme contrast. It looked like the entire staff had been called in. Everyone was utterly focused on TT taking the lead on the reporting about the murder, and they were all busy gathering what little information was available. In a couple of hours, some of them would have already begun writing, but the information gathering would go on for a long time to come, particularly if the police didn't apprehend any suspects. And with every passing hour, the odds of a quick solution to the case decreased. Every police employee knew this, as did every journalist.

After only a few hours, Stieg was given an assignment that would take him all day and maybe into the night to complete, depending on what facts emerged. He was going to make a map of the area around the Grand Cinema and the murder site, which he would fill in later in the day with what was known so far. The fact that he and Eva had just been to the scene of the murder helped, but it wasn't obvious what information should be included in the map. The risk was that they would end up needing to put a lot of text around the scene of the murder and the movie theater, but none around the edges. An English version would also be important, and the translated text would take up more space than the Swedish. They were already under a massive amount of pressure from the foreign press, as TT was one of their main sources in Sweden.

On a map of Stockholm, Stieg traced the places he already knew the Palme couple must have walked past. Before he really got down to drawing, he cleared the old coffee cups and unnecessary stacks of papers from his desk and fetched himself a fresh cup of coffee to replace the one that had already grown cold. He spread out a copy of the map section in the proper scale and then laid a sheet of transparent A3-size paper on top. Using paperweights, a T-square, a razor blade, sheets of self-adhering raster pattern, and all the state-of-the-art tools of the trade, he began mocking up a map of the murder scene by hand.

Information poured in throughout the day, and he and his coworkers persistently sorted through messages from the police, the media, and the public. When Stieg was finally done with both a Swedish and an English version of the map, it was already a couple of hours into March 2.

Sherlock Holmér

Stockholm, March 1, 1986

The police investigation into the assassination of Olof Palme could hardly have gotten off to a worse start. The killer got away without much difficulty, even though there were several police patrols in the area and the first police car reached the scene within a couple of minutes of the murder (though the actual time the police arrived became a topic of discussion that created conspiracy theories for years to come). The area cordoned off at the scene was far too small, so the bullets that had landed outside the police tape were found by members of the public, and not until the day after the murder. Some witnesses' names were not recorded and other witnesses were not contacted for days. Vital information and other evidence was lost forever.

As news of the murder started to get out, leaders at the emergency operations center were paralyzed, and a nationwide bulletin, which stated that there were two perpetrators, wasn't sent out until 2:05 a.m., two and a half hours after the murder.

The night passed in chaos, demonstrating just how necessary it would be to put a strong man in charge of the investigation. There were three choices. The first option was Sven-Åke Hjämroth, head of the

Swedish Security Service (Säpo), which investigated acts of terrorism and other crimes tied to foreign powers. He had been appointed after a turbulent period within the organization in order to calm the troubled waters. His not-so-flattering nickname (the Mailman) resulted from beginning his career in the postal service.

The second option was the hard-nosed Tommy Lindström, head of the National Criminal Investigation Department (Rikskriminalpolisen). This department was in charge of investigating special incidents, and the murder of the prime minister definitely qualified as such. The National Murder Commission was also part of this group, and was where Sweden's leading experts in complicated murder investigations worked. Lindström had quickly become a media darling, earning the nicknames Tommy Turbo (after he was pulled over by the police for driving his Saab 108 miles per hour) and Super Cop (possibly because of his tendency to personally assist in investigations, although his academic background was in law rather than police work).

The third option was Hans Holmér, the Stockholm County police commissioner. The local police, in this case the Stockholm police, were responsible for routine crimes such as, for example, a murder on the street. Holmér also had an academic background in law rather than police work and lacked experience leading a large-scale, violent-crime investigation.

Säpo had abjectly failed in their responsibility to protect the prime minister in the first place. If they were put in charge of the investigation, they would be examining their own failure, which would be closely scrutinized by the media. That left the National Criminal Investigation Department and the Stockholm police as the only viable choices.

Tommy Lindström was not afraid to get his hands dirty and loved being in the spotlight, but when it came to the murder of the prime minister, he chose a different tactic, for some reason. After he was informed of the murder early in the morning, he chose to go back to bed, then stay home to celebrate his birthday. He ate cake, looked for his new floorball stick, the birthday present his sons had hidden some-where in the house, and then took it easy for a while longer. At around ten thirty in the morning, he went into town to his office, but by then, responsibility for the investigation had already been assigned elsewhere.

When Hans Holmér heard the news of the assassination at 7:35 a.m., he was—by his own admission—at the Scandic hotel in Borlänge, 130 miles northwest of Stockholm, with his girlfriend Åsa. He had been planning to ski his eighteenth consecutive annual Vasaloppet cross-country race the next day, but instead he got into his car and returned to Stockholm immediately. By the time he arrived, he had been put in charge of the murder investigation. No one really knew how that deci-sion was reached, but clearly it wouldn't have been possible without support from the country's highest-ranking politicians.

Hans Holmér fulfilled many of the requirements listed for the per-son who would be in charge of the most important murder investigation in Swedish history. He was intrepid and decisive, and he had experience with police work, both as a former chief of Säpo and as the Stockholm County police commissioner. He had extensive political connections, especially within the ruling Social Democratic Party, and he had in the past helped Olof Palme out of his most difficult pinches. The IB affair and the Geijer affair were examples of stories that could easily have resulted in the prime minister having had to step down. Those were cases where Hans Holmér's loyalty and toughness were put to the test. Each time, along with Ebbe Carlsson, he rose to the occasion, show-ing Palme that he could weather difficult crises. Now Holmér's boss of many years had been murdered, and it would be up to him to make sure that the person or persons responsible were held accountable.

***

At 10:50 a.m. on Saturday, March 1, Hans Holmér stepped into police headquarters to officially take over the Palme investigation. He had already accepted the offer of an observer from the Ministry of Justice, so Undersecretary Harald Fälth had sent over a deputy director general to participate in the investigation. The Swedish constitution precluded a government representative from participating, but Holmér's rationale for accepting this offer was that extraordinary circumstances required extraordinary measures.

The press and the public were waiting for information, and Holmér gave the first in a long succession of press conferences. He had time to receive only a short briefing from his colleagues, but he quickly decided that one of the two people named in the nationwide bulletin should be removed, so that the new text contained only one perpetrator. How he reached that decision was something Holmér kept to himself.

It was noon by the time Hans Holmér walked into the press room at police headquarters and began his first press conference in the self-confident manner that by year's end would earn him the title of Swede of the Year.

***

The pressure was enormous. Holmér had accepted responsibility for a murder investigation that trained the whole world's eyes on him, and many people expected him to appoint one of his most qualified homicide detectives to lead the investigation. But Holmér surprised everyone by taking on the role himself. He had no relevant experience with cases of this magnitude, but his investigative team, which after only a couple of days had expanded to include more than two hundred staff members, did.

In the first days of the investigation, there was a lot of uncertainty. The assassination of Olof Palme could have been part of a bigger sequence of events. Maybe it was even the beginning of a coup d'état. The first thing Holmér did was look after his own safety. Instead of utilizing Säpo's compromised security, he hired four bodyguards of his own, whom he trusted completely.

As the head of the investigation, Holmér also needed to make sure that he had the government's confidence. This required meeting with the country's brand-new prime minister, Ingvar Carlsson, and just such a meeting occurred on the second day after the murder.

Hans Holmér met Ingvar Carlsson in a room behind the big auditorium in the Stockholm City Conference Centre at six in the evening on March 2. Ebbe Carlsson also attended that meeting, which was unconventional given that Ebbe's official title was acquisitions editor for a book publisher, but both Ingvar Carlsson and Holmér knew that Ebbe, as Olof Palme's friend, had often been present in situations when he shouldn't have been. And almost as often, he had successfully cleaned up messes that no one else could fix. They might need his services this time, too.

After they sat down, Holmér briefed the new prime minister on the murder investigation, and he also received an important confirmation of his role as head of the investigation. Despite this reassurance, he wasn't a shoo-in for the position yet. The murder could be formally designated an act of terrorism, which should be investigated by Säpo, or a special incident, which would fall to the National Criminal Investigation Department. But as it turned out, things went Holmér's way.

For the first few days, tips poured in, pointing to everything from a foreign conspiracy to the work of a lone deranged gunman. The first tip that the press picked up on concerned a disturbed Austrian, which definitely fell under Holmér's jurisdiction. The media reported that the police were approaching the Palme murder as a street killing. Holmér was in.

On March 2, Hans Holmér held his second press conference and appeared on a live broadcast of the news program *Aktuellt* on the national public broadcast channel, without anyone protesting his having appointed himself head of the investigation. After that, a long time would pass before his position as head of the investigation could be changed.

In an apparent coincidence, Ebbe Carlsson had received a private call from someone at Säpo the day before the murder. This person wanted to speak about a book he thought should be published, but he also revealed that Säpo had tapped a phone call that they interpreted to mean that the Kurdistan Workers' Party (PKK) was preparing a murder in Sweden. The Säpo contact didn't know who was going to be murdered, but after the news of Olof Palme's death broke, Carlsson put two and two together. Hans Holmér, who was by then staying at Carlsson's house, had good contacts at Säpo since he had been its chief. Thus the head of the investigative team learned of this information, and the investigation into suspected PKK involvement began almost immediately after the murder.

***

Work proceeded at a furious pace all weekend, and by the beginning of the next work week, the team had conducted several hundred interviews. Two detective chief inspectors met with Lisbeth Palme at her home on the afternoon of March 1. Despite the interview taking place so soon after the murder, she was not able to describe the attacker's face in the least. She also appeared to have confused the murderer with one of the witnesses, since the clothing and build she described didn't match the other witnesses' descriptions. As if that weren't enough, one witness—called the Skandia man since he worked in the Skandia building right by the murder location—barged in on the scene immediately after the murder, like a bull in a china shop, and may have been confused with the murderer by other witnesses.

On Monday, the investigative team contacted their German colleagues in the Federal Criminal Police Office (BKA) laboratory in Wiesbaden, who were the best in Europe at creating composite sketches for investigations involving unknown assailants. It was arranged that German experts would come to Stockholm on March 5 to produce images based on the descriptions from several of the most important witnesses. Until then, the leaders of the investigative team would work on selecting and prioritizing the most important testimonies.

***

A short while after the murder, a twenty-two-year-old woman named Sarah walked out of the staff entrance of Stockholm's hottest night-club, Alexandra's, to smoke a cigarette. When she opened the door onto Smala Gränd, it almost hit a man nervously rushing by. Their eyes met and he quickly flipped up his collar to conceal his face. The place was relatively well lit, so she got a long-enough look to be able to remember his features. As soon as she heard the next morning that the prime minister had been murdered, she contacted the police and gave the first of her multiple statements to help develop a physical description of the suspect.

The Germans from BKA, detective superintendent Joachim Heun and desk officer Stefan Wagner, brought all the high-tech equipment with them that they needed to produce the composite photos on-site at police headquarters. The most important item was a Minolta Montage Synthesizer, the world's most modern image-processing device, based on a combination of video and optics technology.

It was about the size of a twenty-six-inch television set and weighed fifty pounds. The technology was relatively simple. Photographs of faces were separated into four parts: the chin section including the mouth, the cheek and nose section, the eyes and forehead, and the hair. These sections were placed into corresponding slits on the side of the device. The face cards, of which there were a great many in four rectangular card catalogs sorted by type, were interchangeable.

Based on a witness's basic description—for example, a round face with a big mouth, a receding chin, and a high forehead—a photographic quality face could be created almost magically and then transferred using a video camera to a fourteen-inch TV screen. The witness could then point out differences between the projected image and the face in his or her own memory. The operator could change the distance between various components of the image or swap out individual parts and, in a few minutes, create a new picture for the witness to comment on. That procedure could be repeated any number of times, but usually the entire process took a good hour from when the witness sat down until the picture was finished. When both the witness and the operator were satisfied, the projected image was photographed using a regular camera.

The photo synthesizer that the German colleagues brought with them was the latest model and featured yet another improvement that entailed a fifth card catalog, an additional slit, and two additional wheels on the side of the device. Using pictures from the file, various types of facial markings, such as scars or moles, could be added in the correct locations.

The Palme murder investigation was no common murder investigation, and this witness was no common witness, as it turned out she had extraordinary observation abilities. Instead of one hour, it took just over four hours before the process was completed. The result was a photo-quality black-and-white portrait. This was the first time the term "composite image" was being used in Swedish, so the Swedes borrowed the word for it straight from the German term used by the BKA technicians: "*phantombild*" or "phantom image."

When the picture was done, Hans Holmér personally hand delivered the first copy to his boss. National police commissioner Holger Romander received the first facial composite and a cigarette case as his birthday presents on March 6. A large number of photocopies were made and distributed to the police, customs, and newspaper offices around the country. After that, the German technicians had time to produce some additional facial composites with the less important witnesses, but the only picture that was published to begin with was the one that would for all eternity be known throughout Sweden as the phantom image. Rather fitting, as the suspect seemed to have vanished into thin air like a ghost.

Lisbeth Palme was never asked to help produce a facial composite, because in the first questioning session she hadn't been able to describe the murderer's face and seemed to have confused him with a person leaving the area.

The publication of the composite photo caused the tip lines to start ringing nonstop. In total, the police received more than eight thousand tips. Critics of the decision to release the photo thought this resulted in the police being forced to waste investigative resources on worthless tips and possibly causing people to shy away from calling in tips about persons of interest who didn't resemble the photo.

Instead, later in the investigation, a lot of resources went into explaining away the facial composite and Sarah's testimony when they no longer fit with the investigators' theory.

Victor

Stieg was frazzled. The last nine days had been an inferno of intensive work and—during his commutes to and from work at TT—unceasingly swirling thoughts. Each night, he had a couple of hours talking to Eva and a few hours of uneasy sleep, but it barely helped break the circles his mind was racing in, faster and faster. Everything had to do with the prime minister's murder.

This day, like all others, would begin with the nine o'clock morning meeting. Stieg arrived at a quarter past and stood in the very back of the room as usual, but he immediately sensed that something was different. On the one hand, they had already moved on to other items, but on the other, everyone in the room was full of energy, almost exhilarated, in a way that he hadn't seen since the Soviet submarine *U137* had run aground off Karlskrona five years earlier. Stieg stood with his coffee cup in his hand and tried to stop some of the first people to leave when the meeting ended a couple of minutes later, but they hurried past with a simple nod to indicate that he should ask someone behind them. Once the stream of colleagues leaving the room had slowed down somewhat, he grabbed one of the editors to ask what was going on.

"Seriously? The police brought in a suspect in the Palme murder yesterday."

She slipped away from Stieg's hand on her shoulder and left him looking on with astonishment. He went straight to his desk and called his best contacts for police information. The two crime reporters he knew well had no idea, but his third attempt was a new contact at Säpo. There, he had better luck.

"What do you know about the guy they brought in?" was Stieg's obvious question. After a long pause, the answer came.

"Even we don't know his name yet, and what I know isn't anything you can pass on. But the guy is way out on the right politically, anti-Communist. So not a Nazi, but still a right-wing extremist. Active in a bunch of different organizations, both Swedish ones and abroad. Religious. That's all I've got right now."

Stieg was satisfied anyway. If it had to do with a right-wing extremist or an anti-Communist as they usually called themselves, he had a head start thanks to his own mapping work, which was at his fingertips in a couple of two-foot-high stacks on his desk. He had been in the process of acquiring a mini filing cabinet and hanging file folders, but then he realized that it would be overflowing within a month, so he decided he might as well wait until he had the money to buy a full-size one.

The last few years, Stieg had started mapping out organizations, networks, and individuals that were marked by their right-wing extremist ideas and views. Despite all the time he'd spent on the subject, he was still often flummoxed. How could people in the 1980s, who appeared to be otherwise normal, participate in gatherings and organizations where fascist and racist views were expressed? The same people kept cropping up in political parties that seemed completely on the up-and-up, like the Moderates or the Liberals, and then gradually the boundaries were erased between the right wing, right-wing extremists, and even outright Nazis.

An important step in Stieg's work against the extremist right was when he first contacted Gerry Gable, the editor in chief at *Searchlight* magazine in the UK. They'd had a special bond since their very first meeting, and after that, whenever Stieg wrote for the magazine, which was relatively frequently, he signed his articles, "Our Swedish correspondent," which both fulfilled his need to remain anonymous and allowed him to enjoy the satisfaction of being published.

After all these years spent on his fight against right-wing extremism, it was no surprise that when Stieg found out that the police had picked up a right-wing extremist, his heart skipped a few beats.

There were a handful of people in his materials who matched the description he had received of the apprehended suspect, and he reread the documents he had on those he found most relevant.

Stieg digested the information for a while and jotted down a few items in his notebook before deciding to take a tour through his coworkers on the TT editorial team to find out if they had learned anything more or had found anything that contradicted his own information. It took quite a while since the information exchange had to go both ways. Soon it became clear that he had learned more than anyone else. The police had apparently been somewhat more successful at keeping their information under wraps than they had been on the day of the murder. Stieg shared what he had learned, giving firm instructions that they could not write about it under any circumstances. If so, his source would be toast.

To an outsider, the right flank in Swedish politics could look like it had grown up out of nowhere or merely been buoyed by opinions that had, over time, shifted from the middle. In reality, there was a relatively small but close-knit group of people who were often part of multiple organizations, and there was an unbroken line back to the growing Nazi movements from the interwar period. In the decades following World War II, these movements had not been very active, but they definitely had not disappeared. German Gestapo officers had sought out places of refuge; South America was popular, but also East Germany because the country was still the enemy of the United States and the UK, and because anti-Semitism lived on behind the iron curtain. A handful of die-hard Nazis came to Sweden, where there were multiple layers of hidden adherents and sympathizers. Stieg's own mappings from the last year showed what others had warned of: there were direct and indirect ties between Swedish right-wing extremists, Swedish parliamentarians, and people in the top levels of the Swedish economy.

Stieg decided to go home from work early for the first time since the day of the murder, but he wrote Gerry and his colleagues a short letter to say that a suspect had been apprehended and that he would write at more length once additional information was available. It was unlikely that the police would come out with anything new that night, but the next day was sure to be quite eventful. His journalist colleagues would sit on the info until they had a confirmed name. Everyone knew the police would resist but would still end up releasing the information bit by bit. Maybe the next day would change Swedish history.

***

Just as Stieg thought, the police continued to leak information. The problem was sifting what was true from what was only speculation from individual police officers. There were rumors that the newspaper *Dagens Nyheter* had some kind of monopoly on Holmér and the investigation leadership, while other media, including TT and Stieg, were forced to rely on the next layer down.

Stieg had succeeded in confirming the identity of the person in custody. He continued to be referred to as "the thirty-three-year-old" in the media, but his name was Victor Gunnarsson. Gunnarsson fit all the prejudices of a marginalized person attracted to fringe views and organizations. In his case, one of the organizations appeared to be the European Workers' Party (EAP) which, although it sounded left-wing, was actually a right-wing organization and the Swedish branch of the Lyndon LaRouche movement. Gunnarsson's admiration for the United States was unlimited, and he had often been observed in Stockholm speaking American English or Swedish with an American accent, maybe to compensate for coming from the tiny village of Jämjö in remote Blekinge County in southeast Sweden. After moving to Stockholm, his personal success had been limited, with no real friends and several different jobs, including working as a security guard and a substitute French teacher.

When his connection to the EAP turned up, Stieg thought back to his research into that strange organization from a few years earlier. He remembered having seen a person who looked like Gunnarsson at the organization's book stand at Haymarket (Hötorget) in Stockholm in 1978; he was posed like an onlooker, but he seemed to be more like a barker for those who happened to pass by the table, drawing them in closer. Stieg had observed the same behavior from that man on a couple of occasions and was quite sure that Gunnarsson was affiliated with the organization.

But just as Stieg became excited about a possible link to his own research, the police suddenly released the suspect without charges. Stieg decided to hold off on contacting them about how he had put the EAP and Gunnarsson together. Instead, this was a good time to write a longer letter to Gerry, who had been eager to hear more since Stieg's last one. Almost three weeks had passed now since the murder, and there was more to report than Stieg thought. He was satisfied with his first sentence, which could have worked as the introduction to a novel: "The assassination of the Swedish Prime Minister Olof Palme is, to be perfectly honest, one of the most unbelievable and amazing cases of homicide I ever had the unpleasant job of covering."

The letter ended up being longer than he had anticipated, seven densely written pages in total. With any luck, Gerry would ask him to write an article about it. If not, then at least *Searchlight*'s team would have knowledge that could be valuable later on. Especially in the unlikely event that the murder still remained unsolved in, say, six months.

The Prosecutor's Accusation

Stockholm, April 1986

A good month after the murder, Holmér had managed to strengthen his position as the one who would solve the case. Aside from his role as investigative lead, he was also the highest-ranking police officer in charge. By Swedish law, the important role of leading a preliminary investigation belonged to the prosecutor, but Holmér had said in no uncertain terms that the prosecutor would have to wait until the police decided they had enough evidence to present. Soon enough, Chief Prosecutor K. G. Svensson started showing his frustration, and the conflict only escalated when the police requested that Victor Gunnarsson remain in custody. But that decision was up to the prosecutor, and he decided to release Gunnarsson anyway. At this point, Holmér was furious and broke off all communication with Svensson.

Soon Prosecutor-General Magnus Sjöberg received a phone call from the Ministry of Justice. Harald Fälth wanted the prosecutors to come to the ministry for a meeting. So, on the evening of April 2, K. G. Svensson and Magnus Sjöberg headed off to the art nouveau Rosenbad building, which houses the Swedish government, just across the water from the parliament building and the Royal Palace.

When they were shown in, Hans Holmér was already there waiting for them. It turned out he, Fälth, and Justice Minister Sten Wickbom had just finished a preliminary meeting, and the unexpected result was a compromise whereby Prosecutor-General Sjöberg would alter Svensson's decision in order to comply with the ministry's wishes. Svensson was allowed to retain responsibility for only the Victor Gunnarsson investigation, and his days as the prosecutor in charge were numbered. Holmér had demonstrated that the government was willing to protect him, right up the chain to Prime Minister Ingvar Carlsson if necessary.

The whole production around Victor Gunnarsson had resembled a cockfight and didn't actually matter very much to Holmér, since his interest was really focused on the Kurdistan Workers' Party (PKK). But the Swedish police were finding it hard to map out that group, despite Säpo's having had their eye on them for years. The PKK was private and hard to infiltrate, because the pool of potentially suitable infiltrators was extremely limited. It was just not easy to find a Kurd who was convincing to the PKK and also prepared to betray his fellow countrymen to the Swedish police, especially since former members who were considered traitors had been murdered throughout Europe. But wiretapping and bugging the PKK continued as police waited to find anyone who might leave the group and be prepared to share relevant information. So far, Holmér had succeeded in keeping the PKK line of inquiry under wraps, but he knew it was only a matter of time before it leaked. With three hundred people involved in the growing investigation, it wasn't going to be possible for everyone to keep quiet.

A handful of detectives were assigned to follow other clues, but it became clear that the leaders of the investigative team were not interested in their results. Summary reports went unread. Suggested actions pertaining to other lines of inquiry were rejected by the investigative leads without explanation. There was a lot of frustration, but as is typical with the police, any dissatisfaction was kept within the organization and did not make it past the newly installed bombproof doors of the Palme Room, which contained a trove of materials related to the assassination investigation, or out to the public.

The investigative team leaders were surprised that the few people who were working with Victor Gunnarsson had managed to get so far with a suspect who didn't belong to the main line of inquiry, the PKK. Tommy Lindström, the head of the National Criminal Investigation Department, personally solved this problem. Lindström took control of a key that had been found during a search of Victor Gunnarsson's house and was able to show that it fit a door in a building in which another Kurdish organization had an apartment, an apartment that was located along the murderer's likely escape route, no less. Lindström thought he had shown that there was a connection between Victor Gunnarsson and the police's so far still-secret main line of inquiry: the PKK.

Hence in the spring of 1986, the path was already clear for Holmér to prove the PKK's guilt in the assassination of Olof Palme. What Holmér didn't know was that this was the first step into the labyrinth of bizarre, far-fetched theories that would ensnare the Swedish police for decades to come.

Deeper into the Archive

The moving box had crumpled down on one side, so it was a little more comfortable for me to sit on, but after five hours without daylight, surrounded by dusty paper and cold drafts flowing along the floor, my energy was starting to wane. Even so, I couldn't stop reading Stieg's files. Every box I opened contained documents that took me in a new direction. In one box I found all the daily papers from the days following the murder, all folded up neatly. They looked like they had come fresh off the press that morning, even though the news was thirty years old.

I was transported back to the spring of 1986, amazed at the chaos that had reigned and how everyone was trying to find a new clue or angle. The journalists succeeded in talking to many of the witnesses. The Palmes were surrounded by three men as they walked away from the Grand Cinema. Two were in front of them and one was behind. Lisbeth Palme said that she recognized two people at the murder location whom she had noticed outside their residence the week before the murder. Several witnesses described men with walkie-talkies outside the Palmes' residence, at the Gamla Stan subway station where they had gotten on the train, near the Grand during the movie, and around the murder location.

I realized as I sat with this vast material how much time Stieg must have put into gathering, reading, and organizing it all. My own research material was mostly digital, but I guessed that it only contained a tenth as much information as Stieg's, even though I had already been working on this for four years. Digging into the Palme murder was addictive, as many people could attest. In Stieg's case, that interest went hand in hand with his mapping of right-wing extremists. It was harder to explain why I myself had devoted the last several years to a thirty-year-old unsolved murder. I didn't have a life's mission like Stieg did, no deep-seated passion for the fight against racism and extremism, no single-minded obsession with rooting out injustice and intolerance in our society.

For me, my fascination with the unsolved mystery was a part of it, but that hardly explained why I had put so much time into it. The closest I could come to an explanation was that it provided an escape from my far-too-ordinary everyday life—the monotony, the boredom, and the desire for something more. My hours in the storage facility may have looked like a dark, dusty, tedious slog, but to me they were a visit to a more exciting life.

The descriptions of the motive for the Palme assassination that were published in the newspapers in the months following the murder were unanimous: the murder appeared to be the result of a plot. The map that Stieg had made for TT on March 2, 1986, was published in several papers and gave an overview of the actual course of events. In a way, what I read in the archive was easier to take in than the things people write about the murder now. People truly seemed to know more back then than we do now, thirty years on. By this point, the police and the media have slowly but surely ground away at the facts in order to come up with new truths based on whatever theories they were exploring on any given day.

I kept reading, hoping that Daniel had a lot of work to do back at *Expo* so that I could remain hidden here for a couple more hours among the stacks.

Status Quo

Stockholm, April 2 1986
to Gerry Gable,
SEARCHLIGHT

Stieg Larsson
Axbyplan 34
S-163 73 Spånga
Sweden
Tel. (08) 36 79 74

Dear friend,

It seems the search for the killer of Sweden's PM Olof Palme is as yet fruitless. Perhaps as an indication of the despair mounting in the SweSecPol HQ, the Gods in charge last week ordered the Swedish Air Force into action-in search for the killer.

No, dear fellows, 'twas no joke.

Two "Viggen" types of jet fighters/interceptors almost blasted every window of central Stockholm when repeatedly passing across the city at a low altitude. Their mission: to photograph every roof in the area surrounding the murder, hoping to catch sight of the Smith & Wesson gun used

in the assassination, and which—according
to suggestions from the police—the killer
might have disposed of at the top of a
building.

Nobody cared to explain to inquisi-
tive reporters or mildly surprised citizens why on earth the killer would go to
the trouble of climbing to the top of a
house to get rid of a gun while he was in
a hurry to escape from the scene of the
murder.

Right, your confusion is as great as
mine.

Enclosing a copy of a second "ghost
pic" distributed by the police and manu-
factured on one of their computer graphic
machines. It shows what witnesses describe
as a man who repeatedly (5-6 times) turned
up at the heels of Mr. Palme during January
and February. The police say they believe
he was involved in the murder plot and
spent his time shadowing the PM. They
also say he is probably one of the ring-
leaders and perhaps the brain behind the
assassination.

Witnesses describe him:

Age: 30-35

Height: 195-200 cm

Broad shoulders and a well-trained body
suggesting a former wrestler or boxer type
of sportsman.

Blond or reddish-blond color of hair, some suggested not his original color of hair.

Speaks in languages German and English.

Sharp blue or blue-gray color of eyes.

Also; the reward for giving the police a lead to catch the killers has been topped by an additional half million SKr and is now at a total of one million; appx L 100,000.

Warm greetings,

SL

After Chernobyl

After a couple of warm days at the end of April, it had grown cold once again and everyone was wondering when spring would arrive. Stieg didn't care, but Eva and some of his coworkers seemed to be suffering because of the bad weather. His time outdoors was limited to the short walk between his home and the subway, and the somewhat longer walk from the subway to work—and then the same trip in reverse when he returned home again ten to fourteen hours later, a cigarette always clutched in one hand.

Stieg's thoughts and waking hours were completely taken up with work. If things kept going like this, he wouldn't even notice if the short Swedish summer never happened.

The murder investigation continued to be a hot topic, but the radioactive cloud currently spreading across Europe, which had been discovered in Sweden, was more urgent now.

Soviet officials had made an unsuccessful attempt to keep the accident secret. Bizarrely enough, measurements taken at the Swedish Forsmark nuclear power plant north of Stockholm first revealed the elevated radiation readings and were able to show that the cloud came from the area around the Chernobyl nuclear plant more than seven hundred miles away in the Ukraine. Soon the Soviet Union was no longer able to deny the accident and was forced to admit that reactor number four had suffered an explosion and subsequent meltdown overnight on April 25–26, after which the radioactive cloud had spread over large parts of Europe, only to be discovered two days later by Swedes.

Stieg couldn't help but see the parallels to the Palme murder investigation—the arguing back and forth between the police and the prosecutors, the lack of any results to show from the investigation, and Hans Holmér's press conferences, complete with pretentious statements about lights being turned on and off in tunnels along with numerous Churchill quotations. The only metaphor that really fit the Palme investigation was that it, too, had suffered a massive meltdown.

Stieg read and saved all the major daily newspapers whenever they mentioned the assassination, which was almost every day. It helped, of course, that he worked at TT and could just pick up the day's papers as he headed home. That saved both time and money, but he was starting to run short on space to store them all.

After two months, people began openly discussing the possibility that the police might never succeed in solving the murder, but the largest and most serious of the media outlets—with the newspaper *Dagens Nyheter* (*DN*) and the public TV station Sveriges Television leading the way—still kept Holmér's banner flying high. Somehow *DN* also seemed to have a special hotline to the investigation since they always managed to obtain news from the Palme Room before everyone else. But Stieg didn't actually care if someone had a little leg up. He wanted the assassination to be solved, and he saw his opportunity to contribute if it turned out that one or more of the people involved were from somewhere in the right-wing world he knew so well.

Holmér led the investigation with a strong hand, but an answer seemed a long way off, and criticism of him had begun to fester. If Stieg was interpreting the signs correctly, then it wouldn't be long before the pressure became unendurable. If the murder wasn't solved soon, changes would be in store for the leadership of the Palme investigation.

The Alpha Male

While most Swedes take four weeks of vacation in the summer, Hans Holmér hadn't had much time off. And neither had his colleagues. If he was working, he expected them to be also.

He had assigned a handful of investigators to look into Victor Gunnarsson, the EAP, and a number of other minor clues, creating a desirable smokescreen for investigating the group that, according to Holmér himself, was the real solution to the murder case: the PKK. In the Palme Room, this line of inquiry had been given the code name "main line," which had begun to spread to the rest of the investigative team and was also starting to be mentioned in the press, without anyone knowing for sure what it meant.

Holmér's summer was spent building the case against the suspected Kurds. The police now had the names of a number of people they were convinced were involved in planning and carrying out the murder, but no definite name for the shooter. The most likely theory was that the killer had been flown in from Turkey, kept hidden until the opportunity arose, and driven to the corner near an art supply store. He carried out his assignment and was then whisked away back to Turkey as quickly as possible. An alternate theory was that the PKK terminated the shooter after the murder so that no loose threads could be found.

The motive was easy to reconstruct: Palme had refused to grant asylum in Sweden to the PKK leader, Abdullah Öcalan, and a large number of PKK supporters had been placed under travel restrictions. A tip, which the police considered reliable, had also been received about a possible murder weapon.

The prosecutors wanted to proceed according to their standard process and question people of interest to see if there was any substance to the suspicions. According to Holmér, that would just increase the risk that evidence, witnesses, and the killer would disappear.

But Holmér had an ace up his sleeve. He had started planning the biggest crackdown in Swedish police history and had already decided on the name: Operation Alpha.

Stieg's Tip

Stockholm, End of July, 1986

Sure enough, the summer went by without Stieg paying much attention to it. But on a couple of evenings in early July, after it had rained and then cleared up, he continued past the city hall subway station on his way home from work and walked to T-Centralen, the main station. He noticed that perfect summer air that was so particular to Stockholm. It was absolutely clean air, he thought, mixed with the intoxicating scent of greenery and recent rain, although maybe scientists could explain it more prosaically than that. In any case, those few evening strolls were his only memory of summer that June and July.

Stieg had let what he knew about Victor Gunnarsson and the EAP sit for months now. The police, who had been forced to prioritize something else instead for some time, now contacted him on their own initiative. The officer who called did not want to say how they had gotten his name, but they wanted to hear what he knew about right-wing extremism.

On his way from TT, he walked by three of the monumental buildings that housed Sweden's judicial authorities. Each in their own way, they all wanted to show the nation's citizens that crime didn't pay. First he passed city hall, where the city courthouse was located. The building was designed in a national Romantic style and resembled a medieval castle with a deliberately exaggerated wide tower in the middle. Directly across the park was the old police headquarters. It was only a few years older than city hall and built in a neoclassical style. It also featured a tower in the middle, but significantly smaller, more like an antenna linking the nation's legal authority directly to God.

The buildings were connected by an underground passageway, aptly named the Passage of Sighs, since this was where anyone taken into custody was conveyed from the police building to the courthouse in city hall and then, once sentenced, back to jail again.

The third building, the new police building, was an addition that had been built onto the old police headquarters. It surpassed both the old police building and city hall in its ability to intimidate onlookers. The building was a brutalist 1970s style with disproportionally small bands of windows alternating with the mottled dark-pink facade, which left you with the impression that an enormous, high-quality ribeye steak marbled with streaks of fat had landed on Kungsholmen island in the middle of Stockholm. If the appearance of this building didn't deter criminals, then they probably really were incurable.

Stieg entered through the revolving doors and notified the receptionist of his arrival. A good while later, a police officer came down to fetch him.

Detective Rasmussen kept meticulous notes but appeared to be only moderately interested. Stieg did most of the talking, describing his tip while wondering why he wasn't being asked more questions about right-wing extremists—after all, the police were the ones who had asked him to come in. In just under an hour, Stieg had reported everything he knew about Victor Gunnarsson and his links to the EAP. When he confirmed that he didn't have anything more to add, Rasmussen asked him to wait for a moment. A couple of minutes later another officer came in and introduced himself.

"My name is Alf Andersson. Can you tell me about Sweden's right-wing extremist groups and their hatred of Palme?"

Stieg was surprised; he'd thought the meeting was over but he got out his papers and went through the material with Andersson. Finally, here was a police officer who really seemed to be concerned about the forces at work on the right wing of the political spectrum in Sweden. Stieg left police headquarters almost three hours after he arrived, with the knowledge that at least someone there was on board. The only fly in the ointment was that Alf Andersson had hinted that the investigative lead wasn't actually interested in the right-wing line of inquiry, but Stieg hoped that was just his way of playing down Stieg's tip so it didn't become news.

Stieg was far from sure that the police would do anything with his information, but still he had done something. He also requested a copy of the minutes so he could be sure his meeting had been documented. His goal was to someday become a crime reporter and to get there, he would have to become a frequent visitor to police headquarters and start building a network of contacts. Every journey begins with a first step.

Although the summer had been very calm, Stieg felt sure that things would start coming together in the fall.

The Riddle

Gerry Gable;
SEARCHLIGHT
August 1, 1986

Stieg Larsson
Axbyplan 34
S-163 73 Spånga
Sweden
Tel. (08) 36 79 74

Dear Gerry,

[. . .] There is no hard news on the Palme assassination, but a statement from the police have it that they have pinpointed the killers and know fairly well who carried out the murder. They lack evidence (they say) and do not wish to get carried away and do a premature arrest. They are promising development in the next couple of weeks or months, but refuse to pinpoint a schedule. As far as the statement goes, it could be just another statement to show they are still working on it, but on the other hand there could be some substance in it. Breaking the previous

pattern, the statement was made by members
of the highest body handling the case.
(Formerly it has usually been anonymous
sources inside the police.)

Which direction the investigation is
going is unknown, but the following information I have been able to secure from
rather reliable sources:

* The LaRouche connection is definitely still investigated and of genuine
interest to the police. They do not say so
officially, but I know since I have been
one of the people they recently asked to
provide information.

* One source at the police HQ say what
they are looking for is quote/a group of
people on the right-wing fringe—not Nazi,
but very right wing although not usually connected to rightwing extremism in
the popular mind /unquote. Another source
says it is a quote/ordinary group of people with right-wing connections /unq.

You solve other riddles too?

Cheers,

The Minutes

INVESTIGATION ENTRY
in felony criminal case
number 13082-5
Date
August 5, 1986
Police District
Stockholm
Unit Responsible
National Criminal Investigation Department

Recipient of the Information
Detective K. Rasmussen 7327

Crime This Entry Pertains to
The Palme Murder

Information Provided by
Stieg Larsson

Profession/Title
Journalist

Employer
TT—Graphics

Event
Information about EAP/Gunnarsson

Larsson stated that he first encountered the EAP in
1973 when they "popped up" all over Sweden overnight. They had significant financial assets behind
them and well-oiled machinery. They held meetings
in a number of locations in Sweden and stayed in
each one for a few weeks.

Larsson attended a meeting in Umeå in 1974. He
was planning to stay for only a little while, but ended
up staying half the night and listening to the very
well-rehearsed speeches, including John Hardwick's.
Larsson was interested in them but not committed
to the group.

The speakers spent a couple of weeks in Umeå
and held meetings several times a week. The message then, like now, was a new world order to prevent a total disaster. Larsson's impression was that
a lot of their message and theories lined up neatly
with the scholarly interpretation of fascism. He read
their literature and other published materials, and
everything fundamentally pointed toward the same
outlook on people and society.

The organization is run from West Germany, both then and now. Clifford Gaddy is the one who passes on their orders in Sweden.

In 1978 there was help from Mikel Wale, who is now active in Wiesbaden, at the European Workers' Party's European headquarters. He had a past as an infiltrator and dissident within the American Deserters Committee in Sweden. When they expelled him, he started organizing the NCLC (EAP) with Tore Fredin.

Since 1974, Larsson has stopped by the EAP's book stand and heard them out.

In his job as a graphic designer for TT, he got to study the pictures of the thirty-three-year-old, now famous throughout the country. He thought he'd seen the guy before.

He was very certain because of his good visual memory, but he couldn't place him. Later that same day he remembered where he'd seen the man. He had seen him on three occasions.

The first time was at Haymarket [Hötorget] in Stockholm in 1977–78 when he stopped at a book stand the EAP ran. The man, who was part of the EAP group, spoke to him then. He started asking about Larsson's opinions on the EAP's message, about his job, where he lived, etc. The man began the conversation with, "Hi, how are you doing?" as if they knew each other. At first Larsson was confused about whether or not he knew the guy, but after a while he began to suspect that he was part of the EAP group and seemed to be reaching out to the

audience. Larsson moved on after about ten to fifteen minutes.

Two to three weeks later, he met the man at
a book stand the EAP had outside the Nordiska
Kompaniet department store on Hamngatan. This
time, he avoided walking over there, but saw that
the man was reaching out to the people around the
book stand.

He has thought a lot about this, especially after
the police asked him to come in. He is very sure that
the thirty-three-year-old and the man look very much
alike. He remembers that his hairstyle was a bit different eight years ago because his hair was longer.
Larsson is a freelancer for *Searchlight*, a radical
magazine in London, which strives to write investigative journalistic reporting about extreme right-wing
groups in Europe and the United States.

Severin

All the classic Swedish baked goods sat behind the glass in the pastry cabinet at Nyberg's Café. Next to the green princess cakes there were slices of Budapest roll and strawberry tarts. On the shelf above that, chocolate oatmeal balls, coconut macaroons, and punsch rolls. The coffee had spent a little too long sitting on the hot plates by the window, but it was strong and refills were free. The clientele was quite mixed, but once the morning rush was over, there were mostly elderly men left sitting near me. The conversation touched on everything from global politics to the sound of glass breaking at night at the neighborhood recycling center.

Stieg himself had often sat at various Stockholm cafés and listened to slightly too loud conversations at nearby tables. People who knew him had told me he would sit for hours using the cafés as meeting places for interviews with sources. A splash of hot coffee would warm up the dregs of his previous cup that had grown cold, and then the conversation could proceed again.

One anecdote that spread among Stieg's friends was about how he described a newly discovered café that would go on to become his favorite. It was named Severin, just like his grandfather. Or so he thought until some heartless soul revealed that the red neon sign over the door actually said "Servering," the generic word for restaurant in Swedish, but a couple of the letters were burned out.

Stieg's grandfather remained a massive presence in his life, even so many years after he had lost him. Severin was always red, that was how Stieg remembered him long after his death. Even the rocking chair in Severin's living room was painted red. When Stieg's mom and dad had left him with his mom's parents, his grandfather Severin and his grandmother Tekla, when he was a little boy, his life got easier, despite the extremely modest lifestyle he would soon adopt. They may have lived in a very small house, but Stieg had almost unlimited freedom in the village of Moggliden, not far from the tiny community of Norsjö in the interior of northern Sweden, fifty miles from the county seat in Skellefteå. Only about twenty people lived in Moggliden, and most of the houses were located along one small gravel road. By the age of three, Stieg was able to move freely around the village on his own.

Very soon after he moved in with them, Stieg started calling his grandmother Tekla "Mom" and his grandfather Severin "Dad," quite simply because he had been with them for as long as he could remember. When his parents, Vivianne and Erland, came to visit, he mostly addressed them by their first names, even though he was aware of who everybody actually was.

As a boy, Stieg spent a lot of time with Severin out in his workshop, sitting on a pallet by the workbench where Severin usually stood, fixing someone's lawn mower or filing down the intake port on a carburetor. Just as often, Severin would stand facing the other way, with his back leaning against the bench, and talk politics with some visitor while they drank a pilsner together. Stieg listened to everything and soaked up all the information he overheard.

Severin hated Nazism and, even more than that, he hated the Nazis who had changed their outward masks after the Second World War but still clung to the evil ideology in their hearts. There were a lot of them and they occupied higher positions than anyone could imagine. Stieg listened and learned. There weren't that many little kids in inland northern Sweden who were interested in politics, and a lot of them soon began to think he was precocious.

Stieg spent some of his most important childhood years with Severin, and it was clear early on what ideal he would work toward for the rest of his life. Unfortunately, the time Stieg got to spend with his grandfather was far too short.

When Stieg turned nine, his life changed dramatically. Severin had had his first heart attack in early fall of the year before. He hadn't been feeling well and he had pain radiating out into his arm. He had described it to Tekla and Stieg, saying it felt like he had eaten something that disagreed with him and his arm had fallen asleep. After that, his doctor in Norsjö had given him several stern warnings, but Severin had not heeded them.

A whole year went by, and the fear of a second heart attack had started to fade. It was Saint Lucia's Day, December 13, 1962, and Severin was working hard to finish up a few things and maybe earn a little extra money before Christmas, so they could get Stieg his own kick-sled (like a wooden chair on metal runners). He was big enough now to explore the somewhat larger world of Bjursele and maybe even go all the way to Norsjö.

Severin wasn't feeling well at lunchtime that day and had to lie down on the bench in his workshop. When he wasn't feeling any better half an hour later, and the numbness in his arm had increased so much that he could no longer blame the drafty workshop, he decided to walk home. He managed to put his jacket on, but couldn't button it. Although it was only a few hundred yards back home to Tekla, it took almost superhuman effort to attempt the trip. His kick-sled slid nicely over the hard-packed snow. There was no wind and it was only a couple of degrees below freezing. The sun peeked out from behind the

edge of a cloud on the horizon. But Severin didn't notice the unusually
nice weather as he concentrated on making small pushes with his right
foot. Nor was he able to perceive the world suddenly tipping or his body
landing hard, facedown in the snow. Or maybe that was the last thing
he did perceive as he lost consciousness.

In a way it was still better that he collapsed before he got home,
since he and Tekla had no phone, and she wouldn't have known whether
to leave him and run to the neighbor's house to call for help or to stay
with him. That problem was solved, because the neighbor kids were out
throwing snowballs nearby and saw Severin collapse, not even putting
out his hands to break his fall. They immediately yelled, and a couple
of grown-ups came outside and saw what had happened. As the closest
neighbor ran to his garage to start up his two-door Volvo PV, Tekla and
Stieg overheard a commotion and came running.

Severin came to, but his face was deathly pale. Working together,
the village residents managed to maneuver the big man through the narrow car door, where they tilted the passenger seat back as far as it would
go. Stieg saw how Tekla was shaking with fear, but she still managed to
open the driver's-side door and clamber into the back seat so she was sitting by Severin's face and could hold him so his heart could maybe calm
down a little. Little Stieg squeezed in beside her in the back seat and
hoped that no one would tell him he couldn't go. The neighbor drove
carefully, but as fast as he dared. The sounds were almost completely
muffled by the high snowbanks, and as the low winter sun sparkled in
the snow, it was almost believable that Severin was already dead as he
lay there, icy still, his face ash gray.

By the time they reached the medical clinic in Norsjö, Severin was
unconscious again. They rolled him inside in a wheelchair and left Tekla
and Stieg in the waiting room with a nurse. No one in Moggliden knew
what the doctor did next, but after a couple of hours, he came back out.

"It was a very close call this time, Mrs. Boström," the doctor said. "A few minutes more and I think his heart would have given up. Severin will have to stay here at the clinic for a few days for observation."

Tekla cried with relief, the panic still lingering in her throat. An hour later she and Stieg were allowed to see Severin, who was lying on his back in a basic hospital bed. His breathing was labored, and it was hard to understand that this was the same person who the day before had run into the kitchen and chased Stieg around the small house just for fun. Now he was lying in bed like a baby rabbit. His eyes were steady but vacant, and he hardly seemed to know who they were. Tekla took his limp hand and spoke comforting words, trying to smile through her fear. "It'll all be OK."

Four days later, Severin was deemed strong enough to go home. The warnings were stern: he was to go on short, quiet walks; take his medicine regularly; and do absolutely no strenuous work. It was good that it was almost Christmas so that Severin could rest for the next three weeks before he started working a few hours a day again.

The third heart attack happened in the morning four days before Christmas. Severin was lying on the daybed in the kitchen while Tekla cleaned the rest of the house for Christmas. They had pulled the daybed away from the window a little bit so Severin wouldn't feel a draft. When she came into the kitchen later that morning to ask him if he wanted a sandwich for lunch, he was dead. Tekla stood there, frozen, holding the broom in her hand and not saying a word. Even though she didn't scream or do anything in particular, Stieg could sense that something was wrong and came running downstairs. When he saw Severin lying still in the middle of the room and Tekla walking around and around, sweeping, he realized something was very wrong. He ran out onto the front porch and screamed for help. A neighbor was out shoveling snow and could tell Stieg was serious. The neighbor rushed right into the kitchen.

Severin lay with his hands crossed on his chest and his eyes closed, as Tekla still swept around him frenetically. Stieg was angry and walked around Severin, but in bigger circles and faster than Tekla. Each time around he stopped and kicked Severin's foot while swearing loudly at Severin for leaving him without discussing it first. But Severin was truly dead, and he left a big void in both Tekla's and Stieg's lives.

A couple of hours later, Vivianne and Erland arrived to collect their son. Stieg's time with his grandfather Severin was over, but their years together would leave their mark on Stieg for the rest of his life.

Cafés

Stieg's passion for the fight against right-wing extremism had been part of his life in one way or another ever since his grandfather's death, but only in the last few years had he started to find some way to approach the issue. His grandfather Severin's stories from the Second World War and the years following it had surely sparked Stieg's interest, how Severin had been punished as a suspected Communist while Nazi sympathizers had been able to keep working in neutral Sweden. Stieg was only a child when he started to understand the injustices his grandfather had suffered. Maybe it was a desire for revenge for the way Severin was treated and his far-too-early death at the age of fifty-six that motivated Stieg so strongly. At any rate, he would devote his life to fighting injustice and intolerance, especially when they came in the forms of fascism, racism, and sexism.

But all of Stieg's simultaneous interests and causes took up a tremendous amount of his time. Mapping out right-wing extremists, starting a magazine, writing books. And then there was researching the Palme murder, which didn't leave enough time for several of his other passions or his relationship with Eva. He always needed one more cup of coffee and one more cigarette to keep up. No time to relax or exercise. His weight, which continued to creep up, and his failing health were reminders that his time was limited, just as his grandfather's had been. He left so much good work undone; sometimes I felt that I had been given a crucial job—to breathe life back into these old forgotten documents, in the hope that they would reveal some vital clue.

There was so much to go through. That morning at Nyberg's Café, I said a quick hello to the other customers when I arrived, but unlike Stieg might have done, I didn't interact with anyone more than a polite greeting or a smile and a nod. Instead, I quickly became engrossed in the scanned copies of Stieg's documents I had on my computer. At this point, I had looked at everything that I had digital copies of several times, as well as the useful items that Stieg apparently loved to collect.

I gradually made my way into the 1980s in the documents, which brought me back to an era before cell phones, when Sweden only had two public TV channels, there were only five political parties in the Swedish parliament, and the Cold War was drawing to an end. Having the interior of Nyberg's Café as a backdrop definitely helped, as there had been only minimal changes in there since the 1960s.

The more I read, the more I started to see the connections I knew Stieg had also seen. How the groupings of right-wing extremists in the 1980s were reminiscent of the ones we had now, with their varying degrees of racism, nationalism, and fascism. And how their hostility toward immigrants united them even back then.

A small group of 1980s Swedish right-wing extremists said they were primarily motivated by something other than xenophobia. They were opposing Communism, choosing to fight it either because they or their families had been victims, or because they stood with the West in the Cold War. Sometimes, acceptable opinions drifted into racism, anti-Semitism, or fascism. What made this group extremist was that they were prepared to resort to methods extending far beyond the bounds of what was democratic or legal, and which often included elements of violence.

The group that was openly hostile toward foreigners was more aggressive and therefore more visible. It was clear from the archive that in the years before and after 1986, Stieg was at least as fascinated by the other, less visible group. Maybe because members of that group were also embedded in Sweden's central power structures, where the resources existed for them to cause a great deal of harm.

In his research on Olof Palme, it was clear that Stieg did his utmost, but also that he had turned over relevant portions of his research to the police when journalistic methods couldn't get him any further. It was possible for him to do things that the police couldn't, but he also knew his limits. He could dig up information or infiltrate an organization, but in the end, it was the police's role to investigate crimes, the prosecutor's to bring suspects to trial, and the court's to determine their guilt. If the police did not act on his information, he was still confident that they had done their best, just as he had.

It was my turn to do my utmost, just as Stieg had, to offer the police something they might not have been able to investigate on their own. Because even before I found Stieg's archive, my own research had led me to a person who had initially been suspected but ultimately dismissed as a suspect by the police, and who had never received much attention from the media at all. I would do what Stieg would have done and put together a memorandum for the police on a man I named Jakob Thedelin. The purpose of the pseudonym was to protect his privacy as I began to make connections between him and the murder of our prime minister. Of course, the police would know his real name, but for everybody else he would be known as Jakob Thedelin. In the document I wanted to write for the police, I would outline all the new facts about him that I had found. It was a matter of providing structure, limiting speculation, and omitting unnecessary information. It would take time, but before I began, I would have another cup of overheated coffee. And a cigarette.

Holmér Strikes Again

Stockholm, December 1986

It had been a rough autumn for the police. Journalists had been keeping an eye on the main line of inquiry and had picked up on the fact
that it had to do with the Kurdistan Workers' Party (PKK). The articles
they published resulted in the police feeling pressured to take action.
The worst of the journalists coming after the police was the most powerful of them all. Jan Guillou, who had set the Harvard case and any
other wrongdoings by Olof Palme aside, was working hard to convince
the public that the police were conspiring as usual against immigrants
and people on the left. With the PKK line of inquiry, the police were
trying to kill two birds with one stone, he surmised. With one of his
usual well-formulated arguments, Guillou pulverized the police's PKK
suspicions and turned the sword that the police had aimed at the Kurds
on Holmér himself. Guillou made Holmér look like a self-absorbed,
conspiratorial buffoon, which Holmér in turn considered the epithet
that fit Guillou himself best. The battle between the media and Holmér,
which had started in September, was carried out in public view all the
way into the last weeks of the year. Nobody was prepared to give in.

The quarrel the police had with the prosecutors continued as well. K. G. Svensson had been gone for a long time, and the public prosecutor's office had replaced him with Claes Zeime, a sly old fox who would be retiring soon and didn't have anything to lose by saying what he thought. Holmér continued to systematically pursue his investigation against the Kurds but was constantly under attack from the media, the prosecutor, and—at least it felt this way—parts of his own organization. But he still had an ace up his sleeve. He was going to go all out and bring in all the Kurds who might have had anything to do with the murder, all at the same time. No less than fifty-eight people would be questioned simultaneously. In Holmér's eyes, there was no doubt that these so-called freedom fighters were guilty. Hell, his friend Ebbe Carlsson had gotten a tip about an upcoming murder by the PKK the day before it happened, directly from the secret police. In his worst-case scenario, even if they didn't manage to pin down a shooter, they would at least establish that the PKK was behind the murder. Any other possibilities had been, in essence, completely ruled out by Holmér. There was not a doubt in his mind he was right.

The stumbling block for Holmér was that the prosecutor's approval was required in order to carry out the operation. Even with the government's support, he couldn't tackle Zeime alone. The prosecutors were pigheaded, and they even compared Holmér's intended plan to the military in Chile detaining opposition members in the soccer stadium in Santiago in 1973, an absurd comparison according to Holmér.

After months of negotiations, it was finally agreed that Holmér could carry out Operation Alpha, but he could bring in only twenty people for questioning. But Christmas was rapidly approaching; Holmér really couldn't ask his team, most of whom were already buckling from all the overtime, to work over Christmas break, too. But they were so close now, Holmér felt. All resources should be directed toward the solution—the only solution, he was convinced of it—even if it meant putting everything else aside. He could definitely see the light at the end of the tunnel.

One piece of good news for the investigation in the middle of all the misery came at the end of December. Hans Holmér was named Swede of the Year by the news program *Rapport*. Sveriges Television, the country's most important media company, had awarded him its most prestigious honor; Holmér was thrilled.

***

Operation Alpha was carried out on January 20, 1987. Twenty individuals, mostly Kurds, were brought in and questioned simultaneously. But the prosecutor decided that almost all of them should be released that same day, and the rest were released shortly thereafter.

Operation Alpha was not the success Hans Holmér had planned. To the contrary, it became the prosecutors' chance to restore what they saw as order. Two weeks later, on February 5, Hans Holmér resigned from his position as head of the investigation. A month later, the Swede of the Year handed in his notice as police chief.

But the final word was not in yet. Holmér still had his network of Social Democratic ministers and his friend, the police fixer, Ebbe Carlsson. People would keep toying with the PKK line of inquiry for a while to come, only this time, they would do so in secret.

No, No, Yes

The doorbell at Stieg and Eva's place rang at eight thirty at night. Stieg opened it himself and invited his guest in. Håkan Hermansson had a full beard and was tall, dark, and charming, which probably brought him a fair share of respect in his editorial work at the morning paper *Arbetet*, and surely the attention of the occasional woman. Stieg had expected him to have a Malmö dialect since that's where the paper was located, so Hermansson's thick Göteborg dialect came as a surprise.

"It's quite a schlepp out here to the outskirts of Stockholm, I have to say. You wouldn't have a cup of coffee, would you? I think I smell some."

Stieg was caught off guard but gestured for his guest to follow him to the kitchen from the front hallway once he'd taken off his winter boots.

"Northern Sweden–style cowboy coffee," Stieg said and poured the last of it from the pot without getting any grounds in the cup.

He set his own cup on top of a filing cabinet and forgot about it as he lit cigarettes for himself and his guest. Eva came into the kitchen and took his cup off the cabinet and handed it to him. That wasn't the first time that had happened.

"This is my wife, Eva. Or, well, partner or whatever it's called these days," Stieg said. "We've been together for more than ten years, and there's nothing you can tell me that I wouldn't say to her."

Nevertheless, after fixing herself a sandwich for lunch the next day, Eva excused herself to go to bed, as she was responsible for opening up the construction site where she worked as an architect early the next morning. Stieg showed Håkan into the living room, and they sat down at the combined dining table–desk against the wall.

"What little I've heard sounds exciting, but let's hear the full story," Stieg said.

Hermansson took a deep drag on the cigarette and leaned back with his legs crossed and his cigarette hand stretched out, propped against the edge of the table for support.

"Lasse Wenander and I are on assignment for our newspaper, *Arbetet*," he explained after a brief pause. "It has all the makings of something that will have lingering effects in Sweden for a long time to come."

Stieg sat leaning back with his arms crossed, waiting.

"We're going to map out anti-Palme hatred and opposition campaigns from before his death," Hermansson continued. "I've heard about your mapping of right-wing extremists and I'm positive your work will have some points in common with ours. People also say that you've got a knack for digging things up, so Lasse and I would really like you to join us. If you would be so kind, as they say."

It was hard to resist Hermansson's Göteborg charm and the way he made it sound as if they'd already started working together. If he used this same style when he interviewed people, there was no doubt he'd be able to charm more out of his interviewees than most of their journalistic colleagues. He placed two handwritten pieces of paper on the table in front of Stieg.

"This is a list of the names we want to look at. We don't have that many yet, but we figured you'd have a better idea."

Stieg glanced at the list and needed only to raise one eyebrow to learn more.

"I'm a Social Democrat and quite firmly established in the party," Hermansson explained. "Lasse and I met with the party's . . . well, let's call it their fact-gathering unit. We pitched the idea of writing a series of articles in *Arbetet* and maybe a book if all goes well. The other day we got the go-ahead for our plan, with financing. The most important part of all is that we're going to get free access to the Social Democrats' network. Everyone who knew Olof will talk to us."

Hermansson eyed Stieg expectantly.

"It sounds like a cool project, and obviously I'm familiar with all the names on the list, so it's definitely in line with what I work on. But there's one thing that's bugging me," Stieg said and lit them both another cigarette. "You know that I'm not a Social Democrat, right? I'm a Trotskyist and I write for the *International*. As you know, we're not exactly thrilled with how you're governing the country, so even if we have the same goals in this specific case, I'm not sure I want to be connected to the party of government in this way."

"Yeah, I know you think we're revisionists and all that. But you also thought it was awful that all that hatred was directed at Palme, and indirectly at the democracy as well, right? Or am I missing something?"

Stieg waved his hand to show that he agreed with Håkan but that there was something else.

"It's like this," Stieg said. "I'm going to be fighting fascism and right-wing extremism for a long time to come, probably my whole life. However tempting this may sound, I don't want the other side to get to know who I am, what I investigate, or the methods I employ."

"But if you were to be part of this project, you would become so well known that you could write any articles or books you wanted. It would give your career as a journalist a big boost."

"Sure, but will I still be able to work? My goal is to fight right-wing extremism, not to become a famous journalist. So, the question is: Will I lose more opportunities than I gain?"

Their conversation ran out of steam. They obviously liked each other, but they had gotten off on the wrong foot and Hermansson was asking for something that Stieg didn't know he could give.

"I'm afraid my answer is no," Stieg said. "You're welcome to read my material, but I simply can't risk not being able to keep working on mapping out right-wing extremism after your articles come out."

Hermansson looked disappointed, and so his forty-minute subway ride out to Rinkeby wouldn't be in vain, Stieg opened a bottle of red wine and poured two glasses without even asking. They chatted for quite a while about other things without approaching the issue of possibly cooperating. Maybe that was exactly what they both needed in order to reset. After a second glass of wine, Stieg stopped.

"Wait a minute," he said. "I'm going to do something I've never done before."

Stieg disappeared into the bedroom, where Eva had gone to bed a good two hours earlier. Hermansson sat in the living room by himself for a long time. When Stieg came back he looked serious and determined. He sat down across from Hermansson again.

"Here's what we'll do. I'll help you with the research for the articles. I don't want any credit or payment for my work. Actually, to the contrary, I want you to guarantee that I will not be mentioned in relation to the project. Does that sound like an arrangement you can agree to?"

Hermansson mulled over Stieg's simple solution for a few seconds and then accepted it. Guaranteeing his anonymity wasn't a high price for gaining access to the man who was very likely the best researcher in Sweden. He nodded, reached out his hand, and they shook to seal the deal. Stieg opened another bottle.

Mission: Olof Palme

Stockholm, February 1987

The premise was worded this way: "The work in this series of articles will be based on the supposition that the murder of Olof Palme can be viewed as a logical consequence of changes that happened gradually in the Western world and Sweden."

Stieg's task required subtlety. It was always a balancing act to do research for a series of articles or a book that would be scrutinized closely by all political camps, but when it pertained to Olof Palme, as well, and there was a murder investigation underway, the risk of disapproval increased exponentially.

There was a risk that the murder might end up being solved before the book came out, and it could turn out that there was no connection at all between the murder and the anti-Palme hate campaigns. On the other hand: if the murder *was* solved, that would still be the best outcome. In that case the only risk was that the book would receive less notoriety, which was a price that everyone had to be willing to pay. There was also considerable risk of criticism, but the upside to their plan was that Håkan Hermansson and Lars Wenander would take the brunt of it. All Stieg could do was make sure his research was irreproachable.

Another problem, which was more concrete, was that there was an extremely large number of organizations and people who were engaged in campaigns against Olof Palme. In the material that Stieg was planning to hand over to Hermansson, he had deliberately toned down parts that were interesting but did not have anything to do with anti-Palme hatred, such as links to Stay Behind—the secret network of loosely composed cells that would be activated if Sweden was occupied by a foreign power—and the Swedish part of Operation Chaos. The latter was the CIA's infiltration of, among other things, American Vietnam War deserters in Sweden, which was carried out with CIA director William Casey's consent. Casey was a real piece of work in Stieg's eyes because of his active role in the completely unnecessary invasion of Grenada in 1983.

Another difficulty was that many of the organizations that Stieg had mapped out overlapped each other. They often united, split up, or disbanded. And when you got down to looking at the level of the individual people involved, the picture became hard to understand, at least to everyone except Stieg, who remembered most of it—and if he didn't, he always knew exactly where to look in all his papers. Now he was forced to put all his vast research into an easy-to-grasp format, not only for the journalists he was helping but also for the readers who didn't have any prior knowledge on the subject.

In order to get off to a quick start, he decided to make three lists with brief descriptions: one of organizations, one of people, and one of interesting addresses in Stockholm. The aim of the lists was to give his colleagues an overview of how the right wingers and opponents of Olof Palme were interconnected, without any prejudice that any one of them was involved in the murder. A natural starting point was Anders Larsson, the founder of the organization Democratic Alliance (Demokratisk allians) in the 1970s, who was still very active. He also claimed to have known about the murder of Olof Palme in advance.

ANDERS LARSSON
A bit of a spider in the web who turns up all over the place among Swedish right-wing extremists. He seems to use other identities, made up and real, when he writes letters. Larsson issued a warning before Palme's murder. Anders Larsson was also apparently reported to Säpo because he wanted to kill Social Democratic politicians (not Olof Palme).

CARL G. HOLM
One of the publishers of *Contra* magazine and an employee of the Federation of Swedish Industries (Industriförbundet). Sworn enemy of Anders Larsson because they went into different factions of the Democratic Alliance when it split. Since then, there has been outright war between Anders Larsson and Holm/*Contra*.

FILIP LUNDBERG
Linked to *Contra* and leads "The People's Campaign for NATO" (Folkets kampanj för NATO). He is also connected to Freedom in Sweden (Friheten i Sverige).

ANDRES KÜNG
Seemingly a harmless member of the Liberal Party who moves in the select circles in Freedom in Sweden, but he's also on the board of Resistance International and has been drawing nearer to the *Contra* sphere since he received their Freedom Prize, which should really irritate their archenemy, Anders Larsson, in particular.

BERTIL WEDIN

Former lieutenant who distinguished himself early
with his support of the Vietnam War. Worked for the
Wallenberg sphere doing "information gathering."
Links to Democratic Alliance. Moved to London in
1975 and worked for a group of Swedish companies.
Knows both Anders Larsson and the *Contra* gang,
though he is closer to the latter. He is included on
this list for his genuine opposition to Palme, because
of which, there is persistent suspicion that he might
have been involved in the murder in some way.

HANS VON HOFSTEN

Naval commander who has been on Freedom in
Sweden's board since October 1985. One month later
he led an officers' rebellion in which he openly stated
in a polemical newspaper article in *Svenska Dagbladet*
that people did not have faith in Olof Palme prior to
his trip to Moscow.

VICTOR GUNNARSSON

He was not of any interest until he was suspected of
the Palme murder, but he has been linked to the EAP.
According to a source, he is also often seen with two
people with ties to the Democratic Alliance who both
warned of the murder independently of each other:
Anders Larsson and the former mercenary Ivan von
Birchan.

ALF ENERSTRÖM AND GIO PETRÉ

Enerström has been called the biggest Palme hater
in Sweden. He has backing from some of the

highest-ranking figures in Swedish trade and industry (e.g., Lars-Erik Thunholm of the Wallenberg sphere) and gives money to the EAP and places millions of kronor worth of ads in the daily papers. His common-law wife, Gio Petré, is an actress, and together they traveled throughout the country spreading propaganda against Palme. Their latest book came out recently and is called *We Brought Down the Government, Part II* (*Vi fällde regeringen del II*). In it they compare Palme to Hitler and write that there is only one punishment for a traitor. It's a pity for them, though, that their title was wrong, since contrary to expectations, Palme and the Social Democratic Party won the election.

Even though Stieg worked to keep the number of people on his list down, there were more than he would have liked. He had deliberately dropped all the foreigners—which had included Italian neofascists Stefano Delle Chiaie and Roberto Fiore and professional hitman Michael Townley, who had all shown up on Stieg's radar following tips that they might have been involved in Palme's murder. But they didn't make the cut on this list.

Aside from more or less open hatred for Palme, which they all shared, there was a recurrent pattern: People of a certain standing put themselves at the head of an organization. Behind them, with significantly rougher agendas, were those who were actually pulling the strings. Sometimes there were even Nazi ties. Another interesting phenomenon was that the same names came up again and again, which would become clear in the next list.

Democratic Alliance (DA)

Although the DA split up in 1975 and their activities ceased altogether the following year, it was the progenitor of a majority of the non-Nazi right-wing extremist organizations. Founder Anders Larsson has some type of relationship (positive or negative) with all the organizations below and led the majority faction from the DA after it split up.

Contra

After the DA split up, the minority faction with the most hardened characters started the foundation and magazine (not to be confused with the US-supported guerilla movement in Nicaragua). One of their biggest enemies is Anders Larsson from the DA's majority faction. The magazine's contents are fueled by an admiration for the United States and, until his assassination, a strong hatred of Palme. For example, they sold a dartboard with a caricature of Olof Palme that could be used as a target.

The Baltic Committee

One of about ten strange organizations with Baltic ties, most of which are registered in the Estonian Building at 32 Wallingatan. The Baltic Committee is of interest, among other reasons, because the organization is a member of the WACL (see below) and because Anders Larsson managed to get kicked out of it a good month before the murder of Olof Palme.

WORLD ANTI-COMMUNIST LEAGUE (WACL)

Umbrella organization with roots in Asia in the 1950s and the fight against global Communism as the glue that binds it together, which has attracted a number of dubious right-wing organizations and individuals. WACL's popular conferences are held in various locations around the world and those enticed to attend from Sweden have included a Moderate member of parliament and our notorious Anders Larsson.

EUROPEAN WORKERS' PARTY (EAP) OR EUROPEAN LABOR COMMITTEES (ELC)

An extremely small political party founded by American millionaire Lyndon LaRouche, active in Sweden since the 1970s. This is the organization that went furthest in its hatred; they described Palme as a crazed murderer, drug dealer, and Soviet agent. The EAP may have been infiltrated by CIA operatives posing as Vietnam War deserters living in Sweden. Victor Gunnarsson collaborated with the EAP and their material was copied for distribution in Anders Larsson's office at the Baltic Committee.

RESISTANCE INTERNATIONAL

Anti-Communist organization formed in Paris in 1983 and in Sweden in 1985. Started as an organization for traditional right-wing conservative anti-Communists, but has since expanded to include more strikingly right-wing extremists, people in émigré circles from the Eastern bloc and WACL. On the Swedish board we find Anders Larsson, Baltic exile Andres Küng, the

UNITA representative Luís Antunes, and *Contra* editor Filip Lundberg.

THE FOUNDATION FOR SOCIETAL ISSUES

A secretive society with ties to Resistance International through Anders Larsson and to the Democratic Alliance in that they use the same post office box (which was registered by Anders Larsson). They claim to be anti-Nazi, but are politically right wing. The connection to the old Democratic Alliance might provide a key to the foundation's activities. The Foundation seems to be something of a one-man show.

FREEDOM IN SWEDEN

New organization that was started in September 1985 by Liberal Party member Andres Küng. Squeaky clean on paper with a free Sweden as their goal. But behind the pretty facade, including a member base composed of actors Jarl Kulle and Ulf Brunnberg among others, there are significantly darker forces, such as Contra figure Filip Lundberg and commander Hans von Hofsten. This organization is far larger than the Foundation for Societal Issues, claiming over 1,500 members.

NEW TUESDAY CLUB

Inspired by the ultraconservative British Monday Club, which the colorful Lord Moyne was president of and both Anders Larsson and Bertil Wedin were active in. The group invites big name speakers for innocent evening meetings, but behind the scenes there are the usual ultraconservative names. The seemingly omnipresent Anders Larsson is responsible for their mailings.

UNITA

Guerilla movement from Angola supported by the United States with an office in Stockholm and ties to the CIA. Their representative Luís Antunes shows up in several of the organizations above. Anders Larsson applied for a job here after he was fired from the Baltic Committee.

Stieg thought that these names and organizations were enough to start with, enough to start the two Malmö journalists' heads spinning anyway. But one piece of the puzzle was still missing for them to be able to see the whole picture. The right-wing organizations were linked to a small number of locations, and these locations made it possible to visualize the groups' interconnectedness.

PO Boxes 5817, 490, and 21

One commonality for most of the right-wing organizations is that they use post office boxes. That is one way to run a large number of organizations at the same time, and it also makes them harder to map out. Post office box 5817 was the Democratic Alliance's old box and has also been used by the Foundation for Societal Issues. Post office box 490 is linked to the Baltic exiles' organizations at 32–34 Wallingatan and has been used both for the Foundation and for Resistance International. The most recent post office box to turn up is number 21, but I'll have to come back to that once I've made it further in my research.

32–34 WALLINGATAN

There are countless organizations in the Estonian
Building. Most of them are on the up-and-up, but the
WACL, the Baltic Committee, and a number of other
more shadowy groups are also housed here. There are
also strong ties to Anders Larsson and Andres Küng
here, in addition to the post office boxes mentioned
above.

6B BIRGER JARLSGATAN

Some of the trade and industry lobbying associations
are located here, as well as other suspect firms and organizations, such as Freedom in Sweden. The building
was owned by the Carlberg Foundation (Carlbergska
stiftelsen) with connections to Nazi individuals. The
address is placed in the center of the sketch [p. 103]
of people and organizations I received anonymously
some time ago.

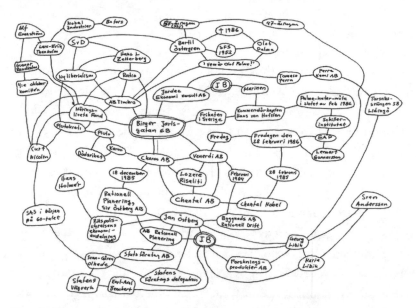

Network of persons and organizations, sent to Stieg Larsson in September 1987.

There were two more names that Stieg thought were relevant to mention to Hermansson and Wenander. The individuals traveled in right-wing circles, but Stieg was convinced that they were working on undercover activities for the Swedish government. Joakim von Braun was on the board of Resistance International but also carried out services for Säpo as a contractor. Joel Haukka was a Baltic exile and knew the whole crew at 32–34 Wallingatan but gathered information for the military intelligence service Special Acquisition Section (Sektionen för särskild inhämtning, SSI). In all probability, von Braun and Haukka would turn up in Stieg's future research for Hermansson and Wenander, so it was good that they knew about them now so they wouldn't confuse them with the most hardened of the right-wing folks.

***

This, Stieg thought, would at least give the journalists a comprehensive view of what the organized Palme haters and the extreme right wing looked like. He made three copies of the lists and sent the originals to Hermansson and Wenander. He kept one set of copies and would give the other two to people he trusted so that the documents could be found in multiple locations in the event of a break-in or fire.

In the material he sent to Hermansson and Wenander, Stieg attached a copy of a letter he had written to Björn Rönnblad in the Socialist Party a year earlier. At that time, no one could have imagined that the prime minister would be assassinated in the open street, but now it was a fact. The letter had to do with materials that had been sent to Rönnblad which were intended to harm Andres Küng's reputation, but it was unclear who had sent them. Stieg had devoted a lot of time to Anders Larsson and post office box 21; he eventually even surveilled the box to see who retrieved the mail from it. He hoped the letter would show the Malmö journalists how he did his research and how much time and effort he put into it. The contents would also get them off to a flying start on the project, which finally had a name—"Mission: Olof Palme."

1987

Holmér's abrupt departure caught the police involved in the Palme investigation off guard. One day they had a boss who decided everything and acted as the head of the investigative team, the police chief, and the leader of the preliminary investigation all at the same time. The next day they had nothing. Coordination between the Stockholm County police, the National Criminal Investigation Department, and Säpo ceased entirely. On paper, department head Ulf Karlsson at the Swedish National Police Board (Rikspolisstyrelsen) was going to head the Palme investigation, but in reality, there were suddenly at least three separate investigations instead. Every group had their own pet theories, which they each happily leaked to the media, creating mass confusion over what was actually going on in the investigation.

Things were easiest for the individual police officers further down the pecking order in all three organizations. That's where the experienced investigators were, and with no one calling the shots from above, they just carried on with business as usual. In each of the three investigations, a list was made of all the theories that were relevant for that department. They started at the scene of the crime and looked at the circumstantial evidence they had before prioritizing which lines of inquiry to focus on. It was an enormous list, and they were fighting their way into the wind, especially since a whole year of valuable investigative time had been lost. If the odds of solving a murder decreased radically after twenty-four hours, then the odds were that much lower after nearly a year.

The theories ran the gamut of possibilities and included a lone madman, groups of Swedish anti-Palme right-wing extremists or police officers, and vast international conspiracies tied to arms deals with Iran or Palme's opposition to apartheid in South Africa.

But 1987 was also the year when the various police units were able to work systematically on the case, following their usual methods and checking with their colleagues in other departments when necessary. Over the spring, the work continued with sporadic meetings between the various units. And somewhere in there, the contours of a plot began to emerge. The answer they reached was not a simple one, but for the first time, the rank and file were participating and controlling the agenda. Many people began to feel optimistic that the murder was solvable. Investigator Alf Andersson, who was particularly interested in the right-wing extremists and had questioned Stieg about the topic months earlier, was one of them.

The Stars Align

Stieg understood that a bottleneck had been cleared. Once Holmér was gone, it felt like everyone dared to think things that they had been unable to before. That was true for the police, but also for the media and the public. Even Säpo had woken up from its lethargy. A couple of weeks after Holmér was gone for good and the new decentralized investigative teams started working on the case, Säpo visited Stieg at TT in a rather conspicuous way. Maybe they had heard from the Palme investigation about his expertise in right-wing extremism. They asked unusually ignorant questions, including what kind of relationship the National Socialists had to other socialist parties, making it clear that they seriously believed that Nazis were socialists—a ridiculously naive conflation of radically different ideologies based on the use of a similar term. Eva had never seen Stieg as mad as he was that night.

For Hermansson, Wenander, and Stieg, their work got somewhat easier since everyone they contacted had read the papers and knew that the PKK line of inquiry had been written off. That meant the path was clear to talk about people who hated Olof Palme.

The coming book and article series were well timed, since several of the lines of inquiry being discussed in the media touched upon their research. Now it was just a matter of getting the book out in time, before public interest faded, the police investigation changed direction, or someone else beat them to it.

Stieg decided to have another go at his research into Resistance International. A year earlier he had staked out the post office where box 490 was located. He knew it was linked to the old Democratic Alliance and a number of active organizations. Although he had given up many hours of his free time outside the post office, he had not succeeded in finding out who picked up the mail from that box.

But this time his focus was on post office box 21, which proved significantly easier to link to both organizations and people of great interest to him. Stieg was convinced that if he could manage to discover who was behind box 21, he would find the person behind the web of numerous groups and individuals in the far-right wing of Swedish politics. But he needed to bounce ideas off someone, and his best bet was Håkan Hermansson. It was time to write another letter.

***

Dear Håkan,
Like you, I have had a little trouble getting going at my typewriter. In my case, however, it doesn't have anything (luckily) to do with lumbago but rather that I've just been so darned busy. I'm simply having a hard time finding enough time for everything. Unfortunately (and I'm almost a little envious of you), I don't have the option of dabbling in these issues during work hours to the extent I

would like. Instead I have to make do with
squeezing it in in little chunks in my
free time. Sometimes it's hard to get it
to add up. I just want to make a few brief
notes to follow up on your letter from
this last week. And apropos that I need
to start by telling you that the material
you enclosed—the letters from the Sweden-
Vatican Association—quite simply could
not have come at a more suitable time.

What I'm working on right now is trying
to map out all the organizations in this
swamp once and for all; in other words,
trying to untangle all the addresses, post
office boxes, phone numbers, cross connections, and all that. At first glance,
this whole field looks like an illogical
ball of loose yarn scraps. This Sunday I
started sorting out all the old notes I
had lying around from when I helped Björn
Rönnblad with information about Resistance
International, and I discovered that I had
a ton of random notes about things that
"ought to be checked" but that I never got
around to.

One of those items that I had put a
question mark by had to do specifically
with post office box 21 at Stockholm 1.
Officially (as I assume you've already
verified), that's the box used by the
Baltic Action Center/Information Archive.
Originally I thought that was the same

thing as the Baltic Archive, in other
words, tied to Arvo Horm/34 Wallingatan.
The problem was that the phone number 20
54 45 didn't match either Wallingatan or
any of the other official Baltic exile
addresses. And, sure enough, the Baltic
Archive on Wallingatan has its own totally
different phone number.

In other words, box 21 seemed to be
different from the many other boxes with
numbers in the twenties that I found which
are linked to Baltic organizations, and I
thought it would be worth doing an extra
check on it.

This Wednesday I went down to Stockholm
1 and checked the registration card for
the box, and lo and behold: the owner of
the box was neither the Action Center
nor the Information Archive, but rather
an organization with the curious name
The Fund for Free Enterprise [Fonden för
Fri Företagsamhet] (FFF). Odd that neither I nor any of TT's financial/polit-
ical reporters had heard of it. Well,
on the registration card I also found a
note about the street address FFF provided when they rented the box, which was
1 Målargatan, a little stump of a street
that crosses Kungsgatan a stone's throw
from Haymarket [Hötorget]. So I walked
down there and checked the address and
got nowhere. You see, 1 Målargatan is

one of the buildings that was part of
the neighborhood-wide renovation project in the Klara district. It's possible
that box 21 belonged to someone at that
address before, but there's no trace of
them left today. It was too late in the
day to start checking if the property
owner had any records of former tenants,
so I stood there scratching my head and
feeling disappointed.

Then I went home and discovered box 21
mentioned in my own mailbox, in the material you sent me. When all is said and
done, it sure is a small world.

Well, thanks to the idea provided
by the letters from the Sweden-Vatican
Association, all there was to do was
keep unwinding. The address I started
checking with of course was the one for
MFS, Kungsholms Kyrkoplan 6, 8tr, which
strictly speaking is the penthouse of
a building in one of Stockholm's most
attractive neighborhoods. Late Thursday
night I managed to get past the key pad
lock for the stairs (I'm telling you, key
pad locks are a menace to free investigative journalism). And had a chance to
take a quick look at the name on the door
for MFS.

Håkan, if someone is sitting behind
that door and cobbling together confused
letters in Gothic script, then in that

case, I think we might have struck gold.
At any rate, we found a completely new
ball of yarn to unravel. And with that
cliff-hanger, you'll have to be patient
for a few days while I check to make sure
I'm not barking up the wrong tree. I'll
send you a letter with all the details
later in the week.

A few marginal notes about the
Sweden-Vatican Association: During the
day on Friday, I went and confessed my
sins to an understanding and forgiving
priest at the Saint Eugenia church on
Kungsträdgårdsgatan. He's been with the
Catholic Church in Stockholm for six years
but had never heard anyone mention an
organization with the name Societas de
Amicitia Suecia Vaticana. However, he was
able to refer me to another (albeit less
forgiving) priest in the Jesuit order, who
said that he knows everything there is to
know about every Catholic association in
Sweden.

The Jesuit priest said that he didn't
know what the Association was, but that
in any case, as far as he knew, it had
absolutely nothing to do with the Catholic
Church. What's funny is that while he
was suggesting that he didn't know about
the Association, I thought I picked up
quite a harsh reaction in him when I mentioned the name. I think that he might

be much more familiar with the name than he let on, but that maybe it brought up some unpleasant memories for him. Did the Association perhaps make itself unpopular on Kungsträdgårdsgatan at some point?

A friendly young woman who works in the Catholic church's bookstore offered me a cup of coffee. She had never heard of the Association, and was also able to inform me that she had never come across any literature, newspaper, or magazine published by them. She also let me look in the Church's internal phone book—which is quite comprehensive and covers all of Sweden—where the Association is not mentioned in any way.

No one at the Catholic parish registrar's office had ever heard the Association mentioned either, but one of the pastoral carers suggested that maybe it might have something to do with one of the small "High Church" lobbying groups that arose in connection with the fuss surrounding the election of Pope John Paul I, in other words, the one who only survived for thirty-three days. My source told me that things got quite heated in the internal debate. Another possibility, he suggested, was that it might have to do with one of the (also High Church) lobbying groups that were very common a few years ago, and which aimed to work on

behalf of seeing Sweden acquire diplomatic connections with the Vatican.

Finally, before I wrap up, I have had
it more or less one hundred percent confirmed that Anders Larsson's telephone
is really tapped. That information comes
from two sources.

I have no info on his Baltic lodger,
but another name on the door of his apartment is Stenbeck. I will see if I can
determine if he has any lodgers, but from
the outside it seems like it's a small
one-bedroom apartment.

I have quite a few comments on your
other thoughts about Taiwan, see unconventional warfare and Baltic Arab African
. . . etc., but they'll have to wait until
later in the week. I'll do my best to put
together a little more detailed information in the next few days, and you'll get
copies of my material as soon as I have
time to type the darn stuff up.

Sincerely,

Warning! Warning!

It was time for Håkan Hermansson's next visit to Stockholm. One of the things that interested Stieg the most was that warnings had been received about the assassination ahead of time. There were up to ten people who claimed that they knew about the assassination in advance and notified the press or the police (and the police then leaked this to the press). Two of these warnings stuck out because they had unquestionably been passed on to the authorities *prior* to the assassination and should therefore have resulted in Säpo raising the threat level for Palme's security team, which might have prevented the assassination from taking place. Säpo was responsible for investigating the warnings and that was surely why they were trying to keep quiet about it for as long as possible. What was most exciting was that there was at least one common denominator between the two warnings.

In January 1986, Ivan von Birchan called both Säpo and an acquaintance in Stockholm's city government and told them that he had been offered a large sum of money to assassinate Olof Palme. Von Birchan was a former mercenary who had worked in Rhodesia, and a person named Charles Morgan, whom he had met during his time in Rhodesia, had asked him to kill Palme. Charles Morgan also went by the name Peter Brown, but von Birchan didn't think either of the names was his actual name. According to von Birchan, Morgan/Brown had been a helicopter pilot in Rhodesia and there had only been a handful of them, so it should have been possible to track him down.

On February 20, eight days before the assassination, another person delivered two envelopes with identical contents to the Swedish government offices and the Ministry of Foreign Affairs. The envelopes contained an article from 1918 with the headline citing the death of an earlier Olof Palme: "Doctor Olof Palme Is Dead" (Doktor Olof Palme död), with the word "Doctor" crossed out. The article was about the prime minister's uncle who had been killed in a war in Finland, but without the word "Doctor," the association to the present-day Olof Palme was obvious to make. The envelopes were left anonymously, but the person who brought in the envelopes was being watched by SSI informant Joel Haukka, so it was possible to determine that his name was Anders Larsson. The very same Anders Larsson who kept turning up in Stieg's research over and over again.

Both von Birchan and Anders Larsson had been involved in the Democratic Alliance. Even if it had been more than ten years since the organization had ceased to be active, it remained baffling. The DA's old post office box 490 was still being used by Resistance International, the Foundation for Societal Issues, and UNITA's Swedish office.

According to Joel Haukka, both von Birchan and Anders Larsson knew the first suspect, Victor Gunnarsson. For those who believed in a conspiracy, that opened up almost limitless opportunities for speculation. And Haukka had also handed over documents to support what he said. Håkan Hermansson was coming to Stockholm to discuss these documents with Stieg.

***

Stieg and Håkan had taken their seats at the kitchen table—a Perstorp plastic laminate table that was so typical of the time that no one minded it, but no one loved it either. They could spread the documents out in front of them, chat loudly, and smoke without bothering Eva since she had already gone to bed.

"Today's yield," Hermansson said, setting a stack of papers on the table.

They split the stack in half and each read their own half before swapping. Stieg had a long list of notes and questions when he was done.

"So, Haukka works for SSI, right?"

"Hmm," Hermansson said as he finished reading his last few pages.

"I don't understand why military counterintelligence would bother tailing a slightly nutty right-wing extremist," Stieg said. "Shouldn't they be focusing on the threat from the Russians and things like that?"

"Hard to know. But Haukka did know Anders Larsson from the Baltic Committee, which is also WACL in Sweden. It is reasonable that he saw, or heard about, how oddly Larsson was acting and decided that keeping a close eye on him was enough."

"I mean, of course, it's good if SSI, or IB, is used for something other than registering Communist sympathizers for the Social Democrats, but—" Stieg bit his tongue. After all, Hermansson was an outspoken Social Democrat, and he had been hoping to avoid getting into topics where their views differed radically.

"No worries," Hermansson said. "But there's one thing that makes it even more complicated. This buddy of Anders Larsson's that Haukka mentions, the parliamentary stenographer, I mean . . ."

"Bengt Henningsson?"

"Yes. Bengt says that he's been keeping an eye on Larsson for Säpo for several years. And that it didn't have anything to do with SSI's surveillance."

"That doesn't make any sense to me," Stieg said. "That would mean that the guy who dropped off the warning before the assassination was being tailed by both military counterintelligence and Säpo . . ."

"And that neither of them acted to prevent the assassination," Hermansson supplied.

The smoke lay heavily in the suburban Rinkeby kitchen. The two men looked somberly at each other until they burst out laughing. This story was almost too good to be true. Big journalism award, here we come!

They kept looking through the material and got into the flow, which wasn't interrupted until Hermansson yawned at around three o'clock in the morning. Before he lay down on the sofa, he threw out one request to Stieg.

"We never did get around to talking about Bertil Wedin from your list. If you have anything on him, will you send it to me? I'm leaving bright and early tomorrow."

Palme's Worst Enemy

Stockholm, May 1987

"How the hell did you pull this off?"

Hermansson's genuine surprise was obvious, as was his appreciation. After most of his coworkers had gone home from TT, Stieg had dedicated a few hours to compiling the material he had on Bertil Wedin to send to Hermansson. It was only a few blocks' stroll from his office on Kungsholmstorg, across the short King's Bridge (Kungsbron), to deposit the thick envelope into the mailbox for the ten o'clock pickup. The day after Hermansson left Stieg's place, he already had a complete background on Wedin in his hand. It made sense that he was amazed, but Stieg hadn't really planned it. It was just funny that someone thought he had supernatural research powers.

Of course, Hermansson didn't know that Gerry Gable at *Searchlight* had called Stieg about this exact same matter a couple of months earlier. *Searchlight* had received information that Wedin was supposedly involved in the murder of Olof Palme and wanted to know what could be found out about him. Stieg had taken it upon himself to put together what he could find in Sweden, while Gerry and his gang were going to continue talking to their source and determine what could be learned in London, where Wedin had lived since 1975.

Gerry's question had only made Stieg all the more fixated on the Palme assassination. Now that Holmér had stepped down, Stieg saw a genuine opportunity to contribute. He regularly chatted about this with a select few, and each week some new person would contact him to ask questions or give him new information. Once the wet blanket woven from thin threads about Kurds in the PKK vanished, everyone was optimistic and engaged in learning about the new possibilities.

Aside from what he and Hermansson discussed during hours-long phone calls and in person when they saw each other, Stieg also intended to produce a memo for each questionable person and organization—basic, concise information that would quickly give Hermansson and Wenander an overview that they could cut and paste from, maybe even borrow entire paragraphs of text from. To produce an example, he started with the memo about the ad-campaign couple, Alf Enerström and Gio Petré. It was only two pages long and contained a background, descriptions of their ties to Sweden's big businesses, their financing of the anti-Palme ad campaigns, and a description of their peculiar book, *We Brought Down the Government* (*Vi fällde regeringen*). Finally, he put in a few brief summaries of the texts the couple had published as ads in daily papers. As usual, Stieg made a couple of extra copies and sent two to Hermansson and Wenander in Malmö for their comments.

Alf Enerström was certainly an odd character, but with his contacts in the highest echelons of Swedish trade and industry—including some of the very richest Swedish expatriates—it was very unlikely that he would be involved in anything as sordid as assassinating Olof Palme. Plus, he had an alibi from his common-law wife, Gio Petré.

Stieg produced memos for some of the people on the list that he had drawn up for the Malmö journalists, and as soon as he was done with a few of them, he sent them off. But one of them took significantly more time—the memo on Bertil Wedin. He made it the most thorough and detailed of them all because Gerry had gotten back to him with more information from his source in London and Stieg was convinced that the police should take a closer look at Wedin. Gerry guaranteed his source's credibility and said that he had contacts in MI6, the British foreign intelligence service. The source had obtained information that Wedin acted as a middleman in Olof Palme's assassination. It was confirmed that Wedin worked for various security services, the most interesting of those being South African—information about South Africa's involvement in the Palme assassination had come from a number of sources as early as the first few days after the murder.

The Middleman?

MEMO ON BERTIL WEDIN

Tip to *Searchlight* from a person with ties to right-wing extremism: rumor that Wedin acted as a "middleman" in Palme's assassination.

Cyprus, spring 1986: a person with a right-wing extremist past, now liberal and for many years an agent for MI6, runs into Wedin by chance. They are casual acquaintances and Wedin believes he is meeting someone "like minded." They start seeing each other, and to the question of what Wedin is doing in Cyprus, Wedin responds that he "is working for the Swedish Employers Association."

Recently the MI6 agent meets with G at *Searchlight* and says that he ran into Wedin. Since the agent is going back to

Cyprus, G asks him to dig up everything there is to find on Wedin. The agent and G have known each other quite well for many years since the agent "leaked" info about right-wing extremists to G, very probably at the request of MI6 or with MI6's knowledge.

In the fall of 1986, G receives a series of documents from the Cyprus source: passport, immigration documents, firsthand accounts from the Cyprus police, etc. The material is sent to Sweden where it is given to (a) the Palme investigation and (b) the Ministry of Foreign Affairs via Håkan Hermansson.

Spring 1987: The MI6 agent goes to see G again, this time upset, and demands to know what happened to the material on Wedin. "Did you give it to some outside party?" The source is nervous and agitated, but doesn't want to talk about why. During the summer and fall, the source lives in England, but gives a fake address to G, who repeatedly tries to make contact again.

Interpretations: The source acted without MI6's knowledge simply as a friendly favor to G. This leaked back to MI6 (through the Palme investigation or the Ministry of Foreign Affairs), which put

the source on the spot, or back to Wedin
who threatened to kill the source.

Spring 1987: Wedin contacts the Swedish
embassy and says that his passport is
missing.

Sources inside the Palme investigation
claim that they have not been in touch
with W, but would really like to be.

By his own admission, Wedin was "chief
of staff" of the Swedish UN battalion in
Cyprus in 1964-65.

Holmér's spokesman, Leif Hallberg,
served in Cyprus in about 1965 with the
rank of major.

BACKGROUND

Press reports say that Wedin previously
worked as a UN soldier in what was then
the Congo and in Cyprus. Multiple sources
report that after that, he began a career
as a mercenary recruiter.

Another source claims that his past
in the private soldiering business was
rather pathetic and unsuccessful, but
that Wedin often tries to appear "macho
and dangerous."

Since the mid to late 1970s, Wedin
had obtained or appropriated a reputation
of being "a gun for hire." One source
described him as a middleman in assassination contracts.

Several sources claim that Wedin has primarily worked for the South African secret police, the Bureau for State Security (BOSS), since the 1970s. The connection to BOSS is confirmed in part by the facts that came to light during the trial in London in 1983 when Wedin was charged for illegally possessing documents that were stolen during a break-in at African National Congress's (ANC) London office.

CYPRUS

For several years, Wedin and his English wife, Felicity Ann, have permanently resided in Cyprus. In their immigration documents, he stated the reason for entering Cyprus as "to live."

In the boxes you check to show if your visit pertains to tourism, business, or education, he marked the "other" box.

Wedin says he is a journalist and that he is registered as a freelance journalist with a Turkish reporter's pass from 1985. His journalistic activities are limited to three spots per week on a Turkish radio station, and to having written (parts of?) a tourist brochure for Cyprus.

When he arrived in Cyprus, he applied for a handgun license. As his reason, he indicated that he "needed a weapon" because he was "afraid of his former South African business contacts" (associates).

His application for a gun license was denied by the local police who handled the matter, but after that, Wedin acquired a shotgun. One source in the local police in Cyprus reports that "somebody very senior is looking after him."

My source's contact person in Cyprus, who is familiar with Wedin's background, reports that Wedin suddenly became aware that the contact person was poking around into his activities. At that point Wedin turned up at the contact person's residence. Wedin had been drinking and threatened to kill him; luckily a local police officer and good friend of the contact person was there and was able to disarm Wedin.

A while later, Wedin was arrested for driving under the influence. A source inside the local police says that they "let him continue drinking in the cell."

FINANCES

Sources in Cyprus describe Wedin's journalism earnings as "modest" in contrast to his "upmarket lifestyle": an expensive private home, frequenting certain exclusive nightclubs, etc.

According to reports, Wedin has assets worth SEK 600,000 divided into accounts

at various local Cypriot banks. There's
an additional SEK 100,000 in a "recently"
opened account in a London bank. The origin of the money is unknown, but in the
latter case, it is thought to have origi-
nated in the US (Note: the source does not
say whether the London money has been or
will be transferred to Cyprus).

PASSPORT

Wedin's passport, which was renewed at the
Swedish embassy in London in 1981, shows
that he regularly travels all over the
world: Tanzania (1981), Canada (1982), a
large number of trips to and from England,
etc.

In February 1985, he was in South
Africa.

WEDIN'S TRIPS

1982

January 7: Heathrow
January 12: Heathrow (possibly from Kenya/
Tanzania)
March 14: Heathrow
March 21: Heathrow (possibly from Greece)
May 6: Heathrow
May 10: Heathrow (from Montreal)

1983

April 19: Gatwick
April 23: Gatwick

1984

May 29: Dover
May 29: Heathrow
July 4: Heathrow

1985

February 18: Heathrow
February 19: South Africa
March 7: South Africa
March 8: Heathrow
November 20: Heathrow (emigration to Cyprus)

Between What and What?

Stockholm, Summer 1987

The memo ended up totaling thirty pages, which Stieg carefully made three copies of. He kept one copy for himself, gave one to Håkan Hermansson, and gave one to a friend as a backup. Stieg knew that Hermansson was in touch with Cabinet Secretary Pierre Schori in the Ministry of Foreign Affairs and thought he might receive a copy from Hermansson. Stieg personally delivered the final copy to the reception desk at police headquarters in an envelope labeled "For the Palme Group."

The next night Stieg couldn't sleep. He kept thinking about the key word in the statement from the MI6 source. Wedin was supposedly the middleman in the assassination of Olof Palme. A middleman would have needed someone on one side, presumably someone who wanted to get the job done, and someone on the other side, presumably someone who assisted with or carried out all or part of the job.

In Wedin's case, one side could have been a security service, most likely the South Africans, since he obviously actively worked for them.

But why would South Africa have been involved in the assassination of a politician halfway around the world? In fact, the South African theory wasn't as far-fetched as it sounded.

The South Africans had a motive: Palme's outspoken opposition to apartheid. And, if it was true, Palme's repeated attempts to stop their arms trading were further motivation for the South Africans to want him dead. They also had a history of demonstrated violence against those who opposed them, violence that did not stop at the level of heads of state.

There were a number of alternatives for who was on the other side of Wedin, but one possibility was that one or more people in Sweden had helped carry out the murder. The South Africans definitely had the ability to shoot someone, but carrying out an assassination on the other side of the world in a foreign city involved countless logistics, so Wedin's network of Swedish right-wing extremists could have come in exceedingly handy here.

Surveillance, transportation, and lodging would have been easier to take care of without being discovered if they had help on the ground from some well-positioned Swedes. Some of the right-wing extremists that Stieg was looking into could certainly have wanted to help, since they had their own reasons for wanting to get rid of Palme. Several of them had also figured in the official investigation.

In this way, the South Africans' motive, regardless of whether it had to do with arms trading or opposition to apartheid, did not conflict with the Swedish right-wing extremists' completely different motives. The right wingers believed that Olof Palme was a traitor, a spy that was going to sell Sweden out to the Soviet Union. And they believed it was going to happen soon. In April 1986, less than two months after he was murdered, Olof Palme was supposed to have gone to Moscow on the first official visit to the Soviet Union by a Swedish prime minister in thirty years. This was a time when the right wingers truly believed that

Sweden was at risk of losing its sovereignty and becoming the sixteenth Soviet republic.

The apparently logical conclusion that the South African security services and Swedish right wingers could have joined forces despite completely different motives helped Stieg finally fall asleep.

It all makes sense. Over and out.

Deep Wedin

If Stieg's South African / Swedish right-wing extremist theory was going to become more concrete, he would need to dig deeper into its various segments. It made sense to start from the middle, or in this case with the middleman, Wedin, and see where the threads led from there, both toward the South Africans and toward the Swedes.

Wedin's résumé was colorful, to put it mildly. He was a UN officer in the Congo in 1963, where he was taken hostage, and then he was in Cyprus in 1964–1965. During the 1960s, he supposedly worked as a mercenary and later recruited mercenaries for Rhodesia, which was confirmed in at least one case.

After he returned to Sweden, he served as an officer, and at one point in the early 1970s, he went to the American embassy and unsuccessfully offered his services in the Vietnam War. When he was forced to leave his military career, he went straight to the Wallenberg group of companies. This conglomerate was owned by the Wallenberg family and was by far Sweden's most influential financial group, controlling a majority of Sweden's multinationals, and still employing 40 percent of Sweden's industrial workforce. Wedin got a job as a journalist in Wallenberg's newly established news agency Press-Extrakt. In 1975, Wedin and his family moved yet again, this time to London.

In his new hometown, Wedin continued working for Swedish trade and industry, and he also began the ultraconservative Monday Club with Lord Moyne as chairman. Gerry and his source had met both Wedin and Anders Larsson, who also frequented the Monday Club, there—the same Anders Larsson who, a number of years later, just days prior to the assassination, would send warnings to government offices that Olof Palme was going to be assassinated. Wedin and Larsson had obviously been acquainted in London in 1975, but Wedin was actually on the same side as Larsson's antagonists in the Contra set. Wedin's ties to Carl G. Holm were stronger than his ties to Anders Larsson, since Wedin had recruited Holm for the Federation of Swedish Industries. In fact, at some point Wedin had begun to consider Anders Larsson an enemy, possibly even a spy working for the Soviet Union.

In 1980, Bertil Wedin made a trip to South Africa, where he went to see Craig Williamson, a South African security services agent who has been widely written about. Williamson, a police officer who advanced within the security services, was hailed as "the Master Spy" in the South African press. For three years he had infiltrated the International University Exchange Fund (IUEF), an international organization based in Geneva, Switzerland, that gave scholarships to students in developing nations. Part of the scholarship money was sent to people who worked to oppose oppressive regimes. One of the regimes that the IUEF had annoyed was the South African apartheid government, which reacted by sending Williamson to pose as an anti-apartheid activist and infiltrate the organization.

The director of the IUEF was a Swede, Lars-Gunnar Eriksson, with direct ties to several high-ranking Social Democratic politicians. He was in routine contact with "the three musketeers"—Bernt Carlsson, Pierre Schori, and Mats Hellström—who all had prominent positions within the Social Democrats. If necessary, Eriksson also had Olof Palme's ear.

Through an ingenious ruse, Craig Williamson convinced Lars-Gunnar Eriksson that, even though he was obviously a white South

African police officer, he was actually opposed to the apartheid regime, and Eriksson recruited Craig Williamson to work at the IUEF in early 1977.

Soon Williamson was second in command in the organization and responsible for handling all the administration, including making payments. The result was that a large portion of the money that was supposed to go to *opposing* apartheid instead went toward *supporting* apartheid. With some of the money, Williamson bought a farm in South Africa a little more than ten miles from the capital, Pretoria. At the farm, Swedes who were in the area could come admire how black freedom fighters were trained. When their visit was over, everyone would go back to their actual activities: torturing apartheid opponents.

Through his position, Williamson also received information about what the apartheid opposition was up to. When black anti-apartheid activist Steve Biko planned to travel to Botswana in September 1977 to meet Olof Palme and the ANC's Oliver Tambo, Williamson passed the information along to his colleagues within the South African police. On August 18, 1977, Steve Biko was arrested at a roadblock and beaten severely during his interrogation. He died of his injuries on September 12. Biko was just one example of the anti-apartheid activists who died as a result of Craig Williamson's actions.

In the spring of 1980, Bertil Wedin and Craig Williamson met in a hotel bar in Johannesburg, which led to a commission for Wedin to work with Williamson's company, Africa Aviation Consultants, that lasted for years. The ample monthly remuneration allowed Wedin to maintain his relatively expensive lifestyle with a twelve-room home in fashionable Kent (near London), England.

The years that followed were intense, including multiple bombings and break-ins that Williamson was responsible for. In March 1982, a bomb exploded in the ANC's office in London, but no one was injured. In August 1982, Olof Palme's friend Ruth First was killed by a mail bomb in her home in Maputo, Mozambique. In June 1984, the anti-apartheid activist Jeannette Schoon and her six-year-old daughter, Katryn, were killed by a letter bomb in Lubango, Angola.

In London, Wedin also worked for South African agent Peter Casselton, a former helicopter pilot from Rhodesia. Casselton was sentenced to prison in 1983 for his involvement in breaking into several black liberation movement offices, but Bertil Wedin was acquitted of the same crimes, even though the British police found documents from the break-ins in his home.

Later, Bertil Wedin called a press conference where he was going to explain his dealings with the South African security services. Instead the press conference grew into an attack on the Swedish government; Wedin said, "I oppose Palme and the Swedish government. I do it in cooperation with intelligence agencies in the Scandinavian countries."

The next interesting event took place in November 1985. Three months before the murder of Olof Palme, Wedin and his family suddenly made a permanent move to the Turkish Republic of Northern Cyprus, a country that had a population of three hundred thousand and a reputation as a sanctuary for criminals, since there were no extradition agreements with other countries besides Turkey. Bertil Wedin was also a personal friend of President Rauf Denktaş, which should have made his life in the country even safer.

***

It was definitely within the realm of possibility that South Africa could organize an assassination on the other side of the planet. If they were going to do it, it's also likely that they would have used their best spy, Craig Williamson, who was also quite familiar with both Stockholm and the Swedish culture from his time as an IUEF infiltrator. Since Wedin was included in Williamson's stable of agents, he could very well have played the role of middleman. But who, then, would have been on the other side?

The obvious reasons to hire Wedin were that he was Swedish, spoke the language, and was familiar with the city of Stockholm, but it had been more than ten years since he had moved to London, so his knowledge was beginning to be dated. But maybe he knew the right kinds of people, such as right-wing extremists who wanted to get rid of Olof Palme. Wedin's network was also old, but Stieg had observed for himself that many of the people involved in 1980s right-wing extremism had a history from the 1970s Democratic Alliance in which Wedin had been active.

Having reviewed the material he had about South Africa's security services and Wedin's boss, Craig Williamson, Stieg felt more comfortable when he started looking into Wedin's Swedish network. This deep dive into the last two decades of right-wing extremism in Sweden couldn't have felt more familiar to Stieg.

Gerry

"A workaholic, he and I had that in common," Gerry Gable said. "A sense of humor, but very dedicated. If he got his teeth into a story, then he wouldn't let go, and that's what makes a good journalist."

I had traveled to London to meet Gerry. He came up over and over again in Stieg's materials, and it was clear that he was one of Stieg's major role models. They regularly sent each other tips and bounced ideas off each other.

Gerry definitely knew how Stieg worked, and if I was lucky, he would tell me something that would help propel me along Stieg's line of inquiry. During our conversation it became evident how important the personal side of their relationship had been. Gerry said that they wouldn't have worked so well together if they hadn't had such a profound respect for each other and been able to lighten things up with their shared sense of humor.

Gerry had suggested that we meet at a greasy spoon, by which he meant a low-key pub, and I enjoyed the typical English atmosphere, although the food less so.

"And how did you approach the inquiry into Wedin?" I asked.

"I had an informant who was a bodyguard for one of the most well-known fascists. That guy helped me get into the conservative Monday Club and introduced me to Anders Larsson," Gerry said. "Out of the blue one day in the early '80s, he wondered if I might like to tag along with him to this really pricey lunch with a person who was big in the Democratic Alliance in Sweden. It turned out not to be Anders Larsson, as I had expected, but Bertil Wedin."

"And what was your impression of him?"

"He looked like a very fit, successful businessman," Gerry said. "Elegant suit, handmade shoes, tie, courteous demeanor. He seemed to belong to the top echelon of the Swedish business world. But he had a vacant look in his eyes, as if he were looking right through you."

"And your informant, that was your source?"

"Yes, I can finally say that now," Gerry said. "His name is Lesley Wooler. He feared for his life when he was gathering the information about Wedin in Cyprus."

"So what he did was a type of infiltration. Is that something you did often?" I asked.

"My job, when we did infiltrations in England, was to find candidates, give them infiltration training, and place them in extremist groups. Sometimes I was forced to talk to our intelligence service. Like when we heard about Nazis who had weapons, explosives, or were involved in some other criminal activity."

After about two hours, I had eaten my fill of fish and chips, and we decided to call it a night. We exchanged business cards, as I knew I would come up with more questions to ask Gerry. But I had already learned one of the most important things. If journalists want to find out something from someone who doesn't want to talk, they need to utilize methods that are more effective than an interview. In Stieg's case, that had included anything from infiltrations to computer hacking. I wondered how Stieg would have used social media if it had been around when he was alive. I knew if I was going to get any further in this investigation, I was most likely going to have to leave my comfort zone and try out some more controversial methods of information gathering. If I wanted to do his work justice, I was going to have to think and act more like Stieg.

The Right-Wing Extremists

Stockholm, September 1987

Stieg took out the lists that he had sent Hermansson at the beginning of "Mission: Olof Palme" to see who had been part of Bertil Wedin's network of contacts before he moved to London in 1975. It was reasonable to assume that if Wedin was looking for logistics assistance for South African agents in Sweden, he would begin with people he already knew and trusted.

Not only had Wedin been associated with the Democratic Alliance, WACL, and a couple of the organizations that were close to Swedish trade and industry, including the Federation of Swedish Industries (Industriförbundet) and the news agency Press-Extrakt, where he worked, but he had also worked as a freelancer for Säpo, where there was relevant experience in surveillance, for example. It was unclear who his contact there was, though one obvious name was Tore Forsberg, who was responsible for counterespionage, but Stieg was not able to obtain confirmation of that.

Among all the people on Stieg's list, there were only a couple whom Stieg was sure Wedin knew and who were relevant to the Palme case. Carl G. Holm was close to Wedin, and Wedin had made sure Holm was recruited by the Federation of Swedish Industries. Anders Larsson and Wedin knew each other from the Democratic Alliance, the Monday Club in London, and another organization called the Swedish Liberty Council (Svenske Frihetsrådet). Both Holm and Larsson had been mentioned in connection with the Palme assassination, but one thing was very sure: Wedin wouldn't have been able to turn to both of them to help the South Africans, because they had been sworn enemies of each other since the Democratic Alliance had splintered. Stieg suspected that Anders Larsson was the anonymous source for the book *To the Right of Neutrality* (*Till höger om neutraliteten*), which was written by Stieg's friend Sven Ove Hansson. That book described how extremist opinions found their way into Swedish trade and industry, with the case of Carl G. Holm described in detail. It also seemed as if Holm himself suspected Anders Larsson's role, because the magazine *Contra* published articles that suggested that Larsson worked for the KGB.

In this case, Wedin could have made an arrangement with only one of them, or maybe both if they had no knowledge of the other's involvement.

Carl G. Holm was relatively easy to investigate. His name came up in connection with the magazine *Contra*, whose Palme-face dartboard cover became an easy symbol of the unbound Palme hatred that preceded the assassination. Holm seemed to be a nasty guy, although many within the right-wing-extremist scene were. It started with their opinions and continued into their personalities, or maybe it was the other way around. But that didn't mean that all the extremists were involved in the assassination; with regard to Holm, there was actually very little evidence implicating him. The situation was different with Wedin's other close acquaintance.

Anders Larsson's name was connected to *all* the organizations on the list that Stieg had put together for Hermansson and Wenander. Since Stieg had written that list, he had obtained more documents, particularly relating to his work with Hermansson and Wenander, which revealed even more remarkable circumstances.

In a letter dated January 20, 1986, just over a month before the assassination of Olof Palme, the Baltic Committee fired Anders Larsson from his position. In connection with his dismissal, one of the organization's representatives had called Larsson "a nobody." Larsson was furious and responded: "Me, a nobody? Soon you'll see: blood will be shed, people will be wading in blood."

That same day, SSI agent Joel Haukka received a letter from Anders Larsson where he described himself sitting with a Jean Duvalier in front of a roaring fire at the Sheraton-Stockholm Hotel bar and said that the fire "reminds me of the future for some people after they were deported to the place where they come from—traitors, crooks . . . and others." The next day, Haukka received a card in the mail in which Larsson asked Haukka "not to worry about the previous letter from the bar."

On February 16, twelve days before the assassination, Anders Larsson and an acquaintance followed Palme when he went to the memorial service for Alva Myrdal at Stockholm Cathedral and ascertained that "Palme's security coverage is bad."

On February 20, just eight days before the assassination, Anders Larsson delivered his warning to the Ministry of Foreign Affairs and the Swedish government offices that Palme was going to be killed.

During that same period, Larsson also said that "the biggest thing in my life was going to happen soon."

After Palme's assassination, two of Larsson's acquaintances—parliamentary stenographer Bengt Henningsson and bookseller Bo Ragnar Ståhl—were convinced that he had been involved in the killing in some way.

Stieg also read that Bertil Wedin himself had recently claimed that he was privy to a plot that supposedly involved Anders Larsson. Wedin claimed that the plan had been to kill Wedin and blame the murder of Palme on him so that he would become the scapegoat. One of Wedin's pieces of evidence for this was a call list from Northern Cyprus's state-run phone company, which he had access to. From that list, also according to Wedin, it was clear that Anders Larsson had been in close contact with an Englishman in Cyprus who worked for the KGB.

The details were numerous and striking, and yet only created more questions. If Larsson was involved in the murder, then why would he pass on the warning? Why would Wedin have hired Anders Larsson, who belonged to the enemy faction of the splintered Democratic Alliance? And would any professional organization really have used such an obviously hard-to-control and unbalanced person as Larsson for anything important whatsoever?

The details about Anders Larsson just didn't seem to add up. If Stieg's nighttime musings a few weeks earlier had concluded with *It all makes sense*, then this new more thorough analysis concluded with *No, nothing makes sense*.

The South Africans would have needed someone who could help them with surveillance, someone who had experience. Other groups would have been much better suited to that than loud-mouthed right-wing extremists—like people from the police, Säpo, or the military. There was also a lot of information that had come out in the first year after the shooting that pointed to surveillance having been conducted by professionals on the night of the assassination. The problem was that there was no proven contact between Wedin and these groups, just several likely connections and startling coincidences, like with Anders Larsson.

Operation Appendix

Stockholm, September 1987

Stieg reread his own letter to Gerry, which he had written on March 20, 1986, not quite three weeks after the assassination. The only significant topic he had mentioned in the letter that he still hadn't had time to look into was what had come to be known as "the police trail."

The "police trail" rubric covered quite a bit of information on ten police officers who had become of interest in the investigation for different reasons. Some of them were interesting for having attended meetings where vitriol against Palme had flowed freely, or having access to potential murder weapons, or having traveled to South Africa, or even having been in the vicinity of the assassination. Several of them had belonged to the Baseball Gang, which was a particular group within the Norrmalm police that was started by Hans Holmér at the beginning of the 1980s to stem street violence. The nickname had come about not because the group played baseball but because the members preferred to wear civilian attire, including baseball caps, instead of their uniforms. Their reputation had taken a blow after several individuals they had arrested complained of mistreatment, and one person even died.

Many of the police officers working on the Palme investigation were also members of Stockholm's Defense Shooting Club, where among other things, people learned to shoot with Magnum revolvers side by side with right-wing extremists.

Carl-Gustav Östling had been a patrol officer in Norrmalm and a member of Stockholm's Defense Shooting Club, and he was the police officer with the longest list of compromising factors.

One week before the assassination, Östling had an operation for a burst appendix with peritonitis at Stockholm South General Hospital and was on temporary sick leave. On the day of the assassination, against his doctor's advice, he signed himself out and went home. He said he was alone at home when Palme was assassinated. Several of his friends confirmed that he was in pain and had a difficult time walking, which meant that he could hardly have carried out the murder, but no one saw him after nine o'clock on the night of the assassination. Säpo wrote off the suspicions against him by March 24, even though he lacked an alibi. Yet the Palme investigation kept receiving tips about Östling. He was an arms expert and sold weapons. He had a documented hatred of Palme, and there were several photos of him doing the Nazi salute.

Despite suspicions of involvement in the assassination and his Nazi interests, a few months after the murder, Hans Holmér entrusted Östling with the task of supplying the Palme investigation with weapons, bulletproof vests, encrypted walkie-talkies, and bulletproof glass. The trickiest part of the order was a submachine gun built into an attaché case. Östling's newly started company, Strateg Protector, which he ran with a good friend, had won the bid. Östling never went back to work as a police officer after his appendix operation.

A year later, the customs crimes investigation police, a different arm of the police entirely, raided Östling's home. They found a number of items of interest, specifically: 218 boxes of ammunition, twenty pistols, four revolvers (several of which were loaded), one pump-action shotgun, one Mauser, one gas grenade, five machine-gun belts, three smoke grenades, five grenades, three smoke bombs, eight tear gas sprayers, miscellaneous German helmets and bayonets, one antitank grenade launcher, one recoilless antitank rifle, antiaircraft ammunition, and four diamonds worth a total of SEK 200,000. The weapons found could be deemed part of Östling's illegal arms dealings, but some of the other items found were more puzzling. In thirteen photos, Östling and his partner in the arms business could both be seen giving the Nazi salute in locations such as a Jewish cemetery, in front of Berlin's Brandenburg Gate, and in Hitler's Eagle's Nest at Berchtesgaden in the Bavarian Alps.

But there were two other items that Stieg thought pertinent to the Palme murder. One was a postcard supposedly sent by Östling's friend from school Claes Almgren, who was on *Contra* magazine's board. The text read: "The pig on the other side is still terrified by the facial composite, but the railroad tracks are heating up. Get in touch with the Enskede man ASAP." It was hard to make any sense of what that meant, but it seemed likely that Östling and some of his right-wing friends were worried about the police investigation.

The other item of possible relevance to the Palme assassination found at Östling's house was a Winchester .357 Magnum 158 grain metal-piercing bullet. It was the same uncommon type of bullet that was used to assassinate Olof Palme.

Almost all of the ten police officers included in the "police trail" line of inquiry had some connection to Östling. If the South Africans used Swedish police officers or military personnel for surveillance and other assistance, that could explain many of the suspicious coincidences surrounding Östling. Or to put it another way, since Stieg was testing the theory about South Africa with Wedin as a middleman: If South Africa had arranged the murder and Östling *wasn't* involved, despite all the aggravating circumstances, then Stieg would eat his hat. Although he'd have to buy the hat first, since he didn't own one.

Sweden's Grand Prize for Journalism

Stockholm, December 1987

"For their article series 'Mission: Olof Palme.' With vast knowledge and a keen sense of nuance, they mapped out various unknown conditions in the society in which the assassination of Prime Minister Olof Palme took place. Their work methods are an example of good investigative journalism. The articles go deep and wide and don't waver in the face of complicated contexts."

Håkan Hermansson and Lars Wenander were awarded the Swedish Grand Prize for Journalism in 1987, in the Daily Press category. In addition to the series of articles, they finally published a book in which the articles became chapters along with minor addendums. Stieg Larsson's name was mentioned very briefly in the preface. He was conscious of the fact that his biggest misgiving prior to the project was his concern about being outed as a contributor, but the mention was so small, he hoped that it would pass under the right-wing extremists' radar.

Stieg was satisfied. He saw how much of the book was built on his research. All the organizations he had mapped out previously were included, and when people read the book in one sitting, the situation that Olof Palme was in before he was killed really hit them. Palme was truly under attack from all sides.

In the chapter on Bertil Wedin, the authors avoided mentioning Wedin by name, but identifying him would take only a couple of phone calls asking the right questions by anyone who wanted to find out who it was about.

Stieg saw his own wording used in places and was able to bask a little in the glow of one of the most widely written-about pieces of journalism at the time.

***

One by one the threads had been woven together. What had mostly resembled a jumble of separate theories and leads in the beginning was starting to form a picture that was certainly still murky but also coherent: South Africa could have used their middleman Wedin to find Swedes who could have, in their various ways, helped assassinate Olof Palme.

It was December 22, 1987, and many of Stieg's colleagues at TT took a long lunch break to squeeze in a little last-minute Christmas shopping. Stieg sat at his desk, deeply absorbed in his work on an illustration he was creating. He had been sitting there for a couple of hours undisturbed and was nearly finished when his phone rang. It was Alf Andersson with the police, and he sounded excited. He and Stieg had exchanged a fair amount of information since their first meeting more than a year earlier. Alf's news was brief.

"We've had a wiretap on Victor Gunnarsson for the last few months. Today we served him a summons on suspicion of participating in the assassination of Olof Palme."

That was fantastic news. Just as Stieg had hoped based on signs he had seen that fall, the police had used the information they'd received from him, Håkan Hermansson, other journalists, and private detectives. The regular investigators had clearly been filling the vacuum that had formed after Hans Holmér left, and it was starting to pay off now.

To Stieg it meant butterflies in his stomach. Perhaps he might finally be able to take some time off over Christmas now that there was something exciting to look forward to after New Year's. The assassination would be solved. And maybe even Stieg himself had contributed in some small way.

Hans II

In December 1987, Victor Gunnarsson was notified for the second time that he was under suspicion in connection with the assassination of Olof Palme. The first time he had been suspected of having carried out the murder. This time, he was suspected of complicity in the murder. There were many circumstances that pointed to Gunnarsson having known that something was going to happen and his possible involvement. Before the murder he had been in contact with other people who were included in the investigation—for example, Anders Larsson and Ivan von Birchan, who had both issued warnings before the murder. Gunnarsson was near the crime scene on the night of the murder, had expressed his hatred of Palme, and a couple of hours *before* the murder, had been quoted saying that "you can be shot in the back in Sweden because of your opinions."

The investigation had heated up over the fall. Expectations were high as Sweden headed toward the Christmas holidays. It was clear that the investigative hierarchy would change again and that the new leader would be handpicked from Tommy Lindström's team within the National Criminal Investigation Department.

The most likely candidate was Hans Ölvebro, an experienced police officer who made a completely different impression than his predecessor, Hans Holmér. Ölvebro did not seek out the spotlight, but he wasn't afraid to face the media when he had to.

Ölvebro's boss, Tommy Lindström, and the prosecutors liked what they saw in him. Just as they themselves had wanted, Ölvebro proposed to start with the location of the crime: Sveavägen. Hans Ölvebro supported the idea that any suspects the police wanted to look into needed to be linked to the time and location of the murder before any further action could be approved. The logic was simple: Whoever shot Olof Palme must have been on Sveavägen, so that was the place to begin. If they tied a suspect to the murder location, then everything would fall into place. The elegance of this strategy was that it was rooted in one of the three pillars of proving guilt in a criminal case—in other words, motive, weapon, and opportunity. At the same time, it limited the risk of further media scandals similar to those surrounding the PKK line of inquiry in the first year, when Holmér had started from the presumption that the PKK was involved despite having found no evidence.

The prosecutors helped clean up the ongoing investigation before Ölvebro started. For example, police requests to wiretap Alf Enerström, his girlfriend, Gio Petré, and a third person were rejected because there was no evidence that they had been on Sveavägen. In January, the prosecutor yet again dismissed the suspicions against Victor Gunnarsson. The police on the team were surprised, but the action was quickly explained once Ölvebro took charge.

"This is no simple conspiracy," he claimed. "It was a lone madman and that is harder to find than a needle in a haystack."

On February 5, 1988, Hans Ölvebro officially became the leader of the Palme investigation and had his team start looking for the lone madman. He applied his interpretation of Occam's razor in full: the simplest solution was the right one.

According to the new leadership team, Ölvebro's professional approach would surely stop the leaks. If anything was going to be leaked to the media, it would be done intentionally in order to achieve results.

The Palme investigation had taken a new turn; now there would be no room for bombastic conspiracies involving South Africa, right-wing extremists, or corrupt police officers.

Ebbe Picks Up Speed

At the time of Olof Palme's assassination, Hans Holmér had been staying at the home of his friend, the publisher Ebbe Carlsson. This temporary arrangement, occasioned by Holmér's divorce, ended as soon as he found his own apartment, but Carlsson continued to be involved in the investigation as Holmér's constant companion, always ready to provide his advice and assistance as soon as Holmér asked for it. And sometimes even when he didn't ask for it. Which is how Ebbe had come to be present at the first meeting with Prime Minister Ingvar Carlsson and in the police's Palme Room with Holmér during those first days.

Most people probably thought that the investigation would stop pursuing the Kurdish liberation movement PKK after Holmér so lamentably failed to produce evidence through Operation Alpha. But Holmér and Ebbe's fixation on the PKK's possible involvement continued; they were convinced that the PKK was the solution to the case. It was unclear whether they were convinced that someone in that organization really was guilty or if that was just a politically expedient solution. Hans Holmér and Ebbe Carlsson had been Olof Palme's and the Social Democrats' "fixers" for a long time, and if they succeeded in producing an acceptable solution to the murder, everyone would be happy. Besides, Hans Holmér had already received the Swede of the Year award. Perhaps Ebbe could hope for the same thing if he helped solve the Palme murder.

On June 1, the media bomb burst. The newspaper *Expressen* wrote that Ebbe Carlsson had been pursuing a secret parallel investigation into the PKK line of inquiry with the consent of leading politicians and officials. The next day, it came to light that, as a private individual, Ebbe had received a personal letter of recommendation from Justice Minister Anna-Greta Leijon to use in contacts with foreign officials. The letter was registered and immediately classified as secret when the press began writing about it. The same day, Holmér's former bodyguard Per-Ola Karlsson was stopped by customs officials as he tried to smuggle illegal wiretapping equipment into the country. It later came out that the South African legation was the buyer listed on the invoice, and the person behind the delivery was arms dealer and former police officer Carl-Gustav Östling.

To the question of why he had specifically written the South African legation as the recipient, Östling responded, "Well, I had to write something." In fact, the equipment smuggled in had been used by Ebbe Carlsson to wiretap and bug the PKK. Day by day, the scandal grew. All the political parties in the Swedish parliament apart from the Social Democrats declared a lack of confidence in Anna-Greta Leijon as justice minister. She quit on June 7, 1988.

In a new twist in the case, journalist Cecilia Hagen wondered in *Expressen* on June 9, "What kind of hold does Ebbe Carlsson have on the men in power?" insinuating a conspiracy of gay Social Democrats.

The political opposition reported several ministers of the government to the constitutional board of the Swedish Parliament. For many months to come, the Swedish public was overwhelmed, disgusted, and entertained by the live TV broadcasts of the parliamentary hearings of a number of the key players—a farcical parallel to the Iran-Contra hearings in the United States one year earlier. The Ebbe Carlsson affair, as it was called, had grown to monumental proportions. Still, for the most part, the patient Swedes went on with their lives. Others started to think that there was something quite rotten going on in Stockholm.

And yet again, complete confusion prevailed in the investigation into the assassination of Olof Palme.

Doubts

The news that the police suspected Victor Gunnarsson of complicity had led Stieg to momentarily relax. He and Eva did not work in the days between Christmas and New Year's. Instead they took walks and had long conversations over bottles of wine at the kitchen table. But the new year began with a nasty surprise when they learned that the police had suddenly written off their suspicions against Gunnarsson—a signal that the investigation was about to move in a different direction once more.

After the initial shock subsided, a thought started to take shape in Stieg: What if he had walked into the most basic of journalistic traps and combined different pieces of information into something that looked like a whole picture, using imagination as the spackle to fill in any gaps? Maybe he had just been carried along by what he'd previously known about right-wing extremists and, along with other people, had begun to see patterns in the information that he received from the police, which he then expanded on and tipped the police off about, who then thought that entirely new information had come in. That sometimes happened when journalists, the police, and the public mistook idle gossip for evidence.

Stieg was a researcher with a specific focus on right-wing extremists, and he had seen a possibility that Olof Palme was murdered by someone from those circles. But how objective was he really, compared to an investigative team leader with years of experience? If Hans Ölvebro looked at all the possibilities and concluded that this was the work of a lone wolf, then that must have been the result of careful analysis of the murder and the available evidence. It was time for Stieg to at least try, based on the scant information that had leaked from the investigative team, to prove the theory the police now considered the most credible.

As summer approached, Eva convinced him that they should rent a vacation cabin. Late one night in June, when the Scandinavian summer sky was still light, they sat out on the deck and chatted over a glass of wine. For the first time, Stieg shared his thoughts about how a lone wolf scenario would have played out and Eva helped him hammer out the details.

When they returned home to Stockholm, it was time to test their theory on an outsider, someone with a healthy dose of skepticism, someone who Stieg trusted to give them a qualified assessment.

He hadn't known Anna-Lena Lodenius all that long, but it was already quite clear that they complemented each other's strengths nicely. Anna-Lena had only recently graduated with her degree in journalism, but she had chosen to specialize in studying xenophobic and racist groups. She shared Stieg's dedication to fighting right-wing extremism, but otherwise they were quite different. Stieg was the eternal researcher who kept digging long after a deadline had passed. Anna-Lena was the one who organized things to make them understandable to an outsider, and she was the one who wanted to complete one project, then move on to the next. Stieg could draw pictures of networks showing the contacts between people and organizations, sometimes based solely on circumstantial evidence or gut feelings. Anna-Lena would question ideas and demand facts. Together, their skills were unbeatable. She would be the perfect devil's advocate for him to test his latest theory on.

Profile of a Killer

Stockholm, August 3, 1988

Hi Anna-Lena,
Here's a slightly odd letter from someone who just got home from vacation. You
should regard the thoughts in this letter as unfounded and purely meaningless
speculations, but it would be fun if you
would take the time to reflect on it a
little bit and let me know if it stirs up
any ideas for you.

It pertains to the Palme assassination,
and my reasoning basically goes like this:
Like most other people, I have assumed
that the murder was an organized, planned
act by some very well-financed right-wing
group—pick whichever one, they're all more
or less the same—rather than it being one
lone crazy person who happened to be out

taking an evening stroll with his pistol. But time is passing, and I think the odds are beginning to decrease that a large group was involved. If it were, somewhere or other, information would have started leaking.

The theory that it was a lone madman has been in the picture from the beginning, but as far as I can tell, the police have shown very little interest in it. Holmér was too busy chasing Kurdish conspiracies and—to a certain extent—EAPers. We who keep an eye on the right wing have scrutinized the better-known organizations: the WACL, Delle Chiaie's gang, etc.

So what I did on vacation was supposition, and from there I let my imagination run wild.

Assume that we were wrong and that it actually was a lone madman or an extremely small group consisting of maybe two or three people. How should we behave in order to identify him/them?

I sat with Eva one night and discussed this, and we did a little thought experiment, tossed ideas back and forth, and tried to work backward by putting together a kind of portrait of the murderer.

Our reasoning went like this—instead of asking ourselves where he went after he ran up the stairs on Tunnel Street [Tunnelgatan], we asked ourselves the

questions: Where had he come from? What
do we know about him?

We came up with the following:

1) He's Swedish, probably living in
Stockholm. (That assumption is motivated
by the fact that it was February and low
season for tourists, that he seems to have
had pretty good local knowledge, and that
Sveavägen isn't the first place a casual
visitor goes.)

2) He's between 30 and 45 years old. (This
is based on basically unanimous information
from the witness statements.)

3) His build is slim rather than brawny,
average height or somewhat taller than
average. (Again, from witness statements. A
chubby guy would have been reported on in a
different way.)

A few days ago, when we were discussing
just this, a coworker at TT said that he
personally was convinced that the solution
to the Palme assassination was extremely
simple. It's hard to liberate yourself
from the idea that while the police are
running around chasing Kurds and other
terrorists, the real murderer is standing around quietly on a street corner,
watching.

To summarize: we are looking for a
middle-aged, solitary, brooding guy with
access to a weapon and who lives near the
scene of the murder or had a specific
reason to visit Sveavägen wearing regular
shoes on that freezing, slippery February
night.

Listen, Anna-Lena, it strikes me that
in Ebbe Carlsson's Sweden, this line of
argument seems almost a little, well,
undramatic. But couldn't you juggle the
ideas a little, talk with your guy, and
see if we can flesh out this profile a
little more? If this is the way it happened, it shouldn't be totally impossible
to stumble across the right person someday. At any rate, the chances would be
a little higher than if we're chasing a
hired professional from Brazil.

Sincerely,

Stieg

***

A few days after receiving Stieg's letter, Anna-Lena came to see him
at TT so they could talk for a while over a cup of coffee. Together,
they concluded that Stieg's new thinking was logical. This theory also
explained the biggest objection to a conspiracy: if multiple people knew
who was behind the murder, surely someone would have spilled the
beans by now. With the latest increase in the reward, there were fifty
million reasons to start talking. In short, Anna-Lena confirmed what
Eva had said a few days earlier, and Stieg reluctantly admitted that the

lone madman theory was the one he believed in most strongly himself at this point. It was time for him to set aside his thorough research into the possible involvement of right-wing extremists in Olof Palme's murder. Someone else would solve the case. Stieg would devote his time and energy to fighting right-wing extremism. At least until something new came to light that suggested a conspiracy . . .

A Suitable Murderer

The last month of 1988 was eventful. On Wednesday, December 14, forty-one-year-old drug addict Christer Pettersson was brought in for questioning with regard to the assassination of Olof Palme. That same night, Lisbeth Palme picked Pettersson out of a video lineup as the one who best matched her own description of the man who had murdered her husband nearly three years earlier.

Rumors had been circulating for a couple of months, but under Hans Ölvebro, the investigative team had succeeded in holding the information close enough that the news hit like a bombshell. What everyone had been hoping for had really happened. The news was everywhere, on the TV news broadcasts *Rapport* and *Aktuellt*, on Ekot's radio news reports, in the local Stockholm and provincial newspapers. The headlines were in the biggest fonts. The global media reported on the miracle.

A couple of tips had come in about Pettersson during the first month following the assassination, but they had been set aside after a brief check. The investigative lead now described how genuine, focused police work had panned out and how they had managed to find Pettersson in the existing research.

Pettersson was a notorious criminal who was well known to the Stockholm police and the underworld. He committed mostly minor crimes like robberies, assault and battery, and shoplifting for money to buy alcohol and drugs, but in 1970 he had stabbed a man to death with a bayonet on Kungsgatan, only five hundred feet from the location where Palme was killed, which showed that he was capable of killing a person.

On December 16, Pettersson was arrested on probable cause for the murder of Olof Palme.

***

Another piece of news of almost equal magnitude was the honor that was always awarded at the end of the year. On December 29, the much-derided editor Ebbe Carlsson was named Swede of the Year, just as his good friend Hans Holmér had been two years earlier. Immediately there were rumors that it was the nail in the coffin for the award. No one would want to be Swede of the Year after those two gentlemen.

***

In the months after the arrest, the police and prosecutors prepared evidence against Christer Pettersson, and on June 5, 1989, his trial began. The court proceedings at city hall on Kungsholmen island in Stockholm went off like clockwork, and the prosecutors' hopes were not in vain. According to the court system, the unsolvable murder had finally been solved. On July 27, 1989, despite pleading not guilty, Christer Pettersson was convicted of the murder of Olof Palme.

It was an enormous triumph. Investigative team leader Hans Ölvebro beamed. Journalists basked in the glory and wrote told-you-so pieces, as if Sweden had just pulled off some phenomenal international sporting win. The Swedish police were applauded for fixing their previous mistakes through dogged persistence.

A minority of voices questioned the ruling, but they were dismissed. To be sure, most people had hoped for a somewhat worthier explanation than a random killing by a shabby junkie, but it was what it was. Sweden's prime minister had fallen prey to his own dream of an open society where politicians mingled with the people; he had been murdered by a drug-addled madman. The Swedish people had closure. It wasn't some big conspiracy. No foreign spy organizations, no groups of Palme haters with offshoots penetrating the Swedish business world, and no military or police involvement. Just a lone madman, without political ties or consequences. In that sense, one could say that Christer Pettersson was an unusually suitable murderer.

Sweden would have been able to return to its quiet, northerly existence if it weren't for the fact that the wheels of justice kept turning.

The Killer

Stockholm, Summer 1989

It was during the time between the euphoria following the city court's ruling and the preparations leading up to the case being heard in appeals court that something began to chafe. No one had expected that the ruling would gain legal force without an appeal or that there wouldn't be critical voices speaking out against the guilty verdict. That was merely part of the game. In the meantime, Stieg read everything that was published about the case and talked to people he thought would be able to flesh out his own picture of what was going on. Somewhere in there, doubt began to grow again in his mind. What remained when you critically scrutinized what was said in the ruling and in the preliminary investigation, which had now been made public?

The first important fact was that for a guilty verdict, the majority of the court members were not as convinced of his guilt as it might seem. It was true that there were six in favor and two opposed, but upon taking a closer look, it was easy to see that the lay judges were the ones who had voted to convict Christer Pettersson.

The way the Swedish system worked, lay judges were politically appointed and were not trained lawyers. The city court's two qualified members had voted not to convict. That meant that the person who had been convicted of murdering a politician had, in fact, been convicted by people who were politically appointed. It was as if only carpenters would form the jury in the case of a murdered carpenter. Lay judges were obviously emotionally engaged in finding and sentencing the murderer. The members of the court with backgrounds in law, who were experienced in considering evidence, on the other hand, had voted to acquit.

The next fact was that there was only one actual piece of evidence, which was Lisbeth Palme's identification. The rest of the evidence against Pettersson had come from people who had not witnessed the actual crime or seen Pettersson at the scene of the murder; in other words, there was only circumstantial evidence linking Pettersson to the crime. Indeed, there wasn't a shred of forensic evidence against Pettersson.

Lisbeth's identification of the suspect had been unequivocal in the city court. But previously she hadn't been so sure at the lineup, and it had been two years and nine months now since the night of the murder. That was a really long time, during which she had been exposed to the effects of questioning, new information, pictures, and the stress of her own thoughts. The photos of new suspects that might have affected her memory had continued to fill newspapers during the years since the murder, if for no other reason than they increased single-copy sales like nothing else.

It was possible to determine from the lineup records how Lisbeth Palme had reasoned her way to pointing out Christer Pettersson. "It's number eight. He matches my description," as she finally phrased it. That was certainly not a definitive identification, especially since she had received information in advance that the suspect was a substance abuser and had then noted that "you can see who's an alcoholic."

The value of the identification as evidence was further diminished because Lisbeth had several unusual and controversial demands. The lineup was supposed to be recorded on video, but she refused to be videotaped. Furthermore, the accused's defense attorney was not allowed to take part. In addition, the records from the lineup were not written down until six weeks afterward and then only as a summary.

All in all, a layperson like Stieg could see that the Swedish police and prosecutors could have done a far better job to ensure the merit of the only actual evidence they presented against Pettersson.

In addition to Lisbeth Palme, there was one witness who was particularly interesting since, just like Pettersson, he lived in Sollentuna, which borders Stockholm to the north, and knew who Pettersson was from downtown Sollentuna, where Pettersson was well known. The archivist, Lars Jeppsson, had been at the tavern The Three Crates (Tre Backar) and was walking down Luntmakargatan toward Kungsgatan when he heard the shots on Sveavägen a block away. He hid behind the construction trailers on Tunnelgatan and saw the murderer run right by him and watched his back disappear up the stairs. According to Jeppsson, the man who ran by didn't look like Christer Pettersson.

***

Sweden's "open wound," a.k.a. the Palme assassination, had just begun to heal, and everyone wanted to put a bandage over it as quickly as possible and let it be. Christer Pettersson had appealed the ruling, and through a joint effort by the appeals court, prosecutors, and police, the preparations were rushed along so that the proceedings could begin only two months after the city court had issued its ruling.

But something was different this time. Lisbeth Palme's demands to testify without the defendant present, without videotaping, without media broadcasts, without tape recording, and without an audience caused irritation throughout Sweden. People's sympathy for her fate was beginning to be replaced by objections to what was starting to be called her queen-like behavior.

The appeals court requirements also differed. Those with legal training were in the majority this time, and the politically appointed laymen
were in the minority.

The defense had utilized their time well and found respected
experts who had serious objections to the reliability of the testimony
of the principle witness, Lisbeth Palme. Witness psychologist Astrid
Holgerson confirmed, with support from world-renowned witness
psychologist Elizabeth Loftus, that even reliable witnesses were often
mistaken, even if they themselves were convinced. In fact, excessive
certainty in one's own judgment and testimony increased the risk of
error. It was also stated that Mrs. Palme had not described the killer's
face until long after the murder, and that her description of the killer's
clothing did not match the majority of the other witnesses at the scene.

On October 12, 1989, Christer Pettersson was set free, which was
a clear sign of an acquittal verdict, which—sure enough—came on
November 2. Christer Pettersson was officially declared not guilty of
the murder of Olof Palme.

When he came home to his apartment in Rotebro in Sollentuna
carrying bottles of alcohol, the photographers were waiting. Christer
Pettersson's favorite drink, consisting of equal parts Baileys, Explorer
Vodka, and ice, if there was any on hand, quickly became a hit in
Stockholm's trendy bars and restaurants. It was called the Killer.

***

There was complete shock within the Palme investigation team. It was
hard to fathom the fact that they needed to start over. A few weeks after
the appeals court ruling, everyone working on the case was invited to a
conference in the mountains, where they would lick their wounds and
prepare to try again.

They were burned out. Despite the acquittal, everyone kept having
to answer questions about whether they thought Christer Pettersson

was the killer. Twenty-seven out of thirty-three of them said yes. Many expected their team leader Hans Ölvebro to request a transfer or even resign from the police after the ruling, but he did not plan to give up for a long time to come. He was convinced that it was possible to get Christer Pettersson reconvicted. He wasn't going to give up when he was so close to putting away a killer.

Trophy

After Christer Pettersson was acquitted, the path should have been clear to find some other solution to the murder. Maybe Stieg should have taken up his old theories, but his years of research and the recurrent missteps by the police and prosecutors had worn out Stieg's commitment. The unsolved murder still fascinated him, but he couldn't approach it with the same intensity.

Plus, there were still a lot of people who believed Christer Pettersson was guilty. Gaining acceptance for any other solution was going to require a suspect that could be tied to the scene or the murder weapon. This would be true for both the legal system and the public.

But one fact baffled Stieg. No one had managed to come up with a satisfactory explanation for why the murderer had taken his revolver with him when he fled. In every beloved spy novel, professional murderers ditched their weapons as soon as possible, because their risk of getting caught increased exponentially if they were carrying the actual murder weapons around with them. In the case of Olof Palme, the murderer brought a Magnum revolver "as big as a suckling pig" away from the scene with him. He couldn't have counted on the Swedish police making the monumental mistake of failing to seal off the downtown area or known that it would take them several hours to even send out a nationwide alert. If the murderer had been stopped with the weapon, he could have been directly tied to the crime, but instead it was easy for him to escape with police constables Kling and Klang (the infamous not-so-competent duo from the Pippi Longstocking stories) in charge of the pursuit.

The killer took the weapon with him, so the question was: What did he do with it? Obviously he could have ditched it for good by chucking it over the railing and into the Baltic Sea on a ferry ride to Finland or something like that. But an equally plausible reason for him to take the weapon with him was that he viewed it as a trophy. The gun that changed Swedish history would have some value to a person who murdered Sweden's prime minister for his politics. Less so if he was a professional killer who had done it for the money. Since the gun had not been found, that increased the odds of a political motive and, therefore, the involvement of some Swedish right-wing extremist.

If the killer considered the weapon a trophy and yet knew that it would be crucial forensic evidence in a murder trial, that would make the choice of hiding place extremely important. A trophy was definitely something he would want to be able to take out and admire on special occasions, perhaps on the anniversary of the murder. At the same time, the hiding place would need to be absolutely secure so that no unauthorized parties could get to it. It would hardly be safe on a bookshelf or in a cupboard in a normal home, but if it were buried in someone's yard or in a public place, the killer couldn't take it out routinely without risking being discovered. The best place would probably be a burglar-proof safe or maybe a safe-deposit box, one that only the owner had the key to.

Stieg realized that he couldn't just *think* his way into knowing where the murderer hid his weapon, but at some point, he would return to this line of thought. With a hard day's work, there was almost nothing that couldn't be tackled. When he had time, he would see where that led him. But in the meantime, another project had become much more important to him.

***

In the many months they had been working together, Stieg had gotten to know his colleague Anna-Lena Lodenius better, and it was becoming clearer that their skills were complementary. As opposed to him, she had a formal education in journalism and had been freelancing for a couple of years before they met. Now she had just turned thirty and had grown almost as passionate as he was about fighting extremists. Another advantage she brought was that as a woman, and a good looking one at that, the right wingers opened up to her and sometimes even wanted to show off for her by telling her more.

Stieg's and Anna-Lena's individual roles were clear. He was the researcher, and she was the one who fact-checked and ensured that the project made it into print. The article series and the book *Mission: Olof Palme* had whetted their appetites; now it was time to take the next step.

Anna-Lena and Stieg's mutual project was a book that would serve as a bible to anyone who wanted to understand how right-wing forces worked in Sweden and their international ties. The title went almost without saying: *The Extreme Right* (*Extremhögern*). Both Stieg and Anna-Lena had other jobs and knew that the project would take years, but that was actually just fine since it gave them plenty of time for the research. At least, that's what Stieg thought.

Lots of Show, Little to Show for It

Stockholm, 1994

The days passed slowly, but the years flew by in the Palme investigation. The investigative team gradually shrank. There was so much confidence within the police force that Christer Pettersson was guilty that a new expression had been coined for the hopeless situation: the case had achieved "police closure" even though the conviction hadn't stuck. The police had done their part, but the prosecutor and courts hadn't upheld their end of the bargain. One explanation heard in the corridors of police headquarters was that if it had been a regular murder, the verdict would have been different.

Four years after the acquittal of Pettersson, Hans Ölvebro was still leading the team. The goal for the Palme investigation had been to find enough new evidence against Christer Pettersson that "the probability of another [guilty] verdict would be high." If they succeeded in finding that evidence, the prosecutor would submit a petition for a new trial to the Supreme Court, which was their last chance to get Pettersson sentenced.

Somewhat surprisingly, another indictment emerged. Tommy Lindström, the head of the National Criminal Investigation Department, who often helped steer the Palme investigation team in the right direction, was indicted for felony fraud. The month after the Palme murder, Lindström had received a check for SEK 115,000 from the Skandia insurance company. The money was supposed to go to his agent Milan Heydenreich to buy back stolen artwork. Instead, according to the court, Lindström used the money to pay for a party for two hundred of his colleagues. In November 1994, he was convicted of felony fraud with a suspended prison sentence of one year. The sentence was lenient, making allowance for the fact that he had also lost his job.

Around the same time, the Palme investigation received a comprehensive and detailed memo written by Swedish journalist Boris Ersson, who had visited South Africa and received new information there that seemed to demonstrate that the South African security services were behind Palme's murder.

After taking a few basic steps, the investigative team set the information aside. Instead, the police were focused on trying to find new evidence against Christer Pettersson.

South Africa, 1996

At nine thirty on Friday morning, the phone rang. Stieg stumbled into the kitchen, picked up the gray receiver, and heard his friend Gerry on the other end of the line.

"Sleeping Beauty woke up after ten years of sleep," he said in his slightly indistinct London accent. "The South Africans have started singling each other out."

Stieg rubbed the sleep from his eyes, trying to figure out what Gerry was talking about.

"Singling each other out? For what?"

"According to Eugene de Kock and Peter Casselton, the Palme murder was organized by Craig Williamson, and Bertil Wedin helped. Just like we thought ten years ago. Dig out your paperwork from back then and start writing."

"Writing? What should I write?"

"I want a told-you-so article for *Searchlight* within the hour."

"A man of few words" wasn't how people would usually describe Gerry, but on this one occasion, that was just what he was. Stieg stood there holding the phone receiver for a while after he'd heard the click of Gerry hanging up. Now he had to hurry to write an article summarizing what he had dug up almost ten years earlier and which had now apparently begun to trickle out of South Africa. Gerry would fax him a few articles—he was a rather traditional Englishman, one who had mastered email but not how to scan or attach articles. That gave Stieg time to go through his old documents.

He opened the bottom drawer of his filing cabinet right next to the doorway into the kitchen. The hanging file labeled "South Africa" was probably in there, and even if he'd filed it under "Wedin," it would be in the same drawer.

Ten years was a long time. He had forgotten a lot, but new facts had come to light that made him read the contents in a different way now. The boundless evil of the apartheid system had faded with time but was clear and concrete as he read the texts together.

The apartheid regime had fallen. Nelson Mandela had been South Africa's president for two years, and the Truth and Reconciliation Commission had recently begun its work. Since it was now possible to receive amnesty, agents from the security services were competing to confess their evil deeds and singling each other out for culpabilities. They were starting to realize that the reason for their existence was disappearing, and it was happening as fast as the last little bit of water draining from a bathtub.

It was three in the afternoon by the time Stieg made it through his old material. He had jotted down some notes in his notebook and pulled out a number of documents, including his own memo on Bertil Wedin and a number of articles about Craig Williamson and the South African security services. It was time for him to go to TT and prepare to work through the night. From experience, he knew that the best way for him to get going on a project was to drive straight through, right to the bitter end, so that all other priorities faded from his head. It was almost evening on a Friday, which guaranteed that he would be nearly alone in the office. Gerry's fax would be waiting for him, and if he needed anything more, he would have access to all the equipment he needed to get ahold of quickly.

Stieg sat down at his desk and leaned back on his felt-covered chair with the worn wooden armrests. On the edge of his desk sat the first of many mugs of strong coffee and an ashtray with a heap of butts and one lit cigarette. In his hand he had his and Gerry's materials from 1986 and 1987 and a ton of articles he had gathered on his own. Stieg quickly read through them and made notes in his little black notebook. He was ready to start writing less than half an hour later.

Craig Williamson and Bertil Wedin had just been singled out, so there was only scant information about them in two contemporary articles—one South African and one British (which merely referenced the South African one and didn't provide any additional information). The article mentioned Eugene de Kock and Peter Casselton, both of whom had worked for the South African security services. They both named Craig Williamson as the person who organized the murder and Bertil Wedin as the middleman assisting; however, they didn't specify what Wedin's assistance had consisted of.

Stieg found no new information beyond his existing research. The only facet that was really new was that white South Africans were now informing on other white South Africans, which might mean that they were getting closer to the horse's mouth, but could also mean that desperate agents were trying to save their own hides and, at the same time, seizing the opportunity to take revenge on former colleagues. Stieg didn't have time to get to the bottom of their motivations since he was supposed to turn the article in the next day. He focused instead on what he knew and on collating the material.

By seven o'clock there wasn't a soul left in the office apart from him, which made conditions perfect for him to focus on his article for *Searchlight*. He worked all night, slept during the day, and finished writing it at home on Saturday night. He faxed it to Gerry the next morning. Stieg was confident that his English was good, but he was still betting there would be a lot of red marks after Gerry had gone over his text. Gerry himself wrote a foreword and assigned the title, "The Finger Points South," but made almost no changes to the language, which pleased Stieg. Even his witty subhead, "Sherlock Holmér," and the nasty description of Säpo as "the mentally deficient stepchild of the Western intelligence services" were allowed to stay.

The events in South Africa were both uplifting and frustrating to Stieg. Uplifting because the pressure from abroad on the Swedish police would be just as strong as during Hans Holmér's time. They *had* to do something about the South Africa line of inquiry now. Frustrating because there wasn't actually any new information.

But soon the investigation would take another surprising turn. Not necessarily closer to the solution that Stieg most believed in, but in a way that would make headlines around the globe for months.

Keystone Cops in Africa

Stockholm and South Africa, Fall 1996

Investigative team leader Hans Ölvebro was on vacation when word reached him that the world's eyes were once again on the Palme investigation because South African agents had started naming names in relation to the murder.

In the wake of the fall of apartheid, the restorative justice effort known as the Truth and Reconciliation Commission demanded that individuals who wished to receive amnesty for crimes committed in the fight for political power tell the full truth about what they had done in the service of the old regime. As part of that process, people who had served as agents of the South African apartheid government started talking. And one event they were talking about was the assassination of Olof Palme.

Ölvebro quickly concluded that because ten years had already passed since the murder, one more week, give or take, wasn't going to make a difference. He lay low until his vacation was over. When the Swedish and international media piled on the pressure, Chief Prosecutor Jan Danielsson agreed with Ölvebro, saying that the men who had been implicated weren't going anywhere.

The media around the world wrote breathlessly about the news, and Swedish newspapers ran the same story over and over again. Few people in Sweden could really grasp what the South Africa line of inquiry was. Why would a security service on the other side of the planet want to murder the Swedish prime minister? Who would have actually done the deed? How would it have played out? There were more questions than answers. Finally, the journalist Jan Guillou cooled things down by asking in a piece in *Aftonbladet* whether all his colleagues had been suffering from collective insanity while he had been traveling in distant mountains. The South Africa line of inquiry was one of the dumbest things he had heard of.

But former police chief Tommy Lindström showed more initiative than his subordinate Ölvebro and was down in South Africa only a couple of days later. Having been fired from the police following his fraud conviction, he now worked as a freelancer for the newspaper *Aftonbladet*. Using his old business card from the police, with a scribbled "ex" in front of the title, he managed to get in to see Eugene de Kock before the Palme investigation team had even bought their plane tickets to South Africa.

After his vacation, Ölvebro contacted journalist Boris Ersson, who had turned in his comprehensive memo two years before, but not to get more background information on his memo. Instead, Ölvebro asked for tips about restaurants and hotels in Johannesburg. Before he hung up, he even asked if Cape Town or Sun City (South Africa's answer to Las Vegas) were worth visiting. He and Jan Danielsson were planning to take a couple of days of vacation time while they were there.

On October 10, Ölvebro and Danielsson finally arrived in Cape Town, then continued to Johannesburg on October 11. They were met by a crowd of media at the airport. The Swedish and international press had been waiting for them.

Ölvebro and Danielsson spent four weeks in the country and were followed around by an entourage of journalists the entire trip. The list of people they wanted to meet with included the head of the security services, Eugene de Kock, as well as Craig Williamson and his former colleagues Riaan Stander and Peter Casselton.

A small success came when Angolan authorities detained Craig Williamson and made it possible for the Swedes to question him while he was in custody. During questioning, Craig Williamson swore that he was innocent and even squeezed out a tear. After questioning, he complained that the Swedes hadn't allowed him to have a lawyer present and hadn't even let him fly back to South Africa in the chartered plane with them.

According to Ölvebro and Danielsson, Eugene de Kock had only second-hand information about Craig Williamson's involvement in the assassination. The information apparently came from a member of the South African parliament, Phillip Powell, but the two Swedes claimed that he had refused to meet with them. They concluded their stay in South Africa with a week in Cape Town before traveling back home to Sweden.

"I hope we came closer to solving the murder mystery, but I'm not sure there is a so-called South Africa line of inquiry," said Chief Prosecutor Jan Danielsson, summarizing their efforts in the southern hemisphere.

Ölvebro and Danielsson had succeeded yet again in derailing the South Africa line of inquiry. Whether they made it to Sun City or not was never part of the official story.

Last Chance

The Palme investigation had yet another eventful year in 1997, though, unfortunately, in a completely different way than many had hoped. Since Ölvebro and Danielsson's trip in October the year before, there had been no new information on the South Africa line of inquiry, but other news related to the case wouldn't wait.

In January, Hans Ölvebro was suspended from his role as the investigative team lead following accusations of tax evasion. He resigned from his position but was later exonerated of the charges.

In December, Prosecutor-General Klas Bergenstrand submitted a petition to the Supreme Court for a new trial in the case against Christer Pettersson. The police and prosecutor were making one final attempt to convict Pettersson, but the application was rejected after the Supreme Court established that there was insufficient new evidence to expect a decision different from the appellate court's. Most members of the investigative team still thought the case had achieved "police closure" even though the lawyers had failed to prove it.

It wasn't until many years later that the door would be open again to the notion that the guilty party was named something other than

Christer Pettersson—the door was opened by a man named Krister Petersson.

Stieg's Most Important Battle

In the 1980s, Stieg learned the tricks of the trade; in the 1990s, he used them. The mood in Sweden had hardened, and confirmation of this came when the xenophobic New Democracy party entered parliament and John Ausonius, "the Laser Man," shot immigrants using a rifle with a laser sight. To Stieg, these were signs that his fight against extremism had become even more important.

When his book *The Extremist Right* finally came out in 1991, Stieg and Anna-Lena had been working on it for three years. Stieg always found more information to dig into, so a year here or there didn't make any difference to him. But it turned out that Anna-Lena thought it was high time they finished the project, so they struggled their way through to a final manuscript. Stieg wanted to add new information at the last minute, and he nearly drove Anna-Lena crazy when he wrote in new connections and facts by hand in tiny print on the proofs.

In the book, Anna-Lena and Stieg hammered home that "right-wing extremism" was an imprecise expression since some of the relevant groups could be considered left-wing and others didn't have any political party affiliation. The right-wing groups could then be divided into "fascists" and "the radical right." The only thing they all had in common was hostility toward immigrants. One of the newer parties described was the Sweden Democrats party, which was formed in 1988 by people from organizations built on racism and hostility to foreigners.

The book was extremely well received, which whetted Stieg's appetite. But before he grappled with a big new project, he allowed himself to write something just for his own sake. It was a short story about an old man who was sent a flower each year but didn't know who sent them. Maybe someday he could turn it into a longer story, even a novel, if he ever had the time.

One of Stieg's other major goals was achieved a few years later when he met a group of younger activists. In 1995, they started the magazine *Expo* together, modeling it on *Searchlight*. Finally there was a group of people in Sweden who were as engaged in the fight as he was. Naturally, Stieg became their leader since he was the oldest and most experienced, which meant that he gradually became responsible for a number of vital tasks that the others didn't care as much about. The financing, administration, bookkeeping, and security took almost as much of Stieg's time as the editorial work. Along with *Expo*, Stieg kept working at TT, which led to Stieg's working many long nights to hit tight deadlines. The burden required almost superhuman endurance.

Security at *Expo* was incredibly important to Stieg since he saw how the mood in Sweden had gradually hardened, and journalists like him and his coworkers had become targets. A few people thought he was paranoid, installing wide-angle peepholes for those who didn't have them and explaining how to open padded envelopes from the wrong end under a phone book to protect against letter bombs.

Expo wasn't just fighting extremists but also financial difficulties. Threats against the staff, hard work, late nights, and financial troubles wore them down, but the biggest ordeal came on June 28, 1999. A car bomb injured a journalist who wrote for *Expo*, along with his eight-year-old son. The man's girlfriend, also a journalist, was traumatized when she found her partner and son among the splintered metal and pieces of glass.

No one thought Stieg was being paranoid anymore, but several employees thought the price was too high and left *Expo*.

Stieg fought hard to make everything work. Openly neo-Nazi groups had grown in number and size as anti-immigrant sentiments gained public acceptance. *Expo* was needed more than ever, and Stieg was the one who could keep it together.

In the final years before the new millennium, Stieg was the one who realized that a large percentage of right-wing extremists were changing their tactics. Instead of shaved heads, boots, and Nazi salutes, they had clean-cut hairdos and well-shined shoes, and they behaved, at least on the surface, like members of the established political parties. They had cleaned up their agenda—although the old Nazis were still there in the background—but they still wanted to get rid of immigrants. One political party that Stieg wrote about as early as 1991, which had grown in each election since, was the Sweden Democrats. Their style was to give well-worded speeches with smiles on their faces. Their vision was to make it into the Swedish parliament, but there was still a long way to go before they got there.

Together with his coworker Mikael Ekman from *Expo*, Stieg wrote the book *The Sweden Democrats* (*Sverigedemokraterna*), which described how the party grew from Nazi soil and transformed into something that looked acceptable on the surface. Mikael had the idea to compile excerpts from the criminal records of many of the leading Sweden Democrats. It turned out that the Sweden Democrats' accusation that immigrants were criminals was considerably more applicable to the party's own representatives. Assault and battery, violence against women, threats, cruelty to animals—the list of the different types of crimes they had been convicted of was long and damning.

The reception of the book *The Sweden Democrats* in 2001 was gushing, as it had been for *The Extremist Right* a few years earlier. But just as it had then, interest waned in the media as soon as the next reality show star did something stupid.

But Stieg had known since back when he began fighting extremism that there was no such thing as a final victory. Democracy was always under threat. It had to be defended all the time.

By the first year of the twenty-first century, all of Stieg's hard work had paid off. He was, indisputably, one of Sweden's leading experts on and fighters of extremism.

Eva

Eva Gabrielsson and I sat quietly in Nyberg's Café as she drank her latte. All I knew about her at that point was what I had read in the press after Stieg died, where she had been portrayed as a kind of victim. But she was far from a victim, more of a fighter. She made that clear when I asked how she had felt in the years since Stieg's death.

"We're not discussing feelings here," she replied tersely.

I tried a different approach and made a note to myself that I should avoid questions that were too personal for her.

"What drove Stieg?" I asked.

"It came from his grandfather, who he grew up with until he was nine," Eva said. "His grandfather was a Stalinist and was definitely anti-Nazi during the war. That's where Stieg learned about World War II and right-wing extremism, from his grandfather Severin."

I took a bite of my pastry.

"How did Stieg go about mapping out these groups?" I asked.

"You study the papers, you check what groups people are members of," Eva said. "How they spend their time, where they work, do they write letters to the editor, are there people who know them, do the

police know about them, do they have criminal records? Normal journalistic mapping, pure and simple."

"And infiltrations?"

I was thinking about Gerry's source, Lesley Wooler, who had risked
his life in Cyprus.

"No, that came about in the 1990s. In the '80s there wasn't really
anything to infiltrate. The organizations were too small. You needed
other avenues."

"Did you participate in his research?"

"Yes, for example, he and I took pictures of apartment directory
signs with all the names of the residents. There were a number of doors
on Kungsholmen with weird interconnections, strange businesses and
organizations."

"And when you didn't go with him," I said, "did he tell you about
what he'd been doing?"

"Oh, yeah. I mean, it wasn't exactly like a monthly report, more like
he would tell me a little each night and we would discuss it."

"And you discussed the Palme assassination, too?"

"It turned out that there were very large networks that stuck
together. You would find one, and then maybe you would find two
or three others, which in turn would expand outward into even more.
Everything slid together in Stieg's research into the Palme assassination
and right-wing extremist interconnections. It all ended up in the same
right-wing groups."

After my clumsy first question, our conversation flowed more easily,
and we talked about other subjects for a while. We found a common
interest in city planning and architecture. Eva told me about architect
Per Olof Hallman, how his city planning for Stockholm in the beginning of the 1900s created some of the best parts of the city, and how he
had been written off, left out of history, replaced by less talented people
who had come after him and dedicated themselves to ruining Hallman's
work. I told her about the book I was planning to write, about how

someone could analyze locations and see how they affected the people who spent time there. Little by little, Eva and I fell into a comfortable conversation.

When I had sat with Gerry, it was obvious how important he had been to Stieg. He was Stieg's friend and mentor for more than twenty years. But Eva had known Stieg for ten years longer than that, and when he passed away, she was closer to him than anyone. She was his life partner. And she lost *her* life partner when he died. I wouldn't ask her again how it felt to live with a loss like that, so I chose a different question instead.

"How much did Stieg work?" I said.

Eva stopped. She leaned forward over the table between us and looked me in the eye.

"It's not possible to work so many hours of the day for so long."

A New Career

Eva had finally managed to convince him. It was time for Stieg to take a real vacation. She found a cabin in the archipelago where they could relax in peace and quiet for several weeks. Everyone knew that Stieg was a workaholic, and at *Expo* they had laughed about it, that Stieg wasn't going to be able to survive for all those weeks without his *Expo* work, but that didn't bother him. He was looking forward to the time off.

After a few days away, he started wondering what to do with himself while Eva was writing. She had started on a big project that would result in a book about the architect and city planner Per Olof Hallman.

One morning Stieg pulled out the short story he had written several years earlier about the man who received flowers on the same day every year but didn't know who sent them. He showed it to Eva. Maybe he could turn it into something bigger? Eva was curious and wanted to find out who was sending the flowers. She encouraged him to spend his summer writing. Stieg put the first sheet of paper in the typewriter and wrote the title of the book at the top: *Men Who Hate Women* (*Män som hatar kvinnor*), which was eventually published in English under the title *The Girl with the Dragon Tattoo*.

Seven Flights

Stockholm, November 9, 2004

There were seven stories for him to climb. The elevator's blinking red light indicated that something wasn't right, so after he had waited for five minutes, he sighed and pushed the button a few more times, then decided to walk up.

His recent success felt like a relief, but it brought its own stress. The three novels he had written were going to be published in Sweden and people were already talking about record sales. There was a lot of interest in the books from several foreign markets, including the US, and the film and television rights had just been sold.

It felt unreal. He was going to go from being an underpaid, down-right impoverished journalist and publisher of one of Sweden's smallest magazines to living a comfortable life as an author. A dream for many, but Stieg still wanted other things as well.

Obviously he would make sure some of the dreams he and Eva had would come true. A small summer cabin was a top priority, but he would also use the extra time and money to drive his own projects ahead at a faster pace. The battles against racism, sexism, and intolerance were vital and had to continue. But that work was actually very easy. There were several good people who could take over large portions of *Expo*'s publishing, and his own role could be limited to attending a few editorial meetings each week and perhaps writing a couple of articles.

Now he could devote the rest of his time to the project he'd had sitting on the back burner for several years. For the first two years after Olof Palme's assassination, he had dedicated a huge amount of time to researching the killing. But needing to earn his daily bread and other practical considerations meant that he could only work on it in his free time, and for several years he had done very little on the Palme murder. But now he would be able to pick it back up.

He had three floors to go when he felt the first jab in his chest. A few more steps and he would be at the next landing. He held on to the handrail, leaned forward a little, and took some deep breaths, which helped ease the pressure in his chest a little, but at the same time, the pain started radiating into his arm.

To be sure, he hadn't done the best job looking after his health, what with the smoking, the lack of sleep, and the many sandwiches eaten at his desk so that he could work a little longer—but surely things weren't that bad yet? He was only fifty and felt like he had at least twenty good years left in him.

A couple of steps into the next flight, things got better. He got used to the weight in his chest and was able to make it up to the next floor without taking a break. One more pause before he went up the last little way.

For a second it felt as if he were standing outside himself and watching the middle-aged man who was just about to make a name for himself. He saw the weight of his shoulders in his stooped posture and his body shaped by the priorities of work rather than health. His skin was an ashen gray, his hair stood on end, and those round glasses were askew with thumbprints on the lenses. The sight made it easy to recognize that it had all become too much for the man to bear.

He gathered his strength and, step by step, he conquered the final flight. He tripped over the last step, but managed to grab the handle of the door to the office. His coworkers' wide eyes turned toward him as he staggered into the editorial offices and collapsed into his chair. In the distance, someone picked up a receiver and called an ambulance. Everything started to go black.

If only he'd had more time. There was so much that remained undone. Who would take over? Where would they go from here?

Stieg would never get answers to any of those questions. But it didn't matter, where he was going. He was fifty years old, and his grandfather Severin had been only a few years older than that when he had his fatal heart attack. Severin would have been proud of him if he had known what his grandson had accomplished.

It was too soon, but it was time for Stieg to go.

Stieg Is Dead

Sometimes a death unleashes effects that no one can predict. Stieg's death was like that. The funeral was the last time everyone who was close to Stieg would gather in the same room.

Even though Stieg called Eva his wife, they had never formally married, so by Swedish law, his biological relatives inherited everything, including the rights to and income from his books. Eva got the right to stay in the small apartment they had bought together and to keep a few personal belongings. Everything else went to the relatives. This produced a public clash between the parties that would continue to play out in the Swedish and international press. Each time it seemed that the wound might heal, some event would thrust the conflict back into the spotlight again.

Several years later, Stieg's three novels had sold more than eighty million copies, and all the books had been made into movies in Sweden. An American movie of the first book, *The Girl with the Dragon Tattoo*, had also been produced, with Daniel Craig playing the lead.

Expo's future was secure at any rate, thanks in part to money from Stieg's estate. When Stieg warned of the Sweden Democrats in 1991, they received scarcely five thousand votes in the parliamentary election. In 2010, in the second election following Stieg's death, they made it into parliament for the first time with 340,000 votes. *Expo*'s work was more important than ever when a party that was founded by racists and fascists was voted into the Swedish parliament and continued to grow.

***

The years also passed in the Palme investigation. In 1997, the prosecutor Kerstin Skarp started working on the Palme murder. Skarp's sister was married to Olof Palme's old adversary Jan Guillou, who continued to write about Christer Pettersson's probable guilt. The expectation that other lines of inquiry would be investigated came to naught. Even though Skarp said that the investigative team would never give up hope, the police had minimal resources to find other suspects. The continued belief that a lone killer with no political motivation was responsible for the death of the prime minister was the most comfortable one for the police and the prosecutors, as well as for the politicians.

Activity on the investigation continued at a slow pace for many years. Ambivalence from the legal system, media, and politicians guaranteed that everyone who wanted to could forget that someone had managed to shoot Sweden's prime minister to death in the street many, many years ago. The standard Swedish solution to difficult problems— "everyone is innocent"—would have to apply for the time being.

Christer Pettersson died in an accident, a normal death for a substance abuser. A tragic life reached its end, said the Swedish prime minister at the time, Göran Persson.

Maybe the Palme case should have been closed, but no politician wanted to be responsible for that kind of decision. Plus, there may have been compromising information in the files about the many blunders that politicians had committed during the various phases of the investigation. If the investigation were shut down, the case files would become public and the sensitive information along with them, which would just add to the public's growing contempt for politicians. Occasionally people insisted that something concrete should be done. The politicians were forced to ask themselves how to proceed, preferably without risking their own missteps coming to light. The solution was ingenious in its simplicity.

On July 1, 2010, just about six months before the investigation into the murder of Olof Palme was going to be closed, the statute of limitations for serious criminal offenses was abolished. Now no one could say that the politicians didn't want to hold the responsible party accountable. And since the preliminary case files remained confidential, none of the politicians risked being confronted with their own mistakes. But the investigation was, for all intents and purposes, all but dead.

Part 2

IN STIEG'S FOOTSTEPS

Space Syntax

Sweden, 2008–2010

Long before I found Stieg's lost notes on the Palme assassination, I had embarked on my own investigation, one that was, at the time anyway, completely unrelated.

They say that after you've written two books, you can call yourself an author, so I wanted to write my second. My first was about dirty dealings in Czechoslovakia by Saab and British Aerospace and was based on things I had observed firsthand. The second book I had planned would be something completely different.

Ages ago I studied architecture, but after a brief and very unsuccessful career, I gave up my professional ambitions in that field. Yet my interest in the subject remained. One of the classes I had taken twenty years earlier made a lasting impression on me: sociologist Bill Hillier's studies of locations. Along with his colleagues at the Bartlett, University College London, he had developed the space syntax theory in which he described different types of locations, how they fit together, and how they influenced the people in them.

From that theory, Hillier then developed tools that architects, city planners, and sociologists used to design environments to positively

affect people. Others used those same tools to make people want to buy
more in shopping malls. Suddenly it was possible to know in advance if
planned residential areas, neighborhoods, apartments, stores, and workplaces would make people feel safe, harmonious, and inspired, or the
opposite, create anxiety and social problems and encourage criminality.

In a popular example, most crimes are not committed in public
squares with a lot of people around. Considerably more crimes take
place in hidden-away locations near those public squares—for example,
around the corner in an alley—close to places with lots of people, but
where the perpetrator won't be seen.

My book was going to be about locations where serious crimes had
been committed and the place itself had been a factor. I was fascinated
by the notion that places could possibly influence people to commit
crimes and that this could be studied but not explained.

After about a month of research, I came up with several locations
where more than one crime had been committed, but one of them in
particular captivated my interest—24 Norr Mälarstrand in Stockholm.

The infamous von Sydow murder had shaken Stockholm many
decades earlier. Late in the afternoon on March 7, 1932, three people
were found beaten to death in a 2,700-square-foot eight-room apartment on the fourth floor of 24 Norr Mälarstrand. The three bodies were
discovered by the family's fifteen-year-old daughter. The victims were
identified as Hjalmar von Sydow, who lived in the apartment, Karolina
Herou, the cook, and Ebba Hamn, the housekeeper. All three had been
killed by blows to the head with a blunt object, probably an iron that
was missing from the household.

Hjalmar von Sydow was the president of the Swedish Employers
Association, a member of the upper house of the Swedish parliament,
and a knight of the Royal Order of Vasa and was, therefore, one of the
most prominent personages in the city and the country. As soon as the
police were called, it was clear that the killer was probably the family's

twenty-three-year-old son, Fredrik von Sydow, who had fled the scene with his equally young wife, Ingun von Sydow, née Sundén-Cullberg.

At around ten that night, the police caught up with the young couple at Restaurant Gillet in Uppsala. The police waited in the front so as not to attract unnecessary attention, but before they were able to arrest the couple, Fredrik shot Ingun in the head. She died instantly. After that, Fredrik shot himself and died just as quickly. It became one of the most widely written-about murder cases in Swedish history, referred to as the von Sydowian murders, and one of the biggest society-page scandals the country had ever seen.

For obvious reasons, the history of the apartment was tarnished, and in the decades after the murders, even though many people wanted to live in one of the most beautiful apartments in Stockholm, none of them stayed at the address for very long. That is, until the summer of 1980 when notorious anti-Palme activists, the physician Alf Enerström and actress Gio Petré, moved into the von Sydows' apartment. Enerström and Petré proceeded to conduct their concerted anti-Palme hate campaign from the very same apartment where three people had been brutally murdered several decades earlier.

Twenty-three years after Alf Enerström moved into the apartment, his relationship with Gio Petré had ended, he was suffering from mental health problems, and he had been sentenced to jail and psychiatric care several times for repeated violent crimes. The elegant apartment had fallen into disrepair, and he was well on his way to filling it with all manner of trash and junk. The rent hadn't been paid in months.

Alf Enerström was to be evicted on November 28, 2003. On that day, he opened the door to the enforcement officials and the police wearing only a shirt and with a saucepan on his head like a helmet. When he realized why they were there, he quickly locked himself in and started shooting his gun through the double doors with their panes of etched glass. A female police officer was hit multiple times but survived. Alf Enerström was sentenced to psychiatric care.

**

I read several books about the von Sydowian murders and everything I could get my hands on about Alf Enerström. I quickly found the Review Commission's 1999 report on the Palme case—a one-thousand-page-long review that more or less accurately summarized all the various lines of inquiry that the police worked on while investigating the assassination. A long series of actions taken against Alf Enerström was described over six pages. It was clear that in the shadow of the PKK and Christer Pettersson inquiries, some police investigators were also interested in Enerström—the most active of them was Detective Inspector Alf Andersson.

During the days after the assassination, tips had poured in about Enerström's involvement. One informant reported that a few months before the assassination, Enerström had said, "I am going to remove Palme from office faster than you think," and that "the day we've gotten him out of the way, the Social Democrats will elect us." The informant was later offered the position of minister of justice in Enerström's future government. Enerström was questioned by the police, but his wife, Gio Petré, insisted he was home with her at 24 Norr Mälarstrand when the murder took place.

One month after the murder, Hans Holmér decided that there was no reason to run surveillance on Enerström, a decision that was confirmed two weeks later by a Säpo analysis: "The entire Alf E. case is designated as closed as far as the security police are concerned."

In the following pages of the report, I read about how tips concerning Enerström had continued to come in, how a few people wanted to continue investigating him, and how these suspicions were repeatedly set aside and any proposed actions halted.

As I planned the section in my book on 24 Norr Mälarstrand, I could hardly get better characters than the flamboyant Fredrik von Sydow and the fanatic Alf Enerström, both intelligent, well spoken, charming, narcissistic . . . and obviously prepared to commit acts of violence. And Enerström had been a suspect in the Olof Palme assassination.

The premise of my book began to take shape. Certain locations could influence people to commit serious crimes. In order for that to occur, it required that a man—always a man, it seemed—with hubris spend a long time at a location that kindled his arrogance. The location had to be secluded and exclusive and provide a sense of invincibility. If all those prerequisites were met, it could happen that a certain type of man would commit a serious crime in that location. It wasn't a convincing enough theory for Bill Hillier, but it would definitely work as the basis of an exciting true-crime book about real-life murders.

And I knew what the next step of my research would be: Alf Enerström had recently been discharged from the psychiatric hospital in Arvika, and I was going to pay him a visit.

The Campaigner

I was a couple of minutes early as I stood outside the door to Thelin's Bakery on Kungsholmen. It hadn't been hard to find Alf Enerström. There was even a webpage with his résumé and an email address. One week after I emailed, a man named Bo, who seemed to be Enerström's companion or assistant, responded, and he and I agreed on a time and place for the meeting. Just before one o'clock, a very tall, very old man came striding toward me. He was wearing a stained quilted jacket in an unusual turquoise hue. Everything about him looked shabby, bordering on possibly homeless. Under his jacket I could make out layer after layer of monochromatic cotton shirts.

"Are you Alf?"

"Yes, yes I am. I was the last of nine children, so my parents wanted a short name. That's what happened. So, Alf it was."

He made a gesture and chuckled, causing me to instinctively take a step back.

"Well, you're certainly tall," I said.

"Indeed, I'm six foot four! I was very fast when I was young. I ran with Gunder Hägg, and he said that if I trained, I would be faster than him."

That was obviously a fantastic appraisal from runner Gunder Hägg, who had broken ten world records in eight days, in every distance from the 1,500 to the 5,000 meter, but it also reinforced the sense that everything wasn't as it should be with Alf. Too much information, too fast. Soon we were joined by his companion, Bo, who was significantly quieter and looked like a friendly man in his seventies; he was wearing a wedding ring and well-kept clothes.

The bakery had been updated since I was last there and had gone from cozy with dark velvet armchairs and marble-topped tables to someone's interpretation of modernist style, with dark-brown designer chairs and square white tables. Alf and his friend each ordered a cup of coffee and a crispy pastry.

"I've read your webpage, Alf. You seem to have led a very exciting life," I said.

"Yes, I was the most intelligent student at school, so I got to attend the fancy school in Gävle, across the river. The only one in my family who had the opportunity to go to high school and college, and I became an aeronautical engineer and an officer in the air force. Luckily I was never forced to fly in the Flying Barrel—that's what we called the Saab 29 fighter, you know—because then I wouldn't be sitting here if I had. Half the pilots died. Then I started working for Saab in Linköping, and when I didn't want to do that anymore, I went to medical school. I've seen over 150,000 patients."

My fears about how I would get the conversation going had been unfounded. Alf clearly liked to be the center of attention and willingly shared a bunch of more or less reliable stories.

Bo was quieter, and as far as I could tell, everything he had said on the phone was true. He had informally taken on the role of helping

Alf with various problems, and such things seemed to arise more often than they were resolved.

We chatted—or rather Alf chatted and we listened—for a good while before we moved on to topics that were more relevant to me.

"Gio and I moved into this amazingly beautiful apartment and made it the headquarters of our political work."

"Was that the apartment at 24 Norr Mälarstrand, where the von Sydowian murders had taken place?" I asked.

"Exactly. It was the same apartment. I mean, just think!"

"You don't seem to think it was that strange to move into a place where three people had been brutally murdered."

"It was a fabulous apartment. And we got a good deal on the rent."

I had confirmed that it was the same apartment and gotten a good quote for my book on locations, but I suspected that there was an even better story here.

"Tell me about your relationship with Gio."

"Ah, Gio, Gio. She was the most beautiful woman in the world. They thought that in America, too, when she was there. They interviewed her for *Life* and *Playboy* and wrote about her beauty. Then she came back home to Sweden and we started working together on politics. I'm a Social Democrat and at first we worked for Palme, but when he wanted to legalize abortion without restriction, then we'd both had enough. We traveled all over the country talking to the people. We became Olof Palme's strongest opposition. But it was Gio that people came to see. She had the knack for bewitching an audience. Regular working folks listened to her."

"Was Palme really the one driving the issue of legalized abortion?"

"Yes. That was part of what started developing, what I called Palmeism. But it was also his fall in 1976 when he lost the election because of Gio's and my campaign. That was what decided that election. If he had stuck to what he had agreed to with us, then he could have stayed in power. But Palme couldn't be trusted. That was part of

Palmeism, too. Only Olof Palme counted. So we wrote a book about how we had influenced the election and why. It was called *We Brought Down the Government—Olof Palme's Downfall* [*Vi fällde regeringen—ett fall för Olof Palme*]."

I had the book with me, the pages dog-eared where I had found items of interest. The texts were alternately signed by Alf and Gio in turn. The farther I read in the book, the sharper the anti-Palme tone became.

"In this section Gio wrote, it says that she realized that she 'had seen the devil' when she met Olof Palme. What did you two mean by that?" I asked.

"Well, that's obvious, isn't it? Are you familiar with Greece? It used to be the best country in the world and now it's the world's worst. If Palme had been allowed to continue, Sweden would have become like Greece. He was ruining this country, and someone had to stop him."

"But surely that doesn't include killing him?" I said.

Alf looked at me quizzically with narrowed eyes that had instantly become cold and hard. He briefly touched his chin without answering my question.

"It was a long time ago, and all the medication they pumped me full of has messed up my brain. I don't remember . . . But Olof Palme was bad for Sweden, I am completely sure about that. If he had been allowed to continue, we wouldn't have any big Swedish companies left at all."

Alf was starting to get tired and I could tell I wasn't going to get any further today. I had met the notorious Alf Enerström and found myself both charmed and alarmed. The thought was inescapable. He seemed crazy enough to have been involved in an assassination and possibly intelligent enough to have gotten away with it. Indeed, the suspicions against Enerström with regard to the murder of Olof Palme had never truly been written off. To the contrary, the section on Alf Enerström in the Review Commission's report ended with a quote from the Palme investigation's memo from 1996: "If one believes a plot was behind the assassination, there is still a lot to poke around in when it comes to Alf E."

But what shook me the most was Alf's description of how Gio and he had begun their long relationship after two dreadful events, how they had met because they shared the same fate.

The person who brought them together was scriptwriter Henry Sidoli, who knew both Alf and Gio. When the two were introduced, it was only three years after Gio lost her two children in a terrible fire and not quite a year since Alf's daughters drowned in a plane crash.

Henry had understood that the loss of two children, and the overwhelming feeling of being responsible for their deaths, was one of the toughest things a person could go through. So he decided to introduce the two of them, these two strangers bound together by their own unspeakable tragedies. Soon after Alf Enerström and Gio Petré met through Henry, they became a couple.

The Dead Children #1

Excerpt from Inquiry Report SE-BZR Auster V. Sigtuna Fjard, Southwest of Sigtuna, Stockholm County, July 12, 1971

In connection with takeoff from the Sigtuna Fjard heading southwest, the witnesses said the float plane seemed to be running heavy and that after an unspecified distance it rose a few yards above the surface of the water, after which the plane once again touched down on the water. The attempt to take off continued for another little while before the plane suddenly rose up very steeply, after which it immediately began banking left. After the left-hand turn, the plane crashed into the water.

Alf Enerström, who lay in the water right beside the almost completely submerged plane, was picked up by a boat that hurried over. After just over half an hour of work, rescue divers succeeded in bringing up the two dead girls who were still sitting inside the wrecked plane where it lay at a depth of

about thirteen feet. The girls were transported by
ambulance to Löwenströmska Hospital where Dr.
Strömstedt pronounced them dead, after which the
girls were transported to the hospital mortuary.

Skans: I'm recording this conversation on tape and
my colleague will take a few notes. Can you explain
what happened?
Enerström: Were you there?
Skans: I came in at a later stage.
Enerström: Did the plane sink?
Skans: It sank.
Enerström: What happened to me?
Skans: You got out on your own. And fortunately
the tail section was partially above the water when
the first boat arrived. You were clinging to the tail
section.
Enerström: I have no memory of that. I remember
everything up until it hit the water. I must have been
thrown out. I didn't climb out.
Skans: What time did you set out?
Enerström: Hmm, what was the time? Four . . .
around four. What time is it now?
Skans: It's five to eight. So about four hours have
passed. You had rented or borrowed the plane from
Scherdin and picked it up from him?
Enerström: Yes.
Skans: Is that your white Volvo Amazon parked
there?
Enerström: Yes.
Skans: Can you briefly explain what happened?

Enerström: Yes. I got into the plane and did the inspection, checked the oil, fueled up, full tank, pumped the water out of the floats. Then I put my youngest daughter in the back.

Skans: What's her name?

Enerström: Laila. Where's this blood from?

Skans: It's coming from a cut on the side of your nose.

Enerström: Yes, I got her seated there and buckled her in. And a suitcase next to her and a coat on top of that. And Eva, my eldest daughter, sat down next to me, buckled herself in and then we pulled out.

Skans: What was the plan? Were you going to fly far?

Enerström: We were just going flying.

Skans: Was it a day trip?

Enerström: Yes, a day trip to Vaxholm.

Skans: And back again?

Enerström: I work at Karolinska Hospital, and I have the afternoon off for having been on-call. And my wife really wanted to join us. We have puppies and a son, who's nine years old, so we were going to pick them up. Evidently my kids didn't make it out?

Skans: No, they didn't.

Map of plane crash area.

The Dead Children #2

From the August 27, 1969, issue of Expressen by Barbro Flodquist

Poor, poor Gio Petré. How much grief must one person go through before life is done with her? First her husband, the ever-charming movie producer Lorens Marmstedt, was taken from her. She was left alone—a twenty-eight-year-old widow with two little children, Pierre and Lovisa. The boy, two and a half, and the girl just a few months old.

Now just over three years later, both of her children have died. It happened right before her eyes as she tried in vain to save them from the burning home. These two children, who were all that made her life worth living after her husband's passing. Doctors are attending to Gio now. She's hospitalized, having been injured herself, but aware of the dreadful loneliness that now surrounds her.

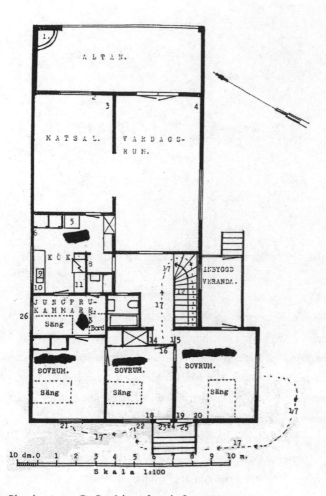

Plan drawing on Gio Petré's house from the fire investigation.

The Double Widow

Värmland, January 2012

The same sound as usual. Has a Volvo ever not started? The road to Örebro was like any old rural highway in Sweden—alternating between highway and arterial with a lot of spruce forest and a few lakes here and there. Then the landscape changed. It grew hillier; the woods became thicker and the lakes darker. Occasional snowbanks became one continuous blanket. Red-painted farmhouses and company towns. After Karlstad, I sped past long stretches of farmland covered in a foot and a half of snow under brilliant sunshine. I hadn't seen many houses for the last twenty miles and even fewer people. Often there were one or more American cars from the 1950s next to the buildings, showing that this was one of the last areas to still cling to James Dean and the rural rebel cause.

I was expecting the building to appear around the next curve. Glafsfjord meandered along with coves and steep cliffs on the other side of the water. And then there it was, Sölje manor. A several-hundred-foot-long tree-lined unpaved private drive led to the house, a yellow country mansion from the 1700s. The pictures I had seen mostly showed a dilapidated building with a bunch of rubbish out front, including about ten cars that Alf Enerström had intentionally put there to keep out any ill-intentioned visitors. Now the house sparkled like the sun. I drove up to the building. There was a circular drive in the front with a somewhat overstated fountain, now drained for the winter, with a balustrade around it and a Greek goddess in the middle. By the front door there was one white and one black Mercedes, both vintage cars from the 1960s and '70s in perfect condition.

But I was mainly preoccupied by the massive dog standing in between my car and the front door. Some kind of Saint Bernard, only bigger. I cautiously opened the car door and the dog immediately turned to look at me, growling deeply. I closed the door again. I repeated the same procedure a few times, and even though the dog didn't budge from where he stood, I didn't dare put a foot out of the car.

I drove back down the tree-lined driveway. It was annoying to come all the way out here from Stockholm without even daring to ring the doorbell. If I succeeded in seeing Gio, it would be worth the ten-hour round-trip drive. I was going to ask about 24 Norr Mälarstrand, about Alf and their life together there, but the notion that she might say something about the Palme assassination and Alf Enerström's potential involvement piqued my curiosity. Gio had lived with Alf for more than twenty-five years, both before and after the Palme assassination. If he was involved in any way, she must know about it.

I followed the rural highway and after a while came up with a plan involving a piece of sausage from the little grocery store in nearby Glava. When I returned to the manor house, the dog was still there, but I tossed the sausage right as I reached the circular drive. I made sure the dog saw me do it, and then I drove around as close to the front door as I could get. As I knocked on the door, the dog was completely preoccupied gobbling up the meat.

"Hi, my name is Jan. Are you Gio?"

"I've been waiting for you . . ."

The words sounded like they had been lifted right out of an Ingmar Bergman movie, but the tone was gentler. Gio was not a big woman, but she had a commanding presence. I knew she was seventy-five years old, but the energy level in her eyes made her seem twenty years younger— although there was a sadness there, too. Her hair was unbrushed and she was wearing clothes obviously chosen for comfort, not for being seen.

"Really? Did you see me when I was here an hour ago?"

"Oh, was that you? I often sit in the front hall by the window and read. I thought maybe it was someone who just wanted to look at the house. That happens a lot. But then I remembered your phone message. Maybe I should have answered, but if it's something important, they always try again sooner or later. It never fails. And now you're here."

Gio had stepped aside to show me in the front door. The front hall wasn't as big as I had expected for a manor house, but even so, there was room for an imperial staircase to the second floor and wall murals that created a cozy, fashionable atmosphere.

"Would you like a cup of coffee and maybe a sandwich?"

I had forgotten the obligatory cinnamon roll tea ring in the car and did not intend to risk a dog bite, so even though I had drunk three cups of black, black coffee on the road, I nodded an eager yes to both.

"We'll sit in the kitchen and you can tell me why you've come all the way from Stockholm to see an almost-eighty-year-old woman."

The coffee kettle sat on the stove, sizzling a little from the water droplets that were trapped between the hot burner and its aluminum bottom. I told her about my book project, how I had become interested in 24 Norr Mälarstrand, and how that had led me to her and Alf. When I was done, the kettle had just started to whistle. Gio poured the boiled coffee into a little porcelain cup, and I waited for her to say something as I let the grounds sink to the bottom.

"A couple of years after Alf and I met, we found the apartment in Stockholm, but we also wanted to have a place we could go to get away, so we found this manor house. Both places were important to us, but in different ways. Alf was already obsessed with politics back then, but I wasn't."

"How was he obsessed with politics?" I asked.

"Well, he started getting involved in election campaigns in the '70s and traveled all over the country. He wanted me to draw people in as a famous actress so he had me read poems. I was never interested in the politics. Where would I have found the time? We had five horses, eight sheep, and then there was a new baby once a year. We had four in the end. He used me. He more or less forced me to go along to his political events."

Gio kept the conversation moving at a faster pace than I'd counted on. She had clearly been carrying this around with her for a long time without anyone to talk to, but now she stopped.

"I've never told anyone this. I don't know if I should . . ."

"Sometimes it can be important to get things off your chest," I said.

"But I was never involved in the politics . . ." Gio repeated herself, as if to gather her strength before continuing. "Alf wanted to be something great. He was obsessed with it. In the end he developed mental health problems from that."

"And when did that start?"

"Oh, I suppose it came on gradually. He had lost two children in a plane crash, and he may have hit his head then. It was never examined. Then there was the business with Palme's assassination . . . and it got worse then."

"What was that about Palme's assassination?"

"It was very uncomfortable. The kids were going to the French school in Stockholm back then, and right after the murder he brought them out here to the manor. They couldn't go to school because of his paranoia. It was very hard. Very hard that was. Later he became violent and the police came and all that. It was awful . . . I was being knocked around more and more. He was extremely aggressive, throwing furniture and things."

"That sounds terrible . . . unbearable."

"And then finally he drove us away, me and the kids, on our daughter's wedding day. We were supposed to have the wedding here at the estate, but Alf was in the middle of election campaigning, so we had to move the whole thing. Then the police came again with the SWAT team and he was arrested for guns and things . . ."

"But that was much later?"

"That was twelve years after the Palme assassination."

"Well that went really quickly. Can you say anything more about his fixation on Palme? When did that start?"

"When Alf and I met, he only talked about Palme and Ingmar Bergman. They were his big idols."

"Palme was his idol?"

"Yes, he was, but then that turned. He became more and more obsessed with politics and jumped from one party to another before he started the Social Democratic Opposition and staked everything on working against Palme."

"Wasn't there anything you could do?"

"From the beginning I thought there was. We were like two wounded birds when we met. Everyone in my life had died. My husband Lorens died, my children died, my father died. Alf said, 'You need kids,' so we bought this amazing manor house and had kids, and horses for the kids . . . It should have been an ideal life, but then something went wrong."

"When did you first sense that?"

"It was very early on. He had a terrible temper. His son Ulf bore the brunt of quite a bit of it."

"Ulf was the son who was waiting with his mother when the girls died in the plane crash?"

"Yes. He lived with us, but Alf beat him, and when child protective services came and took Ulf, then in Alf's head, it was like Palme was behind that." She paused.

"And when our children grew up and started having their own opinions, then they were in a pinch. We finally separated in 1998, and I moved to Stockholm and lived with my mother. Then I happened to run into Lars-Erik, an old banking CEO who had been a friend of the family."

"Lars-Erik? He worked in the Wallenberg conglomerate for Skandinaviska Enskilda Banken and Bofors, didn't he?"

"Yes, but he'd retired by the time we got together."

I let Gio skip ahead in time yet again. It was the first time she had talked about this with anyone outside the family, and it seemed like each time she skipped ahead through her story, a new door opened to the experiences that she had been carrying around inside her for so long.

"But you knew Lars from before, right?"

"Alf had known his wife, May. She collected money for his campaigns from Swedes living abroad, but she had died a few years earlier. Then I ran into Lars and he invited me to the opera. I hadn't been for twenty or thirty years. It became such a great, great love."

"And you two became a couple?"

"Yes. We had eight happy years together. I was able to buy Alf out of the estate. After our separation, I had stayed away from here for a while. That's when the place became so run down, terribly run down. Alf lived here with another person. His name was Rickard."

"Who was that?"

"His actual name was something else, but he wore a wig, called himself Rickard, and was another man."

"Another man . . . What do you mean? Were they a couple?"

"No, no! He wanted to be another person. He was Alf's lackey. He had the same political views as Alf."

"What do you mean?"

"Well, he was writing a book that I helped him with."

"What was it about?"

"Palme, of course."

I flipped through my notes, mostly to win a little time to consider this. The conversation had started out awkwardly, but when I hit the "tell me about your time with Alf" button, it was as if a dam had burst.

"Yes, I took care of the family and the estate while Alf traveled around and collected money for his campaigns," Gio continued. "He picked up big stacks of bills from the bathroom at the Sheraton in Stockholm. And then he had his rich ladies, May Thunholm and Vera Ax:son Johnson, who helped him collect money both abroad and in Sweden. But he never told us who was donating. And the family never had any part in it. He knew the date when the children's scholarship grant funds paid out and he took their money. He ruined so many things for them."

"For the kids?"

"Yes, they're still dealing with it. But in the beginning it *was* really great, with the animals and all."

"But can you tell me about the time at Norr Mälarstrand? I mean, that is what my book is supposed to be about."

"What do you want to know? I've forgotten or repressed so much. Often when I happen to think of something, I tell myself, Don't think, don't think about that, don't think about that. And then I don't think about it."

"Well, for example, what do you know about the circumstances surrounding Alf being evicted from the apartment in 2003?"

"Not much more than what I read in the papers. And what little I heard from the police."

"They contacted you?"

"I called them and told them that Alf had one of those Smith & Wessons."

"Wait a minute. Alf had a gun like the one Palme was murdered with?"

"Yes, he did."

"For how long?"

"I don't know. He's had it for as long as I've known him."

"Since before the Palme assassination?"

"Yes, from long before that."

"And what did the police say about that?"

"They said that they hadn't found any gun. But then our son Johan told them where he used to hide it—in a tiled stove, behind a hatch. Then they found a pistol, but not his Smith & Wesson."

"He had more guns?" I said.

"He had a lot of weapons. Rifles and guns. He was sentenced for that, too. In the evening Rickard had to do the rounds at the estate with a rifle and make sure no one was hiding here."

"What a sight that must have been. But since we're talking about the Palme assassination . . . What were you doing that day?"

"The schools were on winter break and we were here at the estate. We were supposed to go to a cabin we had in Dalarna, but then Alf suddenly had to work on some document about Palme. So on the Wednesday before the assassination, we left the kids at the estate with a nanny and went to Stockholm. I didn't actually want to, but I couldn't disagree. We drove there in an old VW camper and then we swapped out the car in Grums for one of the other beaters Alf had. As I said, he was paranoid and often switched cars. On Friday, the day of the assassination, it was Maria's name day and I wanted to buy a little piece of jewelry for two Marias. First we ate a little something at a restaurant, then we went to Sveavägen right before the shops closed, and then home. That night we watched the nine o'clock news on TV and then Alf said that he was going to go put some money in the parking meter. When I thought back on that later, well, you don't pay for parking on Fridays. It's free for the weekend. Then I went to bed and fell asleep. And when I woke up later, I just saw a shadow standing behind the glass doors."

"Was it Alf?"

"I mean, it must have been . . . ," Gio said, but she didn't seem so sure.

"But do the police know this? I've only read that Alf had an alibi since he was home with you the whole night."

"Yes, I called the police after we separated in 1998 when I was finally brave enough to tell them. I called them twice, but they didn't do anything about it."

"How do you know?"

"They would have been in touch and asked questions, or there would have been something about it in the papers."

"Yes, that's true. Alf said they hadn't been in touch with him for many years."

"Have you seen Alf? Is he alive?" Gio asked.

"Oh, yes. He had only good things to say about you."

"Hmm, well . . ."

I hadn't mentioned seeing Alf because I knew their relationship was troubled, but Gio just raised her eyebrows slightly and drank some coffee.

"Obviously I've wondered if Alf could have run over there in connection with the murder; he was a very good runner. And Rickard was in Stockholm just then, too, I know. But why would Alf have shot Palme? Palme was his livelihood. After the assassination we had even less money."

"Did the police talk to you after the assassination?"

"A police officer came. Alf Andersson was his name, I think. He was here a couple of times to talk to me. And then they dived for the gun just outside there, in Glafsfjord."

"But this was back when you were Alf's alibi?"

"Yes, it was."

The last rays of sunlight shone in the kitchen window, and the conversation was flowing easily. Gio was telling me stories about her time with Alf, but she often came back to things that pertained to the Palme assassination and I was pulled along. She was one of the people whose lives had been affected. Two shots fired on Sveavägen had changed

Sweden, and the ripples from them had ruined a number of people's lives, whether they were witnesses, suspects, or just knew someone who had been involved in the massive investigation.

When there was a natural pause in our conversation, Gio suggested that we take a tour of the estate. We started at the back with the view of Glafsfjord. It was almost indescribably beautiful, but the dark water, the sharp rocks along the shore, and the sun sitting just over the tops of the thick woods made it look cataclysmic.

"In the beginning," she explained, "there was a Carolean-style manor here from the 1600s, but this house is from the region's glory days at the end of the 1700s. Thirteen hundred people lived around here back then, and there was an ironworks and a glassworks here. Things have been up and down for the estate since then. When Alf and I bought it, it was in decline, then it got even worse."

"But it's in really great shape now?"

"I inherited some money from Lars-Erik, so now it's been pre-served. Here's the imperial staircase. My son Johan is an event planner in Stockholm, and when he throws a Halloween party here, a bunch of celebrities come—the murder mystery queen, Camilla Läckberg, and her husband, Martin Melin, and people like that. Then the women walk up the left staircase and the men walk up the right, and they meet at the top up there."

Gio and I each walked up our own staircase and met on the second floor, just like Stockholm celebrities. She showed me through a room where the walls and cabinets were covered with pictures of children and relatives. There was a photo of Lars-Erik Thunholm sitting on a little empire style desk. We walked into a salon with windows that looked out over the front drive from the gable.

"This is by Elsa Stolpe. *Here Lies Palme*," Gio said.

She laughed and pointed to an acrylic painting on the wall and, sure enough, there was a beet-red figure with a hooked nose. Most of the painting consisted of four flowers, each with a stylized face inside it.

"This was the 1976 election, when the nonsocialists beat Palme," Gio explained. "This one is Fälldin and this one is Bohman."

"Wow . . . It's brave to have that on the wall after Palme's assassination."

"Yes, but it was just an election campaign," Gio said.

"Palme looks quite dead."

"You think? I don't think so."

We had completed the tour and Gio seemed tired. We were both tired. My trip to Värmland had been full of impressions, but when I sat down behind the wheel I remembered that I had forgotten to ask one thing.

"What happened to Ulf?"

"Alf's son? He drove his car into Arvika harbor and drowned. He wanted to die the same way his sisters had."

***

I turned the key in the ignition, and the car shuddered to a start. It would take four or five hours to drive back home, which would give me ample time to digest what Gio had told me. I stopped at the burger place in Grums. The gravel lot outside could have accommodated a couple hundred of those big American cars from the '70s, but this wasn't that kind of night. The parking lot was empty. I got a wrap, which settled my stomach, and I pushed in an old cassette tape and turned up the volume to drown out the Volvo's whining as I exceeded fifty miles per hour. Europe's "The Final Countdown" was a suitable song selection after discussing the 1980s with Gio for so long.

There was something about Gio that was different from anyone I had ever encountered before. Her life contained more tragedies than anyone I'd ever met. Her personality, her fate, and her manor house reminded me of an English mystery novel, and it was hard to know where the boundary ran between truth and fiction. She reminded me in a way of Stieg Larsson's character Henrik Vanger in *The Girl with the Dragon Tattoo*, who also harbors countless unspoken secrets as he sits alone in a big manor house.

Although Gio was an actress, much of her role as Alf's victim would surely check out. But the texts credited to her in the book *We Brought Down the Government* were just as aggressive as Alf's, so she must have had some political devotion at some point as well. And who keeps a painting on the wall of their living room of what looks like Olof Palme lying dead, so many years after his death?

Gio had clearly wanted to talk about Alf and the Palme assassination. According to her, Alf had owned a Smith & Wesson revolver, and now his alibi was destroyed, the alibi the police and Säpo had used as their leading reason not to investigate him further. And who was this mysterious Rickard, a man she had emphasized was in Stockholm when Palme was assassinated?

As I organized my thoughts and impressions, I realized that my book on locations with double crimes was slipping away. I was already planning the next step in my research into Alf Enerström and the Palme assassination. The obsession that had, unbeknownst to me, captured Stieg's attention so many years earlier, was about to become my own.

The Librarian

The woman behind the counter in the library had found the book I requested, just as she had promised on the phone, but she had something to say before she let go of it.

"There's someone who wants to meet you. Have a seat and read and he'll be along in a bit."

When Alf Enerström and Gio Petré wrote *We Brought Down the Government* in 1977, the Social Democratic Party, headed by Olof Palme, had just lost the election. Using aggressive language, the couple described how Sweden had them to thank for rescuing them from the tyranny of Olof Palme.

But Palme came back to win the election in 1982, which resulted in Enerström's campaign against Palme intensifying again. Before the September 1985 election, Alf and Gio released a new book, titled *We Brought Down the Government, Part II*. One obvious problem with the title became clear as soon as the votes were counted. Olof Palme had won the election once again; no government had been brought down after all.

The sole available copy of *We Brought Down the Government, Part II* was at the Swedish Labor Movement's Archives and Library. The book's layout was the same as the first. Part of the text was written by Alf and part by Gio. Compared to the first book, the tone of this one was even harsher.

The foreword, which was signed with Gio's name, described how child protective services had taken Alf's son Ulf away from them, because that suited Olof Palme's political goals, and how hard it would be to get rid of Palme: "It took a world war to get rid of Hitler. What will it take to get rid of our own Hitler—Olof Palme?"

The chapters that followed combined articles, ads, and essays; their common denominator was that they were all opposed to Olof Palme. The epilogue was also signed by Gio and concluded by saying that the traitor Georg Heinrich von Görtz, who was executed in 1719, "was a small-fry compared to Palme" and that "Olof Palme, yes, he should be impeached."

Alf must have been extremely disappointed when neither the campaign nor the book had the intended effect and Olof Palme remained in power after the September 1985 election. That was less than six months before the assassination.

I had just finished flipping through the book when a guy around the age of twenty-five walked over.

"I heard we share a common interest," he said.

Daniel Lagerkvist was blond, wore round steel-rimmed glasses, and had just the type of unobtrusive bearing one would expect of someone who chose to work in a library. I asked how he had found the book.

"It was with a bunch of other papers I found when I was researching Alf. I looked after it and added it to the library's collection. I don't know if there are any other copies left at all."

"Why are you interested in Alf? I thought I was the only one," I said.

"No, there are several people. I've been doing this for a few years, and I guess what got me started was the mystery of how anyone could devote so much energy to hating Palme. At first I was planning to write a book about Alf, but so far it's only research. I have gotten hold of most of the official paperwork, from the courts and such. The next step will be trying to see Alf. And Gio."

"But I've seen them, both of them," I said. "Maybe we could swap some notes?"

Daniel and I sat for just over an hour and exchanged ideas and materials. I gave him copies of the recordings I had made of my conversations with Alf and Gio. He gave me copies of the materials from all of the court cases Alf had been involved in. And there were a lot of them: multiple cases of assault and battery, intimidation and harassment, illegal firearms possession and felony weapons offenses. He was sentenced to jail and psychiatric hospitalization, and there was a restraining order protecting his whole family from him.

"This one guy is weird," Daniel said, and pointed to a defense witness statement from one of the trials. "He calls himself Rickard."

"Rickard? Gio mentioned him, too, but I couldn't really grasp who he was."

"He worked for Alf without pay for at least fifteen years. Rickard wasn't his real name. He wore a wig and was one hundred percent loyal to Alf. Even during the trials, as you'll see when you read . . ."

"But what was his actual name?" I asked.

Daniel told me Rickard's real name, which I scribbled down in my notes. For the purposes of this book, I decided to allow him to continue to be anonymous, in order to protect his identity. The name I would use for him from this point forward was Jakob Thedelin.

***

It was not hard to find Jakob Thedelin. There was only one relevant hit in the Swedish search engine Hitta.se. There was no telephone number, but he lived in Falköping in Västra Götaland County. There were three Jakob Thedelins on Facebook, but only one of them was Swedish. In the profile photo and several other pictures posted, he was wearing formal Scottish attire. In one picture he was wearing a short dark-blue jacket like a cab driver would wear, one that would have been fashionable in the 1980s. Other photos were of the British royal family and various Jewish symbols.

His friends included a series of names that were of current interest in the Swedish media: Kent Ekeroth, Björn Söder, and several other Sweden Democrats who were involved in scandals and anti-immigrant events. They were all representatives of the party that Stieg Larsson and others had warned of for more than twenty years, which had now made it past the biggest hurdle by being voted into Swedish parliament.

One person stuck out among his Facebook friends. The profile picture was of an attractive woman, probably not even thirty years old, with the typically Czech name of Lída Komárková. I wondered how an almost exaggeratedly attractive young woman from the Czech Republic had come into contact with a middle-aged Sweden Democrat in a kilt. She didn't fit with the rest of his friends. It seemed likely to be a fake profile, and I wondered who had gone to the trouble and why. Without any specific goal, I wrote a quick personal message to Lída Komárková.

Jakob Thedelin's Facebook posts were public for everyone to read, and I found a number of anti-Palme posts—including how he celebrated the anniversary of Olof Palme's death with a glass of wine. I had definitely found the right person. It was also obvious that he sounded more like a crackpot than a sinister assassin who might be tied to Olof Palme's murder. But Gio had stressed that Jakob Thedelin was in Stockholm on the night of the shooting. Furthermore, in a couple of the photos it was possible to estimate his height at about five foot nine, which was significantly closer to what the witnesses had said about Palme's killer than Alf Enerström's six foot four.

I definitively set my book project about locations aside. Now I had two people to look into regarding the Palme assassination. I was brand new to this investigation and had barely broken the surface. But I was already hooked.

The Analysis

In February at Nyberg's Café, a good deal of the space in the refriger-
ated case on the left was now taken up by semlor, sweet buns popular
around Lent, even though it wasn't even Shrove Tuesday yet. A whole
shelf was filled with the traditional variety—a cardamom-spiced wheat
bun with the top cut off, filled with almond paste and whipped cream
and re-topped with its round lid and dusted with powdered sugar. The
next shelf contained variations on the same theme: minisemlor, puff
pastry semlor with triangular lids, and deluxe semlor with just more
of everything.

I sat quietly over in the corner and gained weight.

If Jakob, or Rickard as he called himself, had been involved, with
Enerström, in the assassination in some way, then the police should have
looked into him at some point. There was no separate section dedicated
to him in the Review Commission's one-thousand-page report, but I
did find a couple of lines about him in the section on Alf Enerström:
"In June 1987, the investigative team lead sought permission to tap Alf
E.'s, his wife's, and Jakob T.'s phones. Jakob T. was a somewhat odd
person in Alf E.'s inner circle."

Clearly the police had had their eyes on Jakob but did not have sufficient information about him to obtain a wiretap. And "a somewhat odd person" was quite a good description of the impression Jakob gave on Facebook.

***

Once I started focusing exclusively on the Palme assassination, I realized that there was basically an infinite amount of written material on the subject. There were newspaper articles, books, investigative materials that had been published, and inexhaustible quantities of relevant or less relevant documents hidden in archives, waiting to be dug up. It was also clear that there were countless theories about the assassination. Many other people had tried to solve the case before, but there was nothing stopping me from creating my own hypothesis.

Since the puzzle contained a million pieces—many of which didn't seem to belong—I chose my own method. I reviewed the few facts that had been established about the murder and came up with my own interpretation. If there were pieces where the connection to my premise was unclear, I would drop them or add to them as I saw fit.

I began where my journey had started: with an analysis of the location.

THE MURDER LOCATION

Olof Palme was shot at the corner of Sveavägen and Tunnelgatan. Was that location selected or was it improvised? Opinions varied from it being a perfect location carefully selected by a professional hitman, to its having been picked at random and not having been a particularly good choice.

Sveavägen was one of Stockholm's widest, longest, and busiest streets. Tunnelgatan, on the other hand, was short and unusual in the sense that it ended with the stairs where the assassin disappeared from sight. There was also a pedestrian tunnel that ran through Brunkeberg Ridge, but it closed at ten o'clock on the night of the assassination. At the time of the shooting, the stairs, the escalator next to them, and an elevator were open. They all led up to the continuation of Tunnelgatan which changed its name there to David Bagares Gata.

Even on a cold night in February, the corner of Sveavägen and Tunnelgatan was a busy place. It was dark, but visibility was good thanks to the streetlights, and there were no obstacles in any direction except along Tunnelgatan to the east. Just after eleven o'clock there were quite a few people on the streets since the movies had ended, people were finished with their dinners, and young people were moving between bars and dance venues. This idea was supported by the relatively large number of eyewitnesses, more than ten people in total. The number of connecting streets was reasonably high, and with each block, the number of possible escape routes increased exponentially. Despite that, the killer had opted to flee eastward, where Brunkeberg Ridge created a high physical obstacle and there were fewer escape routes. The stairs were a risk—the killer would be at a physical disadvantage if he should encounter anyone.

Another factor that very much affected the choice of the location for the assassination was that it would actually have been far more natural for the Palme couple to walk away from the movie theater in the opposite direction to catch the subway at Rådmansgatan or, alternatively, to choose the entrance down into the Haymarket subway station. When the movie ended, the odds were against Mr. and Mrs. Palme passing the corner where the murder would take place. They may not even have known they would go that way themselves.

Conclusion: the murder location was improvised and did not seem carefully selected.

THE TIMING

The next piece of the puzzle was the timing of the assassination. The murder took place late on a Friday night in February. It was dark, cold, and windy. The temperature was nineteen degrees Fahrenheit (–7°C), but it felt like five degrees Fahrenheit (–15°C) due to windchill—good weather conditions for a street murder since many people would have chosen to stay home in that cold. As far as the time of day is concerned, one strike against eleven o'clock at night was the relatively high number of potential witnesses out and about at that hour.

One of the most striking factors to be considered was that Olof Palme did not have bodyguards with him just then, since he had notified Säpo earlier in the day that he wouldn't be needing them. The Palmes had not decided to go to the movies until that afternoon, and they picked the movie they would see even later than that. Because they walked to the movie theater about two hours before the shots were fired, if the perpetrator or an accomplice saw them go in without bodyguards, that would have been just enough time to prepare the weapon and examine the various scenarios for the assassination and the escape.

Conclusion: the timing was relatively good for a street killing, but it had to have been improvised.

THE SHOTS

The assassin fired the gun two times, with the two shots ringing out very close together—most of the witness statements estimated there were one or two seconds between the shots. The first shot hit Olof Palme in the back from a distance of eight inches (plus or minus four inches) and caused him to collapse immediately. The bullet entered in the middle of his back, severing his spine, then tilted to the side and hit vital organs, including his aorta. Olof Palme could have been considered dead before he reached the ground.

The second shot was fired shortly afterward from a distance of twenty-eight to forty inches and entered Lisbeth's coat on the left side, grazed her back from left to right, leaving a scratch in the skin on her back, and exited the right side of her coat. Only through improbable luck did she survive, escaping essentially uninjured.

From the killer's perspective, the first shot had to be considered very successful. The second shot was a miss, regardless of whether he intended to hit Lisbeth or Olof. If you ask me, with only one shot hitting its mark, there was a significant risk that the victim would have survived even though he collapsed. It was impossible for the murderer to know for sure that Olof Palme was dead after just one shot without bending down to check. If the shooter misjudged the location in his back—or if Olof Palme had turned or moved to the side by only an inch or two—the bullet would have missed his spine and could have passed straight through his body without hitting any vital organs. A professional marksman would very likely have guaranteed the outcome with at least one, but probably more, additional shots.

If the second shot was intended for Olof Palme, it would have been easier to aim than the first since the target had collapsed and wasn't moving. With only a couple of steps forward, the shooter would have been standing over Olof and could easily have aimed one or more shots into Olof's torso or head. If the second shot was intended for Olof, in other words, it was a complete miss.

From a technical perspective, the first shot would have been easy to fire accurately with a Magnum revolver if the killer had already cocked the hammer. For the next shot, the shooter would have needed to either cock the hammer again or use the double-action feature, pressing the trigger hard to cock the gun and fire it in the same motion. Using a

double-action trigger would have required more strength but would
have been simpler and faster.

It would also have been easy, however, for an inexperienced shooter
using a double-action trigger to squeeze it too hard, pulling his shot
to the right (for a right-handed shooter)—in this case, in the direction of Lisbeth Palme. So the shot that grazed Lisbeth could have been
intended for Olof.

If the target for the second shot was Lisbeth Palme, it was still a
miss, since she was not immobilized. Regardless of whom he was aiming
for, the perpetrator left the scene without being sure that Olof Palme
was dead and also knowing that Lisbeth Palme had survived and was
an important witness.

Conclusion: the shots were not fired in a professional manner.

THE GUN AND THE AMMUNITION

The two bullets used in the murder were Winchester Western .357 158
grain metal-piercing rounds. Unlike regular ammunition, the bullets
were metal-piercing, which provided the advantage that they could
have penetrated hard material, like a bulletproof vest. They were also
fully jacketed, however, and could have gone straight through Palme's
body and injured him significantly less than semijacketed ammunition,
which would have deformed upon impact and thus done more damage.
Using fully jacketed bullets increased the risk that the only shot that
hit Olof Palme would pass through his body without injuring any vital
organs, which a professional killer would have known.

The marks on the bullets show that the weapon used was a revolver.
The fact that no casings were found at the scene was also a sign that
it was a revolver, since the casings would have remained in a revolver's
cylinder as opposed to falling to the ground where they could have been
recovered as evidence.

The make and model, on the other hand, were more uncertain. The most common .357 caliber weapon was a Smith & Wesson, but there were other manufacturers making revolvers for that type of ammunition. It was also possible to rebore the cylinder of a .38 revolver and use .357 ammo, or alternatively to mount a .357 bullet in a .38 cartridge. In the end, the only thing that could be said with certainty was that a revolver for heavy-caliber Magnum ammunition was used, and that Smith & Wesson was the most common make.

A revolver firing .357 Magnum ammunition has significant explosive force and recoil and is extremely loud—164 decibels. Since the decibel scale is logarithmic, that's the equivalent of something many times louder than the pain threshold, which is 120 decibels. For comparison, a pistol with a silencer makes about as much noise as the pain threshold. The risk of permanent hearing damage is considerable if you find yourself without ear protection in the proximity of a Magnum revolver being fired.

A smaller pistol that made less noise and offered easier handling would have made the assassination easier to carry out and attracted less attention. The gunman would have been able to fire off more shots with greater accuracy in a shorter amount of time and made considerably less noise.

But if the gunman wasn't able to choose, due to a combination of a lack of time and access, then the Magnum revolver could have been the only option. That suggested that the assassination was planned without much lead time and that the killer did not have unfettered access to guns and ammunition.

Conclusion: the killer used an unnecessarily powerful gun and the wrong type of ammo.

The Escape

The shooter's escape could provide information about the process and the killer, but here I had to rely on the witnesses, which increased the uncertainty. By following the rule of thumb that the earlier a witness statement was taken, the more importance it was given, I still hoped to have relatively reliable information.

Almost immediately after the deed, the killer ran up Tunnelgatan, continued to the left of the construction trailers and across Luntmakargatan, and made it as far as the steep stairs. I had already noticed that Brunkeberg Ridge was an obstacle to a quick getaway, but the killer still faced a choice at the stairs. The first flight was actually two separate staircases, one on either side of the pedestrian tunnel through the ridge. The tunnel was closed and the right flight of steps was blocked by construction equipment, which left two options—the staircase on the left or the escalator a few yards farther to the left. Naturally, waiting for the elevator would not have been an option.

If the killer was very familiar with the location and chose to go up Brunkeberg Ridge as safely as possible, the escalator a few yards to the left would have been preferable. There would have been no risk of encountering someone, and he would have been less visible. Instead, he took the regular stairs.

As he ran up the eighty-nine steep steps, his risk of being overpowered increased. Even a physically strong killer could have been stopped by one or more people on their way down the stairs, as they would have had the physical upper hand of being above him.

One of the witnesses who had seen the killer most clearly was Lars Jeppsson. He was standing still on the far side of the construction trailers from the location of the murder, looked over when he heard the shots, and saw the gunman in profile and from behind as the gunman ran toward the stairs. Lars watched the man until he reached the top of the stairs, then decided to run after him. As he went up, he encountered a woman and a man, both of whom had seen a person continue on to David Bagares Gata. Lars went to David Bagares Gata and, from about a block away, saw a man go in between two cars without coming out on the other side. Then Lars was distracted by a police car that drove by slowly without stopping him. He looked for the man for a while but didn't see him again. During questioning, Lars said that he thought the person might have gone to Johannesgatan.

The witness statements that described the killer's escape from that point were more uncertain and conflicted in places. Around the corner from David Bagares Gata, on Regeringsgatan, the couple Gerhard S. and Ann-Cathrine R. encountered a man who muttered something inaudible and then quickly disappeared from view after they stopped paying attention.

The young art student Sarah walked out a back exit from Alexandra's nightclub onto Smala Gränd. She almost hit a man with the door; the man was passing by headed toward Snickarbacken with his arms close in against his sides and his hands in the pockets of his coat. Before he folded the collar of his coat up to hide his face, she saw the man clearly. He was slender and fit but with a hunched gait; he had a slim face and a long, straight, thin nose and short dark hair that hung down some behind his ears. He was wearing a dark-blue half-length coat with a narrow collar, a lighter sweater, and dark-blue pants. Sarah's witness statement served as the basis for the only composite photo used in the investigation. The German police's BKA experts rated the reliability of her witness statement as very high.

Parking enforcement officer Birgit D. was sitting in her official vehicle a few yards into Smala Gränd at the bottom of the stairs on Snickarbacken when she saw a man walking quickly from the stairs toward Birger Jarlsgatan. He was walking in the middle of the street, trying to hide his face with his right hand.

Taxi driver Hans H. was waiting outside the restaurant Karelia on Snickarbacken when he saw a man come running from the

Snickarbacken stairs and open the door of a waiting Volkswagen Passat, probably blue or green. Before he jumped in, he took off a dark coat and switched into a napa leather jacket. The man jumped into the car and drove away with a flying start.

If one or more of these witnesses were describing the killer, then it had taken him a long time to get from the scene of the murder and down to the other side of Brunkeberg Ridge. Several of these observations were made ten to twenty minutes after the murder.

There were more descriptions from witnesses who were in the blocks up on top of Brunkeberg Ridge. Several of them seemed to describe a person who didn't really know where to go. Maybe the assassin had actually wandered around on those blocks for a while. If so, that would be yet another sign that the assassination had been carried out by an amateur, hardly a polished professional who would have left the scene and been on his way out of the country within a few minutes.

Conclusion: the escape was not carefully planned or executed.

***

As I considered the killer's actions, equipment choices, and escape route, I reached the clear conclusion that Olof Palme was not shot by a professional. To the contrary, most of the signs indicated that it had been an amateur. Someone like Alf Enerström, but he was strikingly tall—over six foot four—which the witnesses would have noted.

Or someone like Jakob Thedelin. But it was hard to believe that a person who wore a kilt and was writing anti-Palme posts on Facebook almost thirty years after the assassination could have murdered a prime minister and successfully kept quiet about it for so long.

Or maybe someone like Christer Pettersson. He had been identified by the only witness who had unquestionably been less than a yard away from the murderer: Lisbeth Palme.

Lisbeth #1

I found and quickly read the published transcripts of the questioning sessions with and witness statements by Lisbeth Palme. There weren't many of them and they weren't long. After Olof Palme's assassination, Lisbeth was an injured party, since she had been shot, a principal witness, and a widow. In addition, the former First Lady, a member of the Swedish nobility, was a psychologist by trade. It was clear from the documentation that the police did not know which of these roles applied in this case or how to deal with her. A little over three years after the murder, she became sure of who had killed her husband, but as I went back further through her witness statements, the closer I got to the night of the murder itself, she appeared less and less sure rather than more.

***

On June 26, 1989, more than three years *after* the murder, Lisbeth Palme positively identified Christer Pettersson as the man she had seen at the corner of Tunnelgatan and Sveavägen.

On December 14, 1988, over six months earlier and not quite three years after the murder, she picked Christer Pettersson out of a video lineup, saying, "Yes, number eight matches my description."

On May 5 and 6, 1986, more than two months after the murder, the head of the National Criminal Investigation Department, Tommy Lindström, helped question Lisbeth Palme. Her memory of the shooter's face was detailed. He was reputed to have "an intensely staring gaze; thin, narrow lips with a pale flat upper lip; a straight forehead with straight eyebrows; and a rectangular face with a strong, somewhat prominent jaw and strong cheekbones."

On March 25, 1986, a little over three weeks after the murder, her memory was limited to "the killer has a staring gaze. Candid gaze. His cheekbones are sort of rounded. He has a white upper lip."

On March 8, 1986, a week after the murder, Lisbeth described the killer's face by comparing it to the composite photo: "The man who ran onto Tunnelgatan had a somewhat rounder, plumper face than in the photo. The features otherwise, the mouth and nose, were straight."

On March 1, 1986, the afternoon after the murder, Lisbeth gave no description of the killer's face at all.

On March 1, 1986, early in the morning, immediately after Lisbeth Palme arrived at Sabbatsberg Hospital, she was questioned and didn't offer any description of the shooter's face. She stated that she had seen two people at the scene of the murder who could have been the same men she had observed outside her home two to three weeks earlier.

***

It was hard for me to understand how Christer Pettersson could be convicted by the court when the case rested mostly on Lisbeth Palme's testimony, which was scattered at best. Sure, three years after the murder she was positive that Christer Pettersson was the killer, but the closer to the murder the questioning was, the less she knew about the murderer's appearance. This was the opposite of how prevailing wisdom said witness psychology and memory work.

On the night of the murder, she also said that she had seen two perpetrators but couldn't describe their faces and wasn't sure which of the two had fired the shots. That description had served as the basis for the meticulously verified nationwide alert that went out on the night of the assassination: "Two perpetrators, aged forty to forty-five, dark hair, one of the men is strikingly tall."

At the very least, that statement didn't suggest a lone gunman. It sounded more like a plot. Maybe a muddled, amateur plot involving the strikingly tall Alf Enerström and his average-height assistant, Jakob Thedelin.

Anna-Lena

When I was at the library, Daniel Lagerkvist mentioned that he had spoken to one of Sweden's foremost experts in right-wing extremism and that she might have some material about Alf Enerström and his network. Even though Enerström called himself a Social Democrat, he clearly ought to have been considered a right-wing extremist because of his views and the company he kept.

Daniel wrote down the name and number of the woman he thought I should contact: Anna-Lena Lodenius. At the time, her name meant nothing to me. But she was about to drag me deeper into my burgeoning Palme obsession by introducing me to another name that was only vaguely familiar to me at that time.

***

Anna-Lena lived in an apartment in Sweden's most common type of apartment building, a three-story low rise with a gable roof, three stairwells, and no elevator. This specific building was located in one of the suburbs south of Stockholm. The snow was piled up on the sides of the streets on the day I visited her, which meant that the cars were a yard farther out into the street than usual, with large snowbanks lining the curb and in between cars. I had to hunt a long time to find a parking spot.

Anna-Lena opened the door with an energetic smile and left me standing by the front door while she grabbed the keys to her "archives." From the small entryway, I caught a glimpse of a completely standard Swedish apartment, but this one felt warm and cozy, even though it was full of binders, books, and papers. We went to Anna-Lena's archives, and as she showed me the stuffed rows of Ikea shelves squeezed into the little space, it quickly became evident that she really was one of Sweden's leading experts on right-wing extremism.

Although I didn't know much about her at the time we first met, it turned out that more than twenty years had passed since she and Stieg Larsson had written the book *The Extreme Right*. Some years later their close cooperation ended when she, for her own private reasons, turned down Stieg's offer to join the group that started *Expo* magazine. Stieg and Anna-Lena stayed in contact until his death, but she had continued to build her own impressive career, independent of her work with him. Sure enough, she was now the person everybody turned to when they wanted to ask about extremist groups in Sweden.

"I have the material from the 1980s here. Alf Enerström should be in there. He was already active in the 1970s and continued into the 1990s, but why don't we start here and see what we find?"

Anna-Lena pulled out two thick binders and set them on a table in the little kitchen that was adjacent to her archive storeroom.

"You can sit here and read. I'll be in here if you want to ask me about anything."

I started with the binder labeled Alf Enerström. The pages were yellowed. Some of the documents were originals and others were copies, but they had all yellowed with the passage of time. A lot of Alf and Gio's ads were in the binder: mainly long, rambling texts attacking Olof

Palme, directly or indirectly, and squeezed into too-small ad spaces in order to save money. There were some articles that I hadn't seen before. In one of them, bank CEO Lars-Erik Thunholm from the Wallenberg group of companies, who later married Gio, tried to explain why he, as chairman of the board at *Svenska Dagbladet*, had recommended that the newspaper run Enerström's ads.

One of the documents in particular caught my attention. It was a three-page-long typed memo about Alf and Gio, including a summary of some of their ads. It wasn't signed, but what it said was accurately worded and succeeded in summarizing the most important details about the couple in a few paragraphs.

I switched to the second binder, which said "Mixed 1980s" on the spine. Enerström was discussed on a couple of the pages there, but mostly the material was about names and organizations that were at the time unfamiliar to me: WACL, Resistance International, EAP, Democratic Alliance, Contra, Anders Larsson, Carl G. Holm, Filip Lundberg. Many of the pages had the same slightly unusual typeface and seemed to have been written on the same typewriter. The documents were all about hatred for Olof Palme, and in several cases they mentioned a possible involvement in Palme's assassination.

No signatures, no dates, the same well-worded and efficient language as in the memo about Alf. I couldn't make heads or tails of it. Instead, I got up and walked into the other room where Anna-Lena was sorting through papers.

"Hey, what is this?"

Anna-Lena flipped through the pages I had been holding and read a few lines.

"That's Stieg's," she said.

"Stieg's?"

"Stieg Larsson wrote that. Looks like something he wrote when he was at his peak interest in the Palme assassination."

"You mean the Dragon Tattoo guy? He was looking into the Palme assassination?"

"While he researched right-wing extremism, he was looking into the Palme assassination," Anna-Lena said. "This was a long time before he wrote the detective books. Most of the material in those binders came from Stieg. He always gave me copies of important documents in case anything should happen to the originals."

"Did you work with him on the assassination investigation, too?" I asked.

"No, I had no interest in that. Sometimes he would bounce ideas he had off me, presumably because he knew that my judgment was a little more levelheaded. Stieg loved conspiracy theories and used to sketch out networks of people who were connected in various ways."

"That sounds super exciting," I said.

"I'm sure it is, but to me it's pointless because you start to see patterns that aren't there between people who maybe only met once at a conference."

"Well, that's true, of course," I said, even though I wanted nothing more than to get my hands on his notes and see Stieg's sketched-out networks.

"If you're interested in the Palme assassination, I'm sure there's more of Stieg's stuff around somewhere," Anna-Lena said.

"Really? Where?"

"That I don't know. Try the people he worked with: Håkan Hermansson, Tobias Hübinette, Daniel Poohl, Sven Ove Hansson. And Eva Gabrielsson, of course, his girlfriend."

"Where should I start?"

"I don't know that either. All I know is that that's how it goes with research. You don't really know what you're looking for or where to look and that's what makes it so exciting. Suddenly you find one document and that leads to the next one. You have no idea where you'll go from there. Do you want a copy of these?"

***

When I left Anna-Lena's place, everything had changed. I now had copies of some of the documents that had been written by Sweden's most famous thriller writer about the Palme assassination. Plus, he had written about Alf Enerström, whom I had just started looking into. I had to learn more about Stieg Larsson's research. Less than a year later, I would find myself perched on the edge of that collapsed moving box, in the middle of a snowstorm blowing outside, spending hours digging deep into the piles of Stieg's research, savoring every last word he had meticulously typed so many years earlier.

Lisbeth #2

Stockholm, March 2012

Just like much of Sweden's population, and tens of millions of people around the world, I had read Stieg's books. After *The Girl with the Dragon Tattoo*, which I finished in a couple of days, I looked forward to the next book. But *The Girl Who Played with Fire* was too long and Lisbeth Salander's almost supernatural abilities got to be a little much. The third book, *The Girl Who Kicked the Hornet's Nest*, was my favorite. When I read about the Section for Special Analysis at Säpo, it sounded undeniably like something that could exist in Sweden in real life.

Anna-Lena Lodenius had told me something that I might have previously heard but, if so, had forgotten. Stieg's most important project was his work against right-wing extremism. And that was what brought him to the Palme assassination. Maybe he had used the same research in his novels. Was there a basis in reality for the books and for the third book in particular? I pulled out *The Girl Who Kicked the Hornet's Nest* and reread it straight through with a red pen in my hand.

Along with the obviously made-up story about Zalachenko and Lisbeth Salander, I rediscovered the intrigue that had captivated me the first time I read it. I googled the organizations, people, and books that were mentioned. More of it was based on reality than I had thought.

The book takes place a few years after the Palme assassination and Swedish spy Stig Bergling's escape; both events are frequently mentioned. One group of people at Säpo plays a key role and is part of the Section for Special Analysis, or just "the Section," which is a "microorganization" within Säpo. Several of the people who work in the Section are members of the Democratic Alliance, the former right-wing extremist organization from the 1970s.

P. G. Vinge is the name of the former head of Säpo, both in the book and in reality. The chief of the Section is named Evert Gullberg, which is a fictional name. A real person who matched the description of Evert Gullberg was Tore Forsberg, head of counterintelligence during the years in which the book is set.

In the book, Gullberg worries about the risks of opening up the Section's archives: "Even worse, some ambitious journalist would float the theory that the Section was behind the assassination of Palme, and that in turn would lead to even more damaging speculation and investigation."

It was easy to be enthralled by the thought that one of the world's bestselling crime-fiction authors had been investigating the Palme assassination and had written about it in his books.

Anna-Lena Lodenius had said that there should be more documents from Stieg's research on the Palme assassination, so I decided to look for them. And who knew? Maybe I would find a real Lisbeth Salander in the end, with tattoos, some type of diagnosis, and mysterious friends who could access other people's emails.

To the Archive

Stockholm, March 2012–March 2013

After my meeting with Anna-Lena, I met with several of Stieg's friends and coworkers, who gave me their impressions of Stieg and his work. Sometimes I stopped and asked myself if it was worth all the time I was putting into digging up new leads, since I wasn't even writing a book anymore. The answer was always no, but I kept going anyway. The mystery of Stieg and the Palme assassination became my escape, my obsession.

***

In our conversation, the journalist Håkan Hermansson described working on the book *Mission: Olof Palme* (*Uppdrag: Olof Palme*) and confirmed Stieg's unbelievable research skills, how they had mapped out the intense opposition to Palme, and how Stieg had been researching the assassination on the side.

Sven Ove Hansson, the patriarch when it came to mapping out Swedish extremism, had worked with Stieg and confirmed to me the image of him as a supremely gifted researcher. Hansson was also the one who had connected Stieg to both Håkan Hermansson and Anna-Lena Lodenius.

Tobias Hübinette, who was the research director for and one of the founders of the antiracist magazine *Expo*, said that among other things, Stieg had collected letters that Anders Larsson had written to various people, including Cabinet Secretary Pierre Schori. He told me that the letters and a number of other things could be found at *Expo*'s offices or possibly with Eva Gabrielsson.

Stieg's girlfriend Eva was kind enough to agree to meet with me on several occasions. Our conversations often slid into our shared interest in architecture, but every now and then we talked about Stieg. She said that the line of inquiry Stieg believed in most was the one based on South African agents and Swedish right-wing extremists. But she didn't have any of Stieg's material about the Palme assassination.

I was tremendously disappointed to find out that Stieg believed in a big conspiracy involving the South African security services. That didn't fit with my theory of Alf Enerström being the killer, with the help of one or two other people.

Daniel Poohl, editor in chief of *Expo*, explained that Stieg had still been interested in the Palme assassination when they started working together in 2001. He also mentioned that *Expo* had some papers at a storage facility that might be relevant. It took another few days before he got back to me. We decided we would meet the next morning in the parking lot outside the storage facility where the boxes containing Stieg's papers were stored. It started snowing heavily that night.

Rorschach

It was already early evening and the snowfall had let up a bit by the time I left the storage facility. There were about eight inches of newly fallen snow on my Volvo 780 Bertone, which I brushed off with my coat sleeve. I started the engine and backed out with my rear wheels spinning to get through the banked snow.

My mind was racing, teeming with thoughts. After a full day in the archive, I couldn't absorb any more information. Now I knew that there was a load of information about the assassination in the archive, but not what I should do with it. The biggest stumbling block was that Stieg's theory pointed in the complete opposite direction of my own. He suspected that the South African security services had carried out the murder with the help of a group of Swedes. I personally thought it was the work of two or three Swedish amateurs. It was hard to understand how two such different conclusions could be reached.

Although maybe the Palme assassination was Sweden's own Rorschach test. Instead of symmetrical ink splotches, you looked at the Palme assassination, and what you saw revealed more about you as a person than about the truth behind the assassination. Do you favor the alcoholic, Christer Pettersson, the right-wing extremists within the police, or the South African security services? You see what you want to see.

On the way home from the archive—my windshield wipers struggling as I made my way through a dark, snowy, deserted Stockholm—something else tingled at my fingertips. A couple of years earlier, I had found a thread leading to the Palme assassination. When I tugged on it, it had held and gotten longer and longer, all the way until I found Stieg Larsson's forgotten archive. The prime minister's assassination was the ultimate mystery, and it would take time and energy to solve it. But it was impossible for me to drop it now.

OCR

With permission, I took two big moving boxes full of Stieg's papers with me when I left *Expo*'s storage facility. The selection had been done quickly at the end since I had wanted to read for as long as possible. Even so, I knew what I had was valuable.

When I sorted the papers, there were documents that Stieg had written in the form of letters, memos, or compilations, combined with documents from the police and other officials, some of which were stamped "Confidential."

I turned my living room into a research lab with a desk that was far too big, a combination scanner and copy machine, and a bookcase for my growing collection of Palme books. An old school map of the world mounted on corkboard became a focus wall that could double as a bulletin board.

Stieg had organized all his materials in hanging file folders. Each folder had a handwritten label at the top denoting its topic. As I flipped through the boxes, I saw that there were three different types of folders. Some were brown and others were bright green or blue, and a few titles showed up two or more times. But the vast majority of the folders were brown, and it was easy to tell that the material in these was from the late '70s and the '80s. The brightly colored folders covered part of the '80s but continued into the '90s.

I took two folders labeled Resistance International and laid out their contents side by side. There were letters, reports, articles, and compilations in both folders. The dates overlapped, although one folder primarily had documents from 1985 and the second from 1986 forward. There were no duplicate documents that appeared in both folders. So there were two folders for space reasons—when one was full, Stieg would add a new one with the same name. I did the equivalent check on three folders labeled WACL and two folders labeled Anders Larsson. The conclusion was the same. Stieg had gradually filled the folders and then acquired another filing cabinet along with different types of folders. When it occurred to me how many moving boxes of Stieg's material I had sorted through and left behind as less relevant, I realized how vast the scope of his archive was.

The next step was to start scanning in the papers in the order I had placed them on the table. The loose pages were easy using the document feeder on top of the machine. Bound documents were trickier. Many of those had fifty pages or more. I took apart the ones I thought I could put back together again without ruining them and set the others aside to read later. The work was monotonous, but in doing it, I started to understand not just the scope of Stieg's work but also his method. It was sort of structured chaos. Documents that Stieg had written for himself were sloppily jotted down by hand, while those intended for other people were carefully, almost pedantically, typed on a typewriter with the left and right margins fully justified.

Letters, notes, compilations, and documents that Stieg wrote comprised about a tenth of the total volume of the material I had selected. A little over half was newspapers, clippings or copied articles and documents that were publicly available. The rest were letters, reports, and other records from nonpublic sources that had been sent to Stieg or that he had dug up.

The enormous amount of work Stieg must have put into this was evident—late nights, weekends—when he read, pondered, wrote, and sorted materials. Many hours that he could have spent doing things with Eva and his friends, or something else entirely. He could have had a completely normal family and lived in Bromma. But then he wouldn't have been Stieg Larsson. His books wouldn't have been written, right-wing extremism would have had freer rein in Sweden, and his investigations into the Palme assassination would never have happened.

Toward the end of the process of going through Stieg's archive, I transferred the scanned material to a brand-new computer and picked up some OCR software, which rendered the scans searchable. Ten nights after I started, I was done scanning and sorting Stieg's material. During that process, I found one of Stieg's memos from 1987, about someone named Bertil Wedin. The first sentence read: "Tips to *Searchlight* from a person with ties to right-wing extremism: Rumor that Wedin acted as 'middleman' in Palme's assassination."

That got my imagination working but was just one more thread to pull on. And it didn't contribute anything new to my theory about Alf Enerström and Jakob Thedelin.

Moscow Mule

Prague, April 2013

Co chcete?

After a few months I had completely forgotten that I had sent a brief message to the mysterious Czech beauty Lída Komárková, who had decided to friend Jakob Thedelin on Facebook even though she lived in Prague and was a little too pretty in her profile picture. If it was a fake profile, I still wanted to find out who she—or maybe he—actually was. Now, after more than a year had passed, I suddenly received an answer: *"Co chcete?"*

The personal message consisted of only two Czech words—"What do you want?"—but it was still an opening for communication. That probably made it more likely that it was a fake profile, one that was rarely looked at. But I responded nonetheless, so we sent a few lines back and forth to each other. Lída said very little about herself and mostly seemed to be fishing for information about me. Then again, I was doing the same thing.

I was intrigued by the dialogue with the unknown Czech person that was a Facebook friend of Jakob Thedelin, especially since I had previously lived there for fifteen years and spoke the language. Why would someone set up what I thought was a fake profile and contact a person like Jakob Thedelin in another country? I couldn't stop wondering who the person was, and I obviously wouldn't find out by sending and receiving single-line messages. I had to see her. Or him.

I suggested we meet in Prague, since it was only a two-hour flight from Stockholm, and I knew I had little hope of persuading Lída Komárková to come to Sweden. The answer came quickly:

Blue Light v útery 22. Hodin. 2x Moscow Mule.

The place Lída wanted to meet was close to where Charles Bridge met the Malá Strana neighborhood, the side of the river the Swedish army had occupied for a few years during the Thirty Years' War and plundered of its riches.

I sat in the drab bar and tried to decide if the bar was for tourists or locals. I decided it was a combination. Two Moscow Mules sat in front of me, served in low stainless-steel mugs with handles. It was ten thirty before one of the women circulating around the bar who seemed to know everyone sat down and shamelessly started drinking from the untouched mug.

"Hang on! That's taken," I said.

"Exactly. It's Lída's."

She didn't look like the profile picture. Early thirties, a little shorter than average, hair dyed red, an unusual shade of brown eyes, and a winning smile. Beautiful, yes, but definitely a different woman than in the picture. She had a tattoo on her wrist and one on the back of her neck . . . in Hebrew. Maybe she was Jewish?

"I waited for a while to watch you," she said. "So, tell me. *What's your story?*"

It turned into a dance where I said a little and then waited for her before I told her a little more. It was a little cumbersome, not just because we were cautious, but because she interrupted me frequently. Then, when she was going to say something, she would get stuck on the same sentence, and I would be forced to supply something. But she was easy to like, which was evident when she talked to the staff and the people sitting around us.

Her story was quite simple. The reason she had friended Jakob on Facebook was their shared interest in Judaism. She had been planning to convert for a really long time, and they had several mutual Facebook friends who were Jews. Maybe she—or he—had sent a friend request when they commented on some mutual friend's Facebook post, but they never exchanged any private messages. She had checked that before we met. She had replied to me just now only because she was looking for a different message in Messenger and happened to notice mine.

I asked why her profile had a different picture and a different name, and after some hesitation she said that it was a kind of role playing, where she could meet other people and write different things than in her normal life. She enjoyed getting to be someone else for a while. Besides, she didn't think I needed to know her real name.

That was all I got out of her, though I suspected there was more she wasn't saying.

I described my own research project. Olof Palme and the story of his assassination were new to her, but she had heard of Stieg Larsson. We ended up sitting there for several hours discussing it, and I got the sense she was intrigued. Sure enough, before I could even ask, she beat me to it.

"How can I help?"

"You could help me find out more about who Jakob's friends are, more about Enerström, and especially what Jakob knows about the Palme assassination."

"That sounds like a role for me," Lída said. "Give me a few months and I'll get back to you with something. Maybe I can chat with some friends who also like this kind of thing."

I didn't understand what she meant by that, but Prague is a city full of surprises. The next day, I traveled back to a significantly less surprising Stockholm.

GT

New Police Theories

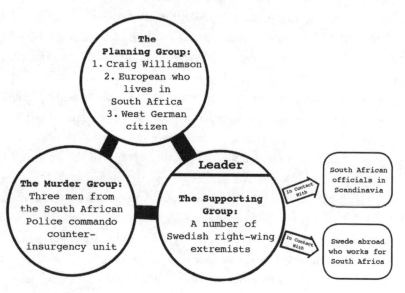

Murder organization according to the article in the GT on May 28, 1987.

Stockholm, Summer 2013

The pushpins in the corkboard on my living room wall made it easy to hang different items I was puzzling over. Sometimes something stayed up for a long time, but other things I swapped out quickly. Every day, I contemplated what had been moving around in Stieg's head many years earlier. The main features of his theory were easy to understand: South Africa, Craig Williamson, South African agents, Bertil Wedin, Swedish right-wing extremists. The details, though, were harder to get at.

One article that stayed up on the bulletin board for a long time had been published in the evening paper *Göteborgs-Tidningen* (*GT*) in May 1987. I thought Stieg must have looked at the article a lot since it described what he himself had been working on so intently at that time. During that same period in 1987, *Svenska Dagbladet* and *Arbetet* also published similar articles. Some of the information came from the same anonymous source that the journalist Mari Sandström had been in touch with in Geneva, where she was stationed. The source was involved in sanctions busting and thus obtained good contacts within the apartheid regime leadership and security services. He could provide detailed information about how the murder of Olof Palme was carried out.

But the *GT* also had at least one source in the Swedish police and had succeeded in using a graphic to describe a coherent theory that the source had contributed to the story. Bertil Wedin also played an important role in the scenario depicted, just like in Stieg's memo about him.

The headline was "Säpo Singles Out South Africa," and the story described how a little over a year after the assassination, Säpo, the National Criminal Investigation Department, and the Stockholm police cooperated to map out a group of right-wing extremists. Several people in the group had been observed with walkie-talkies near the scene of the murder.

According to one informant with ties to South Africa, the Swedes were supposedly accomplices to a three-man-strong South African "murder group." The assassination was allegedly planned by South African agent Craig Williamson along with a European living in South Africa and a West German citizen. They were rumored to have received additional help from a South African official in Sweden and an expat Swede who worked for South Africa. To clarify, there was a typical 1980s-style illustration accompanying the article.

I tried to put names to those who had been anonymized by switching back and forth between the articles, Stieg's documents, and the Review Commission's report, which included a total of two hundred pages pertaining to South Africa and pertinent right-wing extremists. Finally, I had completed a solid list.

THE PLANNING GROUP

1. Craig Williamson.

2. Giovanni Mario Ricci. An Italian with whom Williamson worked.

3. Franz Esser. A West German car dealer who was supposedly responsible for providing the cars.

The only uncertainty in the planning group was Giovanni Mario Ricci, who didn't live in South Africa but rather in the Seychelles, although just as it said in the article, he was European, worked with Williamson, and was deeply involved in business dealings with South Africa.

THE MURDER GROUP

1. Anthony White. Mentioned frequently in articles and documents.

2. Roy Allen. His name was on a travel expense account that might have been faked.

3. Nigel Barnett, a.k.a. Henry Bacon et al. Spoke Swedish and owned a Magnum revolver.

4. Paul Asmussen. School friend of Williamson's and mentioned in a leaked memo.

The article specified three people, but according to another source, the South African "murder group" supposedly consisted of two people. I found a total of at least four possible names.

THE SUPPORTING GROUP

1. Anders Larsson (leader). Contact with South African institutions.

2. Victor Gunnarsson. Dealt with Anders Larsson.

3. Right-wing extremist members of the police. Carl-Gustav Östling and colleagues.

Anders Larsson was that oft-mentioned right-wing extremist from the Democratic Alliance who had delivered a warning about the assassination. Victor Gunnarsson had been suspected of participation at least twice and even picked up by the Swedish police in the weeks following the assassination. Police officer Carl-Gustav Östling was the one who came up the most frequently in the "police trail" line of inquiry. Other interesting individuals included parliamentary stenographer Bengt Henningsson and bookseller Bo Ragnar Ståhl—both close friends of

Anders Larsson—and the so-called Skandia Man who had conveniently showed up at the scene of the murder.

SOUTH AFRICAN OFFICIALS IN SWEDEN

1. Luís Antunes. Angolan UNITA's representative and Anders Larsson's contact.

2. Heine Hüman. Contacted the police in April 1986. Was asked to arrange lodging for South Africans.

3. Jan W. Swedish professor living in Stockholm and an informant for South Africa.

EXPAT SWEDE WHO WORKED FOR SOUTH AFRICA

1. Bertil Wedin.

It was striking that only a couple of months after Holmér left his position as investigative team leader, the police had already investigated Stieg's leading theory of South Africa as the organizer of the assassination. Once Holmér was gone, the police could work as usual and were free to pursue new lines of inquiry, and they had quickly found a theory with concrete information behind it. Several daily newspapers had written about the South African connection as well.

But as far as I could tell, there was no information tying South Africa or Bertil Wedin to Alf Enerström or Jakob Thedelin.

I was still looking at two different theories—Stieg's and my own.

With the Middleman

The police had never questioned Bertil Wedin. According to them, it was because he had eluded them for almost thirty years. According to Wedin, it was because they didn't want to. I could not understand how the police had not been able to get ahold of a person of interest for three decades. What level of incompetence was needed for that?

On the other hand, Wedin could have just walked into police headquarters and said that he wanted to give a statement and the police would have had to receive it. My preliminary conclusion was that neither the police nor Wedin were particularly interested in meeting with each other. I was intrigued. My guess was that Stieg had planned to contact Wedin but died before he had time to attempt it. It was time for me to risk it. What was the worst that could happen?

Before I could change my mind, I booked a one-way ticket to Cyprus. A ticket from Stockholm to Larnaca cost around $150 on Norwegian Air, and the trip took four hours without changing planes. The disadvantage was that I was crammed in with tipsy charter tourists who wanted to make use of the cheap autumn tickets to get some sun before the oppression of winter settled over Sweden.

I landed late in the evening and found a cab that was willing to drive across the border into the Turkish Republic of Northern Cyprus, which is the descriptive name of one of Europe's smallest countries. The country with a population of three hundred thousand was founded in 1966 after the Turkish invasion of half the island. Northern Cyprus is only recognized as an independent state by Turkey and serves as a haven for criminals since it has no extradition treaties with other countries.

I had managed to reserve my first night in a hotel by email and without a credit card. There seemed to be some uncertainty about whether regular credit cards would work, because of the country's non-status, and I had withdrawn $2,000 in Sweden to be sure I would be able to get by for a couple of weeks.

We crossed the border. The cab driver was going a good bit over the speed limit on the winding roads and through the little villages, probably in a hurry to get back to his half of Cyprus. It was already after midnight when we were pulled over for speeding and he handed over the entire sum I had paid him.

***

The first morning was tough. I sat in the hotel's big breakfast room surrounded by British, German, and Dutch charter-vacation tourists who had been lured here by the low prices, not caring whether the country was occupied or not. The hotel was worn down, and the dining room echoed with the sounds of china and silverware bouncing off the walls and tiled floor. The view was probably enchanting, but I didn't devote any energy to it. I tried instead to concentrate on the book I had brought with me: *The Swedish Upper Class and Right-Wing Extremism in the 1900s* (*Svensk överklass och högerextremism under 1900-talet*) by Karl N. Alvar Nilsson. The book was already an inch thicker in the portion where I had dog-eared pages of interest, but on this day, I just couldn't read at all.

After eating a charter-tour pancake with chocolate and some spray-can whipped cream, I took a cab a few miles to Kyrenia, or Girne as the city is called in Turkish, to go on a stroll. The small town had a picturesque downtown with a relatively small fishing harbor where a string of restaurants made it obvious that one of the biggest sources of income here was tourism. At one end of the harbor, there was a castle, which was built in the sixteenth century but was still almost intact. I continued in the opposite direction, along the street that ran along the water. Several hundred yards ahead, I spotted the classic Dome Hotel where Bertil Wedin was interviewed in 1996 by journalists from a number of countries after he was identified by his South African colleagues as having been involved in the Palme assassination. The Dome Hotel was a beauty, built in a functionalist style, which had worn down into a so-so state of disrepair over the years.

I walked around the city for a half hour and got a relatively good impression of its size. I thought it shouldn't be a problem to find out where Wedin lived. I knew from pictures that it was a villa on the outskirts of Kyrenia, but the city had grown. I walked back to my hotel to extend my stay by a night and then took the rest of the day off.

The next day I got more work done. By the end of the morning, I had managed to plan out what I needed to do to locate Wedin, rented a car for a week, and sent an email to the editorial desk at *Svenska Dagbladet* to find out if they would be interested in publishing an interview with Wedin. As an attachment, I included Stieg's memo about him, which I thought ought to make them raise their eyebrows. For safety's sake, I signed it with a different name than my own, using the one I was planning to use when I got ahold of Wedin—Fredrik Bengtson.

Before the day got too hot, I spent an hour driving around in my rental car in the neighborhood that seemed to be the most likely candidate and found three houses that might have been Wedin's. Outside the one I thought was most promising, there was a junkyard-ready

Renault 12 from the late '70s, a make of car I thought I had seen in a picture accompanying an interview with Wedin. The yard around the house was overgrown, bordering on jungle-like, and the little you could see of the house indicated that it was in desperate need of maintenance.

Instead of visiting, I decided I would give it a day or two. Bertil Wedin had lived in the same place for almost thirty years. He was hardly going to sneak off because I had come here from Sweden to see him. But when I saw how easy it was to locate him, it did seem inconceivable that the Swedish police had failed to question him, even though they'd had so much time and so many opportunities.

The main post office was on Mustafa Çağatay Avenue. Beside a row of teller windows, there were some wooden phone booths where an operator could still direct international phone calls. Right next to that, I found what I was looking for: a row of phone books mounted to a rack with their spines up. With only a few hundred thousand inhabitants, it should have been easy to find the phone book for Northern Cyprus. I pulled up the thinnest one first. Bingo. I was right. It was several years old and well thumbed through. Under *W*, I found two phone numbers for Bertil Wedin and jotted them both down.

On the way back to the hotel I took a couple of spins past the house. It was dusk. Now two Renault 12s stood parked out front, and I could make out a few dim lights through the dense vegetation. The evening had begun at the Wedins'. One of the ten thousand evenings they had spent there since November 1985.

***

The next day I was full of energy. I worked on my story and tried out a couple of versions of it before I decided on the simplest one. I sat on the bed in my spartan hotel room and picked up the landline phone. The Do Not Disturb sign was hanging on my doorknob and my balcony door was closed. I dialed Bertil Wedin's number. After a few rings, a voice answered: "Hello?"

"Good day, my name is Fredrik Bengtson," I said. "Am I speaking to Bertil Wedin?"

"That depends on who's asking. What are you calling about?"

"I'm a journalist and I'm fascinated by you. I'd like to interview you."

I clutched the phone hard and waited for his reaction.

"Aha, well that's flattering. Who do you work for?"

"Various newspapers. I'm a freelancer and this article is one I've been talking to *Svenska Dagbladet* about."

My alter ego wasn't entirely made up. Fredrik was one of my actual middle names and my father's middle name had been Bengt, so strictly speaking I was Bengt's son or "Bengtson." I had practiced speaking in a friendly, straightforward way in the polished Swedish I was guessing Wedin would value. I had selected the conservative paper *Svenska Dagbladet* because it was the only daily paper in Sweden I thought he might find politically acceptable. Also, the paper's response to the email I had sent the day before was cautiously positive: "Get in touch once you've done the interview. Don't consider this a purchase order." I also knew that I had to tell the truth as much as possible, otherwise Wedin would surely catch on to me.

"What would you like to talk about?"

"Your exciting life—in Sweden, in the UK, and here in Cyprus."

"Do you want to ask about the Olof Palme assassination?"

"Yes, I'd like to. If that's possible."

I could almost hear him thinking now. I knew that he had turned down a lot of interviews over the years.

"Is there any chance of remuneration to any extent?"

I had suspected that that question might come up, although maybe not so soon. The dilapidated house and the beater cars outside showed that Wedin's private finances were no longer shipshape. What would be a reasonable amount?

"I can pay two hundred and fifty British pounds for an interview," I finally said.

"That sounds good," Wedin said after a brief pause. "Two hundred and fifty pounds for a one- to two-hour interview. I'll see you tomorrow at eleven o'clock sharp at the Dome Hotel."

Well, that worked! I had just accomplished something that the Swedish police supposedly hadn't been able to pull off in almost thirty years. The next day I would meet one of Sweden's most notorious and mythologized right-wing extremists and secret service agents.

Wedin—First Day

The next morning I dressed in a neatly pressed, striped long-sleeved shirt, light gray chinos, and dress shoes. I frantically jotted down questions on my notepad. I stuck out among the charter tourists in their colorful linen, shorts, and flip-flops.

I made sure I was at the Dome Hotel's bar, which faced the street, ten minutes before eleven, to give myself time to calm down. The plainly furnished interior—brown tables and armchairs upholstered in burgundy plastic—was devoid of other patrons. I wondered if I had come to the right place.

At eleven on the dot, Bertil Wedin showed up dressed just as I had expected, wearing neatly pressed, light-colored slacks, an impeccable long-sleeved shirt with the sleeves folded up, and shined shoes. Bertil's face still looked as if it had been chiseled from a block of granite, just like the relatively old pictures I had seen, although with more wrinkles. I didn't see even a hint of a smile; it appeared I had arranged a meeting with a very severe man. I gently pressed the top of the hidden-camera pen, nestled strategically in my shirt pocket, to start the recording. I had purchased it before arriving in Cyprus in the hope that, with a little luck, I would have both pictures and sound from our meeting.

"Fredrik Bengtson, I presume?"

"Yes, that's me. Nice to meet you, Bertil."

"Why don't we sit outside and have a beer?"

"Sounds good."

Wedin led me through the lobby and the back bar to the patio by the pool. I recognized the railing along the edge overlooking the water as where he had been photographed almost twenty years before. We sat down at a table in the shade of an umbrella. I set down my iPhone, which I had set to airplane mode so the recording wouldn't be interrupted by anyone calling, a backup in case the pen stopped working.

"I took the liberty of calling *Svenska Dagbladet*," Wedin said, "to confirm your information. They said that they had never published any articles by a Fredrik Bengtson."

My pulse sped up and I felt my neck flushing red.

"But then they confirmed that they were interested in buying an article from you, so we can begin," Wedin continued. "Did you bring the money?"

I thanked my lucky stars that for once I had been careful with my preparations. Clearly *Svenska Dagbladet* took this story seriously enough to confirm it to Wedin as well. I picked up my wallet and set two hundred and fifty pounds in crisp banknotes on the table. Wedin quickly stuffed them into his pocket without counting them.

"So, what do you want to talk about?"

"Let's start from the beginning. Tell me about your time in the Congo."

"You are thorough. We'll see what we get to in two hours," Wedin said. "We'll start on August 6, 1963, which was an important day in my life. I had been a lieutenant with the UN in the Congo for a while at that point. The UN secretary general, Dag Hammarskjöld, had died in a plane crash a few years earlier. Officially there were no rebel troops left, but our assignment was to make sure that was really true. The CIA was working on the same mission from the air and had notified us that they couldn't see any troops. But the area we were covering was larger than Sweden, and we had heard rumors that there were still rebels in a certain village. So a small group of us UN soldiers flew there. To show that we came in peace, we didn't bring any weapons with us, although I did have a Husqvarna pistol. As we stood chatting with the village leader, suddenly we were surrounded by a hundred and fifty soldiers with machine guns."

"So you pulled your pistol?"

"Everyone had been taken prisoner, including our commander, Axel (Hugo) Munthe-Kaas, a Norwegian. I stood with my pistol pointed at two Katangese with submachine guns, and at the last minute, I received an order from the commander to hand over the weapon."

"But why did you even draw the gun when you were so outnumbered?"

"I was an intelligence officer, but also the commander's bodyguard. It was my duty. In any case, we were taken prisoner and quickly sentenced to death for spying. We were lined up against a wall several times to be executed, but each time they started debating how to actually carry it out. Finally someone came up with the idea that they should cut off our penises so that their leader's first wife could dry them and hang them around her neck."

"What a very primitive idea."

"You could put it that way," Wedin said. "I had decided that if they started cutting off penises, I would jump on the first Katangese I could so I would be shot. But Munthe-Kaas had diplomatic training and kept managing to stall for time. They served us our last meal, which consisted of Coca-Cola and tinned sardines. I didn't like the Coca-Cola, but the sardines were good. The agreement with headquarters in Élisabethville was that if we weren't back by four o'clock, then they would send two thousand men to the area. For their part, the Katangese said that if any reinforcements came, they would shoot us. Luckily our duty officer at headquarters had fallen asleep after lunch and no troops came. By the time it was six o'clock, the Katangese interpreted that to mean that no one was coming to help us, and they let us fly back."

"So you made it through without any injuries or . . . losses?"

"Yes, but the rebels didn't. Major Munthe-Kaas tried to stop it, but the UN general gave orders to send troops there and kill all the rebels."

"And what did you do after that?"

"That event had two results. Every year on the sixth of August, I eat a tin of sardines to celebrate having survived my death sentence in 1963."

"And the second?"

"Since then, I have dedicated my life to fighting Communism."

The waiter came and asked if we wanted anything else and we nodded.

"Large beers?"

"No, today we go for lady beers," Bertil replied, with his proper but slightly stiff smile.

Bertil rhapsodically recounted his time after the Congo, and I had a hard time keeping up with the twists and turns. He had been an assistant in Vienna for conservative journalist Arvid Fredborg who arranged anti-Communist conferences. He had also been close to Alvar Lindencrona, the founder of Stay Behind, a secret defense organization that was the last line of defense if Sweden were occupied, which was made up of independent cells consisting of a few people each. Bertil had been part of "the conservative branch" of Stay Behind, as he put it.

He continued to talk about events I had already read about in Stieg's material, though I listened carefully to his version. How he was working for the Defense Staff in Sweden when he was accused of being too close to the South Vietnamese government and how Marcus Wallenberg put him in charge of an office called "Business Intelligence." It was new information to me that the Business Intelligence office had carried out internal investigations and projects, as well as external ones for organizations like Säpo and the Defense Staff's security department. If this was true, a private company with connections to the Wallenberg group of companies would have been carrying out services for the Swedish secret police, which would be a scoop in Sweden, I thought to myself as I continued to listen.

It was a varied job, Bertil told me. One day he would sit debating with Ebbe Carlsson at The Opera Bar and the next he would attend a conference and participate in an official debate.

"Wait, you knew Ebbe Carlsson?" I asked.

"I didn't know him any more than the other people who used to go to The Opera Bar or to press conferences. We said hello and exchanged a few sentences. That's how it was then," Bertil said.

He paused, took a drink of his beer, and lowered his voice.

"Then the next event that steered my life in another direction occurred. A colleague at the office asked me to meet his son to discuss his desire to travel to Rhodesia and become a mercenary. I had never been to the country, but obviously I was familiar with Africa. We decided to meet at the Tudor Arms pub in Östermalm, which I used to frequent. We ran into another acquaintance there who sat with us."

"And who was that?"

"He was a diplomat at the American embassy. And with that my fate was sealed. The magazine *Folket i Bild Kulturfront* published a story that involved me recruiting mercenary soldiers for Ian Smith's racist regime in Rhodesia on assignment for the CIA. I had walked into a trap."

When Bertil mentioned the trap, my pulse picked up. I quickly took a swig of cold beer straight out of the bottle, hoping I'd be able to get out of there before he realized that our meeting was also a trap in its own way.

"The result was that I once again lost my job. I got tired of everything and wanted to avoid spending Christmas in Sweden, so I decided to go to Saigon in South Vietnam."

I had to think about that.

"But wasn't this during the Vietnam War? Why would you go there then?"

"I knew a Buddhist monk in a monastery there that I wanted to visit."

If Bertil's stories were often within or at least on the boundary of what could be believed, then this one was way beyond that. Bertil was one of a few supporters of the US efforts in the Vietnam War, for which he had been named and shamed many times in the Swedish press. If he had told me he wanted to go to Vietnam to fight, that would have been easier to believe.

"But you went?"

"No, I changed my mind at the airport and flew to Cyprus instead. And a couple of weeks later I met the woman who would become my wife there. After a few more years in Sweden, we moved to London in 1975."

I raised my hand slightly at Bertil, as if to pause him. In Stieg's archive there were several maps of organizations and people that Bertil had ostensibly had dealings with.

"You skipped over a couple of things. I want to hear about the organizations you were part of. Democratic Alliance, for example, that was before you left Sweden, wasn't it?"

"I wasn't a member. I was there a lot but was never a member."

"But you knew Anders Larsson from the Democratic Alliance?"

"Oh yeah."

"What do you have to say about him?"

"Nothing nice. Anders Larsson was a deceitful person. He was a bad person. I don't like to say it, but he wasn't what he said he was."

"Meaning?"

"KGB. The whole time. A bit weak mentally, so to speak. He had a keen intellect, but he had certain problems, schizophrenia or whatever it's called. There was something not totally healthy about him. He couldn't get a normal job, so he was allowed to be the librarian at the Baltic Committee and live on a government allowance. The Baltic Committee got a free librarian and Anders Larsson got a job."

Those were strong words about someone who was dead. I thought it best to see what Wedin himself would continue with from there. I silently counted to ten so that I wouldn't be the first to start talking. After a long pause, Bertil continued.

"I was very active in the Baltic Committee, which was in turn part of WACL. And in the New Tuesday Club. And in the Swedish Liberty Council. Anders Larsson was active everywhere."

Bertil and I had been sitting for almost four hours and had drunk just as many beers. We hadn't even gotten to his time as a South African agent for Craig Williamson, but he was telling fascinating stories about a Sweden that had been gone for a long time and about his time in London. He was a good storyteller, and I sank into the comfortable role of listener. If this were the last time we saw each other, it would be a mistake for me not to ask more questions. If there were to be another meeting, then this was a good way to build trust, letting him say what he wanted to. At five o'clock, Wedin stood up.

"It was nice to meet a civilized Swede. Are you going to pay for the beers or should I?"

"Of course I'll get them. I was the one who requested the meeting. See you tomorrow?"

It was unclear whether it was my paying for the beers that did it or if he actually wanted to, but we decided to meet at the same time the next day.

I drove carefully back to the hotel, tipsy from the beer and euphoric at having succeeded. I remembered to drive on the left. I remembered to change gears with my left hand. Whoops, that was the windshield wipers.

***

When I walked into the dining room at eight o'clock for dinner, I was sober but still high on adrenaline after meeting Bertil Wedin. I had many impressions, but the biggest one was probably that he was human. I had been imagining a personality as hard as his tough facade. Instead I sensed that he had the same needs we all had, to be appreciated and needed. But during his self-imposed thirty-year exile in Northern Cyprus, there didn't seem to have been much of that.

I got the last table and was immediately joined by two Turks who didn't speak a word of English. In another situation, that would have made for a quiet meal. But on this night, those two crane drivers from Ankara and I consumed copious amounts of raki while we ate just as much meze and solved the riddle of life without a common language. Tomorrow was another day.

Wedin—Second Day

Kyrenia, September 2013

I got up, but not much more than that. Ironing a shirt was an almost superhuman feat, and I asked for extra, extra-strong coffee in the dining room that morning. When I listened to the recording from the day before on double speed while I frantically took notes, only then did I realize that Wedin had played an old trick on me. At the beginning of the conversation he asked how old I was. About an hour later he asked what year I was born. If I had lied about my age, surely I would have hesitated at the second question. On the surface this seemed friendly, but we both knew what it was about. We were going to talk about his work for the South African security services and his potential involvement in the murder of Olof Palme. He was being very careful.

Wedin was punctual, but my lack of self-discipline was evident. I had to search for parking for a while and arrived fifteen minutes late. Bertil was sitting at the same patio table as the previous day. Even though I started at a disadvantage, I decided to try to get right to the issue, which seemed to suit Wedin fine. And he didn't react when I placed my phone on the table. It was recording.

"When did you first meet Craig Williamson?"

"That's a story in itself. When I moved to London in 1975, I started doing some jobs for Brian Crozier after a while. He was an amazing journalist who worked for the *Economist* and Reuters, but his most important contribution was to the independent intelligence organization with the unassuming name The 61, which he started in 1977 along with senior people from the CIA and MI6."

"And you did jobs in England?"

"No, in the US and later in South Africa. It was the late '70s and I mapped out Soviet espionage in American territory. That was actually the FBI's job, but the CIA wanted to know more and couldn't do it. As a journalist, I could do it. If I had problems, I had the support of the CIA, but my employer was Crozier and The 61. When I was done with my assignment, the CIA wanted the report directly from me, but I gave it to Crozier who personally submitted it to Ronald Reagan, whose comment was 'This will kill the Soviet Union.'"

This immediately became information overload for me. I had a hangover and was sitting in an almost nonexistent country with a former South African agent who was accused of playing multiple roles in the assassination of Olof Palme, but who had never been questioned by the Palme investigation team. Now he was telling me about top-level political developments where his work purportedly influenced US policy with regard to the Soviet Union. There was no way for me to check the information right then and there. Probably not later either, I assumed. I kept listening to see where Wedin's story would take me.

"My next assignment for The 61 was to travel to South Africa and look for information about what the Soviets were up to. I was quite good at that, since I was used to that type of work. And then I wrote articles that Crozier placed in big newspapers under another name. I was assigned to cover South Africa, Namibia, and Rhodesia—which was just changing its name to Zimbabwe."

Wedin took a drink from his bottle of beer, as if to give himself a moment to consider.

"Well, on one of the trips, this was in maybe 1980, I was in Johannesburg when I read an article with a Swedish connection. A South African spy named Craig Williamson had infiltrated an organization called IUEF, which was being managed by Swedes. I got in touch with him right away and we arranged to meet."

"And this was still in Johannesburg?"

"Yes. We met in a hotel bar. I had a drink, but he drank Pepsi-Cola Light. He was very fat."

"Yeah, I've seen pictures."

"But he was very interesting and helpful. He more or less confirmed everything that was in the papers. A while later I called him and asked if he had any interest in the kind of studies I was good at. Soon someone called me from his front company, Africa Aviation Consultants, and offered me a thousand pounds a month, quite a lot of money at that time, which I accepted. So I started working for Craig Williamson."

"And that was when you organized the break-in at the South African liberation organizations' offices? I mean the ANC [African National Congress], PAC [Pan-Africanist Congress], and SWAPO [South West Africa People's Organization]."

Wedin recoiled.

"Everything I did for Africa Aviation Consultants and Craig Williamson was legal. My work consisted of gathering information, like any old journalist. I was also acquitted on all charges for the break-in. Which is to say: I'm innocent of illegally collaborating with South Africa's security services, of knowingly receiving stolen documents, and of the break-in. Completely innocent."

"But you were working with Peter Casselton?"

"I knew him. He was sentenced to four years in jail for the break-in and pre-served eighteen months."

"Served."

"Maybe that's what it's called. After forty years abroad, I sometimes forget my Swedish."

Wedin leaned forward and spoke in a quieter voice, as I had heard he was accustomed to doing when he wanted to emphasize something. I paid close attention.

"When I was acquitted and my victory was complete, then a bunch of journalists came. I was a member of the Foreign Press Association. Everyone came up and congratulated me. But there were some journalists who didn't come up to me and that was the Swedish group. They were led by a first secretary from the Swedish embassy and they just marched out, pretended not to see. None of them congratulated me. None of them wrote a word about my victory, about the outcome of the legal case."

Wedin leaned back again.

"As you understand, I don't think so highly of the Swedish media. *Svenska Dagbladet* is possibly an exception."

"And what was Craig Williamson like as a person?"

"Since I assume he will read this, maybe I shouldn't be critical. He was . . . I had chats with him and he was pleasant."

"Was he dangerous?"

"Dangerous . . . Well, he didn't shoot me at any rate, but I do recall that when we would get into politics then . . . I described myself as liberal and he claimed he was liberal, too. But I suppose people can be that in different ways."

"So what did you do for Craig?"

"Not that much, actually. I've been described as an agent for the South Africans, but I was no more an agent for them than I was for the KGB when I was in Sweden, actually."

"Did you hear from Craig later, when the South Africans started implicating each other in Palme's murder?"

"No, he's never called. Peter Casselton called, but he must have been drunk. Shortly after that he died in an accident."

"How?"

"I think he was at a friend's house, fixing a truck when the engine started, and he was crushed against a wall. Nasty business."

"Yes, truly, truly."

Wedin ran his hand over his chin, hesitating.

"Well, Fredrik, I'm going to have to finish up now unless you have any more questions?"

What I had been worried about was happening now. I hadn't had a chance to ask the necessary questions about the Palme assassination and Bertil obviously wanted to go. Impulsively, I took a chance.

"I actually have a couple more questions. But it's going to take a while," I said. "I have a memo that Stieg Larsson wrote about you."

"Stieg Larsson? The crime writer?"

I nodded.

"He wrote a memo about you and submitted it to the Palme investigation at the end of 1987."

"Let's see it!"

Wedin eagerly reached his hand toward me and looked at my case, as if he could see that the document was actually there, but my white lie was easy to maintain.

"It's back at the hotel. If we see each other tomorrow, then I can bring it and ask any final questions."

Vanity could be a strong motivator. If one of the world's foremost crime writers had written a memo about him, then obviously he'd want to see it, I thought. There was a battle going on inside Wedin, but in the end he gave in.

"OK. But tomorrow is the last time. And I'll have to wrap up early since it's Friday."

It didn't matter how long we could spend. The main thing was that I managed to get one last meeting. This time, I had to find a way to film again. My phone recorded the sound surprisingly well, but the spy pen's video function was jammed. It was time for a little shopping trip in Kyrenia.

A little over an hour later, after a visit to the local camera shop, I was back at the hotel as the proud owner of a burgundy-red, Canon digital camera. It could film without any red light being on and it only cost $150. Tomorrow, I would be ready.

Wedin—Third Day

Kyrenia, September 2013

After eight hours of talking with Wedin over two days, I was still worried for my own safety, but I was also starting to feel some sympathy for him. Even if I didn't know where the truth lay, in a way, he had atoned for his former deeds through a sort of house arrest on this island. His life had frozen in 1986 in his own personal Pompeii, stranded in a country that didn't exist, in a house that was gradually falling into disrepair and becoming overgrown by weeds. All he had left were his memories of the Cold War era when he had been close to the center of the action. Paradoxically, he had fought for the West against the Soviet Union and been on the winning side, and yet once the war was over and the smoke cleared, he was still forgotten.

Then doubt came over me, having seen the man behind the rumor. Could he really have helped murder Sweden's prime minister? But I had also seen the uncompromising look in his icy-cold blue eyes, which made me believe that Stieg's memo about Wedin was still mostly true.

For the last day, I was better prepared than I had been the day before. I arrived on time, brought all the necessary equipment, all the documents, and had made notes about everything I needed. The location was still the patio section of the Dome Hotel's bar. My phone was recording and the digital camera sat on the table, filming at the chair where Wedin sat down. By sitting upright at the edge of the chair, he indicated clearly that we wouldn't be talking for long today.

"Did you bring Stieg Larsson's memo?"

"Yes, but I was thinking of starting with a list of names that I picked up from various sources and seeing if you knew them."

Wedin did not look happy, but he didn't refuse either. So I started reading from my list, which extended over three pages. I had intentionally included both names that I knew he knew and others that I was almost certain he'd never had contact with.

Anders Larsson and Ebbe Carlsson were already clear; he had already admitted to having contact with them. But I was surprised to hear him deny that he knew parliamentary stenographer Bengt Henningsson, since several newspapers, including the *GT*, had written about how Bertil Wedin, Bengt Henningsson, and Anders Larsson had been in contact before the murder.

Wedin was familiar with most of the people at *Contra* and had even been their Middle East correspondent for many years. Wedin was the one who discovered editor in chief Carl G. Holm and recommended that the Federation of Swedish Industries (Industriförbundet) hire him. He was familiar with the names Hans von Hofsten and Joel Haukka but wasn't sure if he had met either of them.

Wedin's reaction to Palme's close coworker Bernt Carlsson was interesting. The reason I asked about him was that Bernt Carlsson was one of the people who had directed the IUEF's work during the time when Craig Williamson infiltrated the organization. Wedin didn't know Bernt Carlsson but said that he was convinced that the plane over Lockerbie had been blown up because Bernt Carlsson was on board. At the time, Carlsson was the UN commissioner for Namibia and had promised to come after anybody who was looting the country of its natural resources before its coming independence. I was listening in awe. Would the target of one of the largest terrorist attacks in history have been a Swede who I had hardly heard of? Once again, I had to remind myself that I was speaking to someone who had been working for several security services; there was no guarantee that anything he said was true.

A couple of weeks before the disaster, Wedin said, Bernt Carlsson had invited his closest friends to his place for dinner and, crying, told them he was going to die soon. Wedin squeezed out a few crocodile tears to show how Bernt Carlsson had cried. I was impressed. Agent Wedin could cry on command, demonstrating that he was a better actor than I had thought.

"Can we look at the memo now?" he asked once we'd gone through the names on my list.

He had crossed his legs and turned to the side. There was no doubt that he was ready to leave and the only thing keeping him here was the promise of getting to see the document. I couldn't hold out any longer, but as luck would have it the waiter came to ask if it was time for another round, which gave me enough time and distraction to have a chance to check that the digital camera on the table was really filming.

"I thought I would give it to you page by page so you have a chance to react to what it says."

Wedin took the first page, read through the text carefully and asked for the next, and the next, until he had finished the memo. I observed both surprise and pride behind Wedin's stiff expression. Then he started denying things.

"I don't know what 'middleman' means in this context, but I wasn't any kind of 'man' at all. I was never asked to help in any way. No one in the whole world ever said anything to me about Palme or plans to assassinate him. I have never been asked a question that could even lead to helping anyone and was never given an assignment that could have led to anything. Not a single one. Not a single one. Did nothing along those lines. Nothing at all, there's no . . . I know, people always say where there's smoke, there's fire, but there's nothing to this. I know what reputation I have—right winger and conservative and doesn't like Palme and every possible thing—but I haven't done any of this. Not a single bit. And no one asked me to do anything either. So whoever it was, they had no knowledge about me, or they didn't trust me. I wasn't asked."

Wedin's denial was persistent and convincing. A simple "I wasn't involved" would have been enough, but it was understandable that he wanted to say more since time after time, year after year, he was subjected to the same accusation. Wedin vehemently denied it. I didn't ask any more questions about his potential role in the assassination of Olof Palme. That was unnecessary. But I didn't want to give up on the topic quite so easily.

"Who did kill Olof Palme?"

"I wrote an article in *Contra* about that, which I'm guessing you've read. Just like I describe there, I've done my own investigations and compiled a body of information. I've tried repeatedly to turn over my information to the Swedish authorities, first to Cabinet Secretary Pierre Schori and then to the Swedish police. No one has been interested. To the contrary, they've impeded me."

"But you could have gotten around that just by sending in the material by registered mail and contacting the media at the same time?"

"These issues are too serious to have the media pulled in. And with registered mail there's no way to verify what I sent. But very briefly, I think it was a Turkish citizen from what I later found out was called PKK. He did it on behalf of, among others, a woman from East Germany, who was in Cyprus to frame me for it. Anders Larsson was probably involved in some way or other."

I had asked everything I wanted to, and Wedin had been trying to walk away since the previous day. It slowly seemed to dawn on him that he had said too much, which in that case meant my efforts received good marks. No one else had ever interviewed Bertil Wedin for eleven hours, as far as I knew. I was satisfied with myself and relaxed a moment too soon.

"What's your email address?"

I had thought of this earlier, but when everything got going, I hadn't done anything about it. Now, I needed to pull myself together and invent an email address that fit with my made-up name. Fredrik Bengtson was far too common for me to take a risk on a straightforward Gmail or Yahoo email address. I hoped the red flames I could feel flaring up on my neck weren't visible. I stuttered out an answer.

"Four thirty-seven Bengtson dot Fredrik at Gmail dot com. Bengtson with one *S*."

"One *S*. How snobbish."

He seemed to have bought my last white lie, but it clearly showed me that my safety was fragile. It would be enough for Wedin to ask some of his local friends to follow me to the hotel to find out that there was no one named Fredrik Bengtson staying there. The first thing I needed to do the moment I escaped was to set up that email address so that Wedin didn't smell a rat too soon. The next thing was to back up the eleven hours of audio recordings from my iPhone and several hours of video from the spy pen and digital camera. Then, I would leave Cyprus as quickly and quietly as possible.

***

I booked a seat on a Norwegian Air flight home the next morning. The taxi ride to Larnaca went off without any unexpected stops this time. I started wondering about when Wedin had actually been telling the truth. It was evident to me that at times he was trying to remember old lies, like when he told me his own theory of who had assassinated Olof Palme. When he was lying, I noted, he spoke more slowly, as if he had to dig deep to find the memory of what he had once made up.

The Delivery

Just inside my front door lay a pile of ads and bills, on top of which was a small padded envelope with no sender, postmarked Prague. The parcel bombs that Craig Williamson once sent, which had killed two women and a child, flitted through my mind. I opened the envelope from the wrong end, a trick one of Stieg's friends had said he learned from his colleagues at *Expo*. But it was just a USB flash drive, which I immediately inserted into my computer.

The dialogue window that popped up required a password, so I went through the envelope it had arrived in. Nothing. Who would send me an encrypted flash drive? Prague. Lída Komárková. I could still taste the ginger and lime from our Moscow Mules. When we said goodbye outside the bar, Lída had confirmed that she would contact Jakob Thedelin on Facebook and ask him questions about Enerström and the Palme assassination. I didn't know what to expect, but Lída seemed to be a person who kept her word. Maybe this was the result.

I checked my phone messages. The text from her was brief: "Wedin." Yes, that could definitely be the password. But how could she know about Bertil Wedin? I was almost positive that I hadn't even mentioned Wedin's name when we talked about Stieg Larsson, because I wanted her to focus on Jakob, Alf, and Gio. Nothing more.

I tried "Wedin" and the contents of the flash drive immediately became accessible. A PDF and a PST file. Google told me that PST was a format for saving messages, such as emails from Outlook. It would probably be a bit of a hassle to view the email file, so I started with the PDF. It was a hundred pages of private Facebook messages in English between Lída Komárková and Jakob Thedelin. My jaw dropped open as I began to read.

***

Hello Jakob, you have many friend with me. Tell me you and family?
    Best regarding,
    Lída Komárková

Dear Lída Komárková,
Nice to hear from you. You asked about my family. Well, my father is still alive, but my mother died in 1994. My father lives in another city but we call each other from time to time, the same as my friends. I have a small number of friends but they are good friends. One is a real gentleman.
    Love,
    Jakob

Lída had started cautiously, but seemed to have quickly sensed that Jakob was easy to lead. Maybe she had exaggerated how bad her English was, but Jakob had answered every message. It felt like I was intruding on a private dialogue between two people I didn't know, which was also close to the truth. But one of them, Lída, had actually agreed to my reading the dialogue. A pretty profile picture and friendly messages seemed to be the modern era's equivalent to Mata Hari, but significantly easier. After a few weeks and several messages, Lída had indeed gotten closer to Jakob.

Hello Jakob,
I am writing in Word now and that helps me to write in more correct English. So I can tell you more about me and my life. Some time I want to come to Sweden. Maybe this summer?
   I am very interested in the fact that you converted to Judaism! After what I did many years ago, I have thought a lot about converting to my grandfather's (my mother's father) religion. How can I convert? When did you convert? Is it different for girls?
   Big hug,
   Lída

Dear Lída,
You asked how to convert. You can do an orthodox or a liberal or a conservative conversion. I did a conservative conversion. You have to know what foods are Kosher and the basic Jewish laws. It isn't hard at all. A girl doesn't have the religious obligations that a man does. A girl's conversion is less strict. But you should ask your local synagogue for more information.
   Big hug,
   Jakob

Lída had found out that Jakob had converted to Judaism, which explained all the Jewish symbols on his Facebook timeline. His messages gradually got longer and longer, while Lída's got shorter and more straightforward. Usually she asked him to tell her more. Sometimes she asked concrete questions and often received concrete answers, but they were embedded in long messages filled with Jakob's thoughts. She urged him to always tell the truth; she said she had been betrayed and demanded absolute sincerity.

> Dear Jakob,
> I really like that you use "dear". Maybe you are the gentleman you mentioned? Or does your friend really exist? Olof Palme was Swedish, was he a gentleman? A hero?
>> Big hug,
>> Lída

> Dear Lída,
> Nice to hear from you.
>> You mentioned gentlemen—are there still any? Well, I know a few. One of them still lives by the old mottos and speaks quite a bit about chivalry. I do my best to live up to it.
>> Olof Palme was the leader of the social democratic party in Sweden. Palme was assassinated in 1986. He was honored by the Soviet Union with an official stamp bearing his portrait. The only other foreigner who has been honored in that way was Kim Philby, a Soviet spy and British citizen.
>> And by the way I'm not surprised that Palme is viewed as a hero outside of Sweden, not much is said about him in a negative sense.

But there is an exception. The Italian newspaper
La Stampa had an article in 1982 with the headline,
"Palme: A Dictator in Collusion with Moscow."
Love,
Jakob

As expected, Jakob wrote about Olof Palme as a traitor, a KGB
agent, and described how he himself used to "celebrate the anniversary
of the death of that traitor to his country with a glass of wine" each year.
Lída kept fishing for information, but mostly about who Jakob's friend
was. He wrote long messages about his thoughts and Lída shepherded
him closer.

Dear Lída,
Thanks for your message!
You ask if I've shot with a Magnum myself? Yes,
I have. I leaned my arm against a window frame to
achieve a better shot. The result went according to
expectation.
You also write about trust in your letter. I don't
care for lies either, not even little ones are OK, ever.
Lies ruin relationships.
I'm glad you hate lies. I myself have taught
myself the importance of the truth.
When I talk about important things, then I will try
to be as precise as possible.
My chivalrous friend is Mr. Bertil Wedin. I got
to know Mr. Wedin many years ago, over the
phone. He was one of the people who contacted
Dr. Enerström. I've never met Mr. Wedin face to
face. He lives in Cyprus. But we talk every week by
e-mail. Our contact was established for the first time

in 1998 if I remember correctly. I'll tell you more
another time.
     Love,
     Jakob

So that was how Lída became aware of Wedin. She had established
that Wedin knew both Jakob Thedelin and Alf Enerström! I was floored.
I hadn't found any connection like that, not in Stieg's extensive archive,
in the Review Commission's report, or in any other documents.

"My friend who met Otto von Habsburg was the
leader of the Social Democratic opposition. His
name is Dr. Alf Enerström. Unfortunately the pressure on him, political pressure and other difficulties,
caused him to lose his grasp. I met Dr. Enerström
through his wife, whom I contacted. I was interested
in the campaign Dr. Enerström was running against
Palme. I met him at his medical clinic the first time.
We became friends. You asked about eyeglasses.
I wear them almost all the time, except when I'm
reading or writing."

"Well, the good doctor rented a six-room apartment
in the capitol city, Stockholm. He paid half the rent
and his underground party the other half, but that's
not important to the story.
     "What's important is that Dr. Enerström had a
secret bank account in Luxemburg. The money in it
came from donors who supported his cause, mostly
from expat Swedes. One of the people who collected money was Vera Ax:son-Johnsson from one
of Sweden's leading business families. The money

was then used to place ads before parliamentary
elections."

It was impressive to read how Lída led Jakob with questions she
thought were relevant. Little by little she got him where she wanted.
He kept writing and explaining.

". . . the Swedish diplomat Bernt Carlsson at the U.N.
had information about the Palme assassination in his
U.N. safe. The case was forced open and Mr. Carlsson
told his friends that he 'was going to be murdered
soon.' It happened, too. In the Lockerbie massacre
over Scotland. Several hundred people died!"

"You also asked me about the CIA. The CIA man
I worked with worked outside the U.S. embassy
as a newsman. He gathered information from
Eastern Europe on trips there. He also traveled to
Czechoslovakia since he spoke the language as well
as German. You asked if he is American? He isn't.
    "That's how I met my contact. He was a news-
man. I decided I would talk to him after an article in
a newspaper. At our first meeting, I gave him information for him that I received from Dr. Enerström
about a visit of an important intelligence officer who
met Olof Palme in 1982. My contact found the information valuable and later I continued giving information to the CIA.
    "The CIA once did an assessment of the mate-
rial I was providing them. The CIA decided that they
could use 75% of my material, but for those who
were CIA-trained at their headquarters in Langley,

the same number was 50%. Guess if I was proud of myself! That motivated me even more."

Jakob repeated several times that he reported to a CIA handler and provided clues to who the handler was. It seemed too outrageous to be true, but I made a note to myself to keep my eye out for a person who worked as a newsman who could speak Czech.

"You asked me who assassinated Palme, a group or an individual? To summarize: It seems that Palme had a meeting with Soviet GRU officers a day before he was killed."

"You ask how many people would be necessary to handle something like that. That question was asked in a TV interview in the context of whether a larger group could keep quiet. I've heard that to put a tail on someone you need let's say 20 people just to watch the person, but more of course to have fresh people to work in shifts while the others sleep or need to eat. For 20 people to keep quiet it would require self-discipline, professional motivation, honor."

"In Palme's case, I wonder if his telephone wasn't bugged. The question is, who knew he was going to the movies that night? Well, if his GRU handler knew, then it would be easy for them, the GRU, to kill Palme. Take him, kill him, before he took the subway home. Palme was murdered right across from the entrance to the subway. So only one or two killers would have been needed, one in reserve if the first one got sick."

"You wrote that you don't believe me and you're not finding the answer you're looking for in my letter. I'm searching parts of my letter again and looking for what I could have left out or been unclear about?"

Lída had gotten Jakob to write about the Palme assassination, but his answers were confusing. A plot, yes, but the Russians? If Palme was a Soviet agent, then why would they kill him? There wasn't any logic to be seen in that. But Lída was approaching the big question, which was obvious from Jakob's messages.

I want you to know this: I like you a lot. And I don't want to lose you either.

With that, I'll bring up the other subject, about Olof Palme. Oh, I wish I had shot him when I was a 12–13-year-old boy and thus saved my country from a lot of trouble. (See the whole story below).

I thought then, when I was 13, that I could use my friend's dad's pistols that were 200 years old, load one of them with metal things and see if I could get close enough to the prime minister. I thought that as a little boy I could hardly be sent to jail and would also be allowed to get close to Palme. That way, I could succeed with my plan.

I'm not sure if Palme would had survived with the medical care of the day, depends on how good and how lucky I would have been.

King Gustaf III was shot with a pistol like the one I was planning to use. The king died of an infection sooner than from the gunshot itself. And I knew that when I was 12–13, so I knew that I had to do it right—aim for the chest, at close range, stop

the heart from beating. Impossible to save him. I
remember I was worried about the ammunition,
what I would use.

But since it was a long way from where I lived to
the capitol, my teenage plans didn't materialize. I
regret that. Besides, if I had shot Palme, when I was 13
years old, I would have been loved not just by my parents but also by half the country, easy to take a year in
jail if anything at all, maybe I was too young for that.

As I had it planned, I would tell the press, as
a teenager I mean, why I had shot Palme. It was
because I was convinced that Palme was a traitor. I
was expecting support for shining light on the facts.
I know now that some of the people I know today
would have testified in support of me about Palme's
treason. That way, Sweden's history would have
been changed compared to how it was.

Since I didn't shoot Palme, I felt guilty to such a
degree when I grew up that it didn't make sense and
I decided that I should gather evidence and write
about it and publish, as well as do everything I could
to work against Palme and everything he stood for.
That's why I contacted Dr. Enerström in 1980–82.

Love,
Jakob

Dear Jakob,
Important to tell the truth and not to keep anything
back. But the question, I don't see the answer to the
direct question:

Did you shoot Olof Palme?
Love,
Lída

Dear Lída,
So that was the question! I thought I answered it,
the question about Palme. Here is my answer now.
I didn't shoot Palme in 1986. I wasn't involved in his
death on February 28, 1986, either. I heard the news
just like everyone else, astonished at the (good)
news, even if it was 15 years too late to make any
difference when it came to the country's progress
and the damage he had already done.
Hug and love,
Jakob

Jakob,
I'm very sad. This is why I'm afraid of losing you.
I feel that your answer about Palme is a trick. I
understand that it's a problem to tell the whole truth
after a long time. But I can tell that your answer isn't
honest. I said before: just the truth, no withholding
things. Because of what I've been through, the bad
things I've been through.
Jakob. I can't come and see you with trust. I'm
sorry. I'm losing you.
Goodbye,
Lída

Lída had guided Jakob to the question of whether he had shot
Olof Palme, but he had avoided it or answered indirectly until she
explicitly said that he had to answer and be truthful. Jakob's answer

was unambiguous. He had not murdered Olof Palme or been involved in the murder. But why had he felt obliged to add the year in the first answer? And the day and year in the second? Maybe it was a way of emphasizing his innocence, but it had almost the opposite effect. Especially since Olof Palme was declared dead six minutes after midnight and thus he didn't die on February 28 but rather on March 1.

Jakob's reluctance to answer and his mysterious way of wording his answers didn't get rid of the question marks for me. Quite the contrary, my suspicions that he was involved in the murder in some way increased.

But Lída's dialogue with Jakob had ended abruptly there. She broke it off after noting that she didn't trust him. Jakob's desperate attempts to continue their contact went unanswered.

Rockets That Will Never Come Again

Stockholm, September 2013

The second file on the USB flash drive from Lída was harder to open but every bit as interesting once I managed it. I installed Outlook on my computer and eventually succeeded in importing the PST file. After fifteen minutes, I was searching freely in Jakob Thedelin and Bertil Wedin's email history.

I suspected that someone other than Lída must have gotten access to the emails. Maybe it was the friend of Lída's that she had said she was going to ask for help. Regardless of who had done it, I now had the opportunity to read what two people who might have been involved in the assassination of Olof Palme had written to each other. Two people that the police and others interested in the Palme assassination, including me, had not realized knew each other, let alone been close.

I went through thousands of emails and gathered a few things. Jakob felt like he was being watched, so Bertil gave him tips on how he could check to see if anyone was following him and if his apartment had been bugged. They often mentioned that they needed to be careful with what they wrote since someone may be able to read their emails. *You have the right idea there,* I said to myself. They considered phones somewhat safer. Important things that they didn't want anyone else to read, they sent by regular mail.

Some topics came up frequently. Of those, the Palme assassination came in first place. They often wrote about what was being reported on the investigation and what the police were doing or not doing. They described a theory that involved Olof Palme being an agent of the Soviet Union and that the KGB had assassinated him because he was about to be exposed. That theory recurred frequently in their emails and differed from what Wedin had told me in Cyprus, but fit better with what Jakob had written to Lída. Even so, it was hard to see the logic. Why would the Soviet security services murder their own agent who was also a prime minister? The fact that nothing had come out after Palme's death suggesting that he had been working for the Russians made that theory even less likely. Plus, the discussion about the KGB often felt tacked on, when the messages were actually about something else. My interpretation was that the emails about that theory were an agreed-upon smoke screen for uninvited readers like myself.

Another recurrent topic was the Lockerbie bombing in December 1988, which Wedin had also mentioned to me in Cyprus. He had given Jakob an assignment to report back to him as soon as it was written about in the Swedish media. According to their theory, the target of that terrorist act was Bernt Carlsson, and at least part of the motive was that he knew who had murdered Palme and why. If you assumed Wedin and Jakob's theory about the Palme assassination was true, it would have been the KGB that carried out the bombing but, strangely enough, they never wrote that.

Obviously Wedin didn't believe the official version that Libya was behind the Lockerbie bombing, and as I kept reading, I realized there was a possibility that he was right. The Libyan, al-Megrahi, who was the only one jailed for the bombing, was released on compassionate grounds in 2009 after it was revealed that one of the key witnesses had lied and the negotiations concerning a new trial would take so long that the fatally ill al-Megrahi would have died before they were done.

It was clear from the rest of Jakob's emails I read that there was no one closer to him than Bertil Wedin. Almost all the personal-sounding emails that Jakob wrote were sent to Bertil; there was no one he trusted more. Not even himself, it seemed. It appeared from their communication that Jakob looked up to Bertil almost unquestioningly. When Jakob wrote that "the gears are turning" about the Swedish media coverage following Anders Breivik's attacks in Norway, Bertil clearly stated that "there is no excuse for killing women and children." Jakob gave in and seemed to use Bertil as a moral compass, which he himself appeared to lack. It was harder to tell what Bertil was getting out of the dialogue, but maybe the simplest explanation was the most likely. Both of them had become isolated people and craved human contact, even if just by email, regular mail, and sometimes phone. Maybe they simply felt lonely.

The email that I couldn't scrape out of my mind was Jakob's response to Bertil's first email ever.

September 1, 2009
Dear Jakob,
Please tell me about the musical activities in Västra Frölunda.
    Sincerely,
    Bertil

September 5, 2009
Bertil!
In Västra Frölunda we have no musical life to speak
about, but an IDF spokesman can report that thun-
der and crashes in a bunker, with other sounds that
are heard after the bombs fall, remind of rockets
that never come again.
   Sincerely,
   Jakob Thedelin
   (IDF = Israel Defense Forces)

Bertil was asking about musical life in the concrete suburbs of
Göteborg, where Jakob sometimes lived, and where hip-hop music
ruled the scene. Even I knew there was no musical scene for Bertil and
Jakob to be talking about in Sweden's concrete-slab suburbs, as they
were unlikely to be rap fans. Bertil was most likely asking about something else, which Jakob understood.

Jakob's answer was even more cryptic. I sat for a long time, trying
to sort out what he might mean. The email seemed playful, as if filled
with some kind of symbols or code where only the sender and recipient
are in on what they mean. I checked the other emails and didn't find
anything similar expressed anywhere else.

Finally, I realized there were two possibilities. The first was that
it was an innocent, joking email about some everyday thing that no
one needed to worry about. The second was that it was the opposite—
something that they were forced to conceal. I pondered for a while
and then wrote down what it might mean, if I deciphered it as far as
possible:

Jakob (a spokesman for the Israeli army) talks about weapons (rockets) that are stored safely (never to come again) in
a space without a window (bunker) where there's thunder

and sounds (crashes, other noises that are heard after the
bombs fall).

This was a comprehensible and conspiratorial meaning, construed
from a coded email that could just as easily have been completely
innocent.

The left half of my brain thought I was becoming just as obsessed
as the other folks who had taken an active interest in the Palme assassination. The right half was starting to think that Jakob Thedelin might
have hidden the gun that was used to assassinate Olof Palme somewhere
in Västra Frölunda.

***

The next email exchange that captured my attention was significantly
more recent. Two days after Lída put the kibosh on their relationship
in that Facebook exchange, just when I was preparing to go down to
Cyprus, Jakob felt the need to ask Bertil for advice on how he should
handle the situation. He wrote several emails to Bertil about Lída and
their exchanges. Finally he shared how interested she was in the Palme
assassination. Bertil Wedin replied immediately. He could not fathom
that Jakob had discussed such serious topics with anyone else. Bertil
wrote that he didn't trust his friend anymore and that he was forced to
break off contact with Jakob.

Jakob Thedelin had suddenly lost two people close to him in just
a couple of days.

***

I wrote to Lída on Viber to thank her for the materials and asked out of curiosity how she had accomplished it. I received an answer a couple of days later.

> Hi,
> No worries. You got it on one condition: that you never ask me again who helped me. It's my secret. The person who did it wants "källskydd" [protection as a source].
>> Have a good life!
>> Lída

She had obviously looked up the term for "protection as a source" since that was written in Swedish while the rest was in English. Or maybe her source was Swedish and had taught her the term. I sent a response and confirmed my promise never to ask. She didn't reply. A few weeks later I called her. No answer. I sent a few messages but did not receive a response from her. Maybe "Have a good life!" meant that she wasn't going to talk further with me ever again. Or maybe she was just traveling or had a new number. But I didn't worry about it too much. I had something else to think about.

The New Yorker

Svenska Dagbladet turned out to be very interested in my interview with Bertil Wedin, but even more so in the Stieg Larsson memo. Their news director, Ola Billger, and I wrote four longer articles together about Stieg and the assassination of Olof Palme, including my interview with Bertil Wedin. When we published them, we had two of the articles translated into English, which turned out to be a big hit.

News of Stieg's interest in the Palme assassination spread around the world in twenty-four hours, and we were temporary celebrities. *Svenska Dagbladet*'s editor in chief, Fredric Karén, thanked us and strictly instructed me not to mention what had happened when I discovered and opened Stieg's archive. This was an investigation by *Svenska Dagbladet*, I had to understand that. And I would get paid, so why should I object?

A couple of days after the first publication, my cell phone rang.

"Hi, I'm Nicholas Schmidle. I write for the *New Yorker* magazine," a voice said in American English.

At that point I didn't fully grasp the reputation of the *New Yorker* and its position of power and prestige in the US and globally. If I had realized that, I probably would have started stammering, but instead Nicholas and I spoke intently for a good hour about Stieg Larsson's archive, his theories, and my work.

Nicholas wanted to sell an article about my work to his editor. It would take a year, but that became the beginning of a collaboration and exchange of materials that, among other things, would debunk a key lie and take us both to South Africa.

The Composite Photo

There were still aspects of the Palme investigation that I didn't understand, and that Stieg must have been just as bewildered by. One of them was the controversial composite photo that had been produced in the first week following the assassination, based on the witness Sarah's testimony.

Stieg had written about the composite photo in a letter to *Searchlight*'s editor in chief, Gerry Gable, on March 20, 1986. Later in the investigation, the police claimed that both the photo and Sarah's testimony were irrelevant. I decided to analyze how the composite came to be, what role it played in the investigation, and whether it was of interest to my research.

***

Eight days after the assassination, the police seemed sure that the composite photo depicted Palme's murderer. The witness Sarah had been selected as the most reliable to create a picture of the killer. The photo was distributed widely around the world to the police, the media, and the public.

Later, Tommy Lindström, the head of the National Criminal Investigation Department, determined with the help of a police colleague that it was irrelevant because it supposedly depicted an innocent man whom Sarah had seen earlier the same night. They were so sure about this that they decided Sarah didn't even need to be asked about the matter.

On the anniversary, thirty years after the assassination, the police called a press conference and stated that it was "not very likely" that the man in the composite photo was the killer and that the police weren't interested in the photo. This time, the argument was that there was no unbroken chain of witnesses who had seen the killer run all the way from the scene of the crime to Smala Gränd, where Sarah had seen the man. Also, ten minutes, possibly up to twenty minutes, had elapsed since the murder, which was an improbably long time for a fleeing assassin to take to get to that location. The police opted yet again to ignore the composite photo.

Eight days after the assassination, the photo and Sarah's testimony were the most important leads the police had. Thirty years later, the opposite was true—without any explanation being given about who the man was or what he had been doing there.

***

When I did my analysis of how the assassination unfolded, one of the pieces that led to my conclusion that it was an amateur killer was that it would explain the contradictory witness statements from the area at the top of the stairs on Brunkeberg Ridge.

Smala Gränd, where Sarah saw the man, was only one block long and led from one stump of a street to another. The only way to continue on from there was out onto Birger Jarlsgatan or via the stairs up onto

Brunkeberg Ridge. If it really was the killer whom Sarah saw, then the most likely reason for him to be there was that he was lost. If so, one possible explanation for Lars Jeppsson's last glimpse of a man between the cars on David Bagares Gata was that the fleeing gunman was looking for cover because he didn't know where to go. In that case, the same would apply to the other witness statements from up on the ridge. If the killer had wandered around, he could very well not have been on Smala Gränd until ten to twenty minutes after the assassination. If that were the case, it would have created some real confusion for any other people who were waiting for the gunman.

More important to me was the fact that the police could have been just as wrong to dismiss the composite photo as they had been so many times previously in the investigation.

I decided to see what I could find out about it. The composite might resemble one of the people I was interested in. Since Alf Enerström's height of six foot four didn't match Sarah's description, I started with Jakob Thedelin.

To make sure I had the right picture, I requested an original copy of the composite photo from the police. A few weeks later, I received a high-quality copy in the mail.

I had several photos of Jakob Thedelin from his Facebook page and chose a picture that showed his face almost straight on with a neutral expression. Using Photoshop, I straightened the picture so that his face was vertical, erased his eyeglasses, and made the picture black and white. Then, I zoomed in so his face was the same size as the one in the composite photo, then increased the transparency to 50 percent. Finally, I overlaid Jakob's face over a scanned-in version of the composite photo.

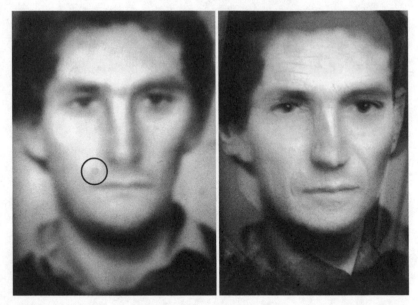

LEFT: *The composite image shows a distinct mole on the right corner of the mouth.* RIGHT: *Combined image of the composite and a photograph of Jakob Thedelin.*

I noticed two things:

1. Jakob Thedelin looked very similar to the composite photo.
2. Jakob Thedelin had a congenital mole on his face just over the corner of his mouth on the right side, in the same location that the composite photo had a circular mark.

The Palme investigation team couldn't explain the circular mark on the composite photo to me. Nor did they answer my question of who the man might be who wandered into Smala Gränd after the murder. They made do with stating again that they did not think the person was relevant.

To me it seemed like another sign of what was widely said about the investigation: Anything that didn't support the case against Christer

Pettersson was considered irrelevant by the police. He had been freed but was still guilty in their eyes. It would be hard for me to convince them that there was another possibility, but I had to try.

***

I used the material I had received from Lída—the Facebook conversation and the emails with Bertil Wedin—Jakob's similarity to the composite photo, and a number of other circumstances to put together a memo, a memo much like the one Stieg Larsson had written about Bertil Wedin. In total there were twelve pages about Jakob Thedelin's possible involvement in the Palme assassination, with quotes from witness statements, illustrations, timelines, and quotes from the Facebook conversations and emails. I submitted my memo to the police, and I waited for them to act. And waited. And waited . . .

A Study of
Assassination

Stockholm, Spring 2015

The information that Stieg submitted to the police the year after Olof Palme's assassination included Bertil Wedin's possible role in the murder and a tip about the EAP. Maybe he had submitted additional information, but no one could really know if there was more, since over the years, the police had lost a lot of material in the black hole that was rumored to be the world's biggest murder investigation.

In his letter to *Searchlight*'s editor in chief, Gerry Gable, Stieg described a professionally carried out assassination; only in passing did he mention the possibility that it was done by an amateur. In the last document in Stieg's files about the murder, an article in *Searchlight* from 1996, the assassination was still described as having been carried out by a professional, with Swedish right-wing extremists playing an unclear role. I knew that Stieg's interest and investigative work continued right up until his death eight years later, but I hadn't found anything concrete that suggested that he had gotten any further than that. But maybe I hadn't searched carefully enough? Were there documents in his archive that I had missed?

I had been through what I'd scanned several times, but there were some bound reports that weren't scannable and therefore I couldn't search in them. I still had them at home and decided to take the time to go through them to see if I had missed anything.

One of the reports was called *A Study of Assassination*. That sounded academic but still got my imagination working. I found no clue as to how Stieg had come across it, but that was true of most of the documents in his archive.

It was a nineteen-page document that was neither dated nor signed, and although it wasn't made public until May 15, 1997, its preparation date was estimated as December 31, 1953. The CIA was behind the document and had used it to destabilize President Guzmán's government in Guatemala between 1952 and 1954.

The CIA operations PBFORTUNE and PBSUCCESS had striven to topple Guatemala's democratic government led by President Jacobo Árbenz Guzmán. The first attempt at toppling President Guzmán was authorized by US president Truman in 1952. At the beginning of the same year, CIA headquarters started producing memos with titles like "Guatemalan Communist Personnel to Remove During Military Operations." The A-list of people being considered for "removal" included fifty-eight people.

***

A Study of Assassination was written in simple language and was laid out like any old report or guide. The document began with a brief background defining the term "assassination," and then provided the limited occasions that would necessitate assassinations. The body of the document described how decisions concerning assassinations should be

made and how sensitive people shouldn't attempt them. It gave pros and
cons for the individual techniques that could be used to kill a victim.

Manual. It is possible to kill a man with the bare
hands, but very few are skillful enough to do it well.
[. . .] However, the simplest local tools are often the
most efficient means of assassination. A hammer,
axe, wrench, screw driver, [. . .] or anything hard,
heavy, and handy will suffice. A length of rope or
[. . .] a belt will do if the assassin is strong and agile.
[. . .] The obviously lethal machine gun failed to kill
Trotsky where an item of sporting goods succeeded.

Accidents. For secret assassination, either simple or
chase, the contrived accident is the most effective
technique. When successfully executed, it causes little excitement and is only casually investigated. The
most efficient accident [. . .] is a fall of seventy-five
feet or more onto a hard surface. [. . .] Falls before
trains or subway cars are usually effective, but
require exact timing and can seldom be free from
unexpected observation. [. . .]

Drugs. [. . .] If the assassin is trained as a doctor or
nurse and the subject is under medical care, this is
an easy and rare method. An overdose of morphine
administered as a sedative will cause death without
disturbance and is difficult to detect. [. . .]

Edge Weapons. [. . .] A certain minimum of anatomical knowledge is needed for reliability. Puncture
wounds of the body cavity may not be reliable

unless the heart is reached. [. . .] Absolute reliability is obtained by severing the spinal cord in the cervical region. This can be done with the point of a knife or a light blow of an axe or hatchet. Another reliable method is the severing of both jugular and carotid blood vessels on both sides of the windpipe. [. . .]

Blunt Weapons. As with edge weapons, blunt weapons require some anatomical knowledge for effective use. Their main advantage is their universal availability. A hammer may be picked up almost anywhere in the world. [. . .] Even a rock or a heavy stick will do, and nothing resembling a weapon need be procured, carried, or subsequently disposed of. Blows should be directed to the temple, the area just below and behind the ear, and the lower, rear portion of the skull. Of course, if the blow is very heavy, any portion of the upper skull will do. [. . .]

Firearms. Firearms are often used in assassination, often very ineffectively. The assassin usually has insufficient technical knowledge of the limitations of weapons, and expects more range, accuracy, and killing power than can be provided with reliability. Since certainty of death is the major requirement, firearms should be used which can provide destructive power at least 100 percent in excess of that thought to be necessary, and ranges should be half that considered practical for the weapon. Firearms have other drawbacks. [. . .] Their use as a murder weapon is consistently overrated. [. . .]

(e) The Pistol. While the handgun is quite inefficient as a weapon of assassination, it is often used, partly because it is readily available and can be concealed on the person, and partly because its limitations are not widely appreciated. While many well-known assassinations have been carried out with pistols (Lincoln, Harding, Gandhi), such attempts fail as often as they succeed (Truman, Roosevelt, Churchill). If a pistol is used, it should be as powerful as possible and fired from just beyond reach. [. . .] In the hands of an expert, a powerful pistol is quite deadly, but such experts are rare and not usually available for assassination missions. The .45 Colt, .44 Special, .455 Kly, [. . .] and .357 Magnum are all efficient calibers. Less powerful rounds can suffice but are less reliable. [. . .] In all cases, the subject should be hit solidly at least three times for complete reliability.

Explosives. Bombs and demolition charges of various sorts have been used frequently in assassination. Such devices [. . .] can provide safety and overcome guard barriers. [. . .] The charge should be so placed that the subject is not ever six feet from it at the moment of detonation. [. . .]

The handbook's classification of various types of assassination was straightforward: "simple" meant that the victim was unaware of the operation, "chase" that the victim knew about the threat but was unguarded, "guarded" that the victim was guarded, "lost" meant that the assassin would be sacrificed and preferably killed, "safe" meant that part of the plan was for the assassin to escape, "secret" meant that the assassination would look like an accident, "open" that it wasn't necessary to hide that it was an assassination, and "terroristic" that the assassination required subsequent publicity.

Applying these terms, the document said that the assassination of Julius Caesar could be considered simple, safe, and terroristic since the victim was unaware of the operation, his killers escaped, and the assassins wanted publicity. On the other hand, the assassination of American politician Huey Long was lost, guarded, and open since the assassin was killed, the victim was guarded, and there was no need to conceal its having been an assassination.

In all types of assassinations that were intended to be "safe," the assassin should have the same properties as a "clandestine agent." He should be determined, intelligent, resourceful, and physically active. If special equipment such as a pistol were to be used, he would need to have exceptional skill in using it. He should have as little contact as possible with the rest of the organization. Apart from terroristic cases, the assassin should spend as little time as possible in the area.

In "lost" assassinations, the assassin must be a fanatic of some kind. Politics, religion, or revenge were nearly the only possible motives. Since a fanatic would be psychologically unstable, he would need to be handled with extreme caution. He must not know the identities of the other members of the organization, for although it is intended that he die in the act, something could go wrong. While Trotsky's assassin has never revealed any significant information, it was unsound to depend on this when the act was planned.

The planning should only occur through conversation and everything must be memorized. There should be no written evidence of the operation.

***

When I read the report about the CIA's methods in the 1950s, I was aware that they probably differed from the ones the security services were using in the 1980s. But it was also likely that knowledge about how to effectively perform assassinations had been refined and spread to more countries, especially if the collaboration between the security services was as established as Stieg and others had written about. The question was whether their methods had become more legal. Had they simply stopped murdering people? As far as the South African security services were concerned, it was a fact that they assassinated people in the 1980s. Many of the guilty parties had already testified openly about that before the Truth and Reconciliation Commission.

I compared *A Study of Assassination* with Stieg's theory about a professional organization and my own conclusion that the assassination was probably carried out by an inexperienced perpetrator. There was a possibility that both were actually correct. A professional organization could have used an inexperienced perpetrator.

If the Palme assassination was supposed to be a "lost" killing, then it would have been carried out by some kind of a fanatic. That would explain many of the mistakes the killer made and how I had concluded that the killer was an amateur.

He didn't hit the victim "at least three times" which was the explicit recommendation. He also used a type of ammunition that increased the likelihood that the victim would survive, and he missed Lisbeth Palme, thereby allowing a witness to survive. I went through the analysis of the killer's behavior, which I had done a couple of years earlier, and noted all the other factors that suggested that he was an amateur.

Based on the report, my conclusion was that if the assassination of Olof Palme were organized by a security service, with access to knowledge equivalent to what the CIA had in the 1950s, then the arrangement had been lost, simple, and open, meaning that the killer was a fanatic, Olof Palme was unaware of the threat, and the assassination did not need to be concealed.

With that hypothesis, Stieg's theory about South Africa, Wedin, and Swedish right-wing extremists could fit quite nicely with my analysis that the assassin was an amateur. To find out if that was true, I had to meet more of the people who were involved. I had to go to South Africa.

The Dead Children #3

In the instant before the collision, the front of the truck loomed like a wall in front of the windshield of the family's vehicle. The shadow temporarily blocked the sharp light of the South African sun inside the car. That was the instant when Franz Esser and his wife, Emily, realized that their car was inevitably going to be hit by fifteen tons of metal traveling at forty-five miles per hour. It took the oncoming truck about a tenth of a second to crumple their hood, which didn't leave the two in the front seat any time for further reflection. The girls in the back seat didn't notice the impending mortal danger, as they were deeply absorbed in squabbling about something that was about to not matter at all. The eldest daughter, Emily, was five years old and had been named after her mother. Sally was two years younger and had just started to discover the world outside her nuclear family.

In April 1986, barely four years earlier, the mother, Emily, went to the hospital in Johannesburg after being shot in the leg by an unknown gunman. Everyone assumed that the reason the young beauty queen had been shot was her husband's shady business dealings with people at the highest levels in the apartheid regime. The young housewife's gunshot wound was probably just a warning that worse things could happen. At the hospital that very day, Emily had learned that she was pregnant with Sally.

Four years later, Franz Esser's business dealings once again seemed to be the likely reason that a truck was crossing over into oncoming traffic to demolish their BMW.

Thirteen years earlier, despite the criminal allegations against him, Franz had succeeded in buying South African citizenship for 550,000 South African rand. Since then, the unscrupulous businessman had tricked many people in his new country. In his old homeland of Germany, he was wanted for rape, extortion, assault and battery, fraud, and tax evasion. In his new home of South Africa, he had long been protected by his ties to the security services agents and the highest political leaders, including the foreign minister Pik Botha.

There were persistent rumors that Franz Esser had supplied South African agents with the cars they needed to assassinate Olof Palme. His wife, Emily, being shot about a month after Palme's assassination was a warning, and it had recently become clear that the South African officials' patience with his criminal business dealings was starting to wear thin. He was going to stand trial soon for crimes committed in South Africa, which would put his political loyalties to the test.

Clearly his loyalty had been deemed insufficient to protect him from the kinetic energy of the fifteen tons of steel now being leveled at him and his family. The truck's uncalled-for lane change on the road bore every sign of one of the South African security services' favorite methods of getting rid of inconvenient people.

The metal that crushed Franz's and Emily's bodies effectively killed them instantly. Five-year-old Emily died at the scene of the accident. When the emergency workers arrived, they found little sister Sally severely injured with a broken back.

If the goal of the planned accident had been to wipe out the entire Esser family, then it almost succeeded, but not quite. Three-year-old

Sally survived and would spend the rest of her life in a wheelchair without a family.

And Franz Esser would never tell anyone about his relationships with top leaders in South Africa, or if he had been responsible for organizing the necessary vehicles for the assassination of Olof Palme. He had been efficiently quieted.

Crossing the Rubicon

South Africa, December 2015

It was a big step to take, but if I seriously intended to go any further with Stieg's research into the Palme assassination, South Africa had to be my next stop. Bertil Wedin had worked for their security services. The names of Craig Williamson and a succession of other agents came up over and over again in Stieg's papers. There was a report in Stieg's archive about contacts between the Swedish police and South Africa during the period before the assassination. South Africa had come up far too many times in my and Stieg's research to be overlooked or ignored. A trip there was basically unavoidable.

As I was getting used to the idea, I contacted several people who had long been interested in South Africa's role in Palme's murder. One was journalist Boris Ersson, who had given me a copy of his previously unpublished memo to the Palme investigation team. He wrote the memo in 1994 after putting his own life in peril to meet with a number of South African agents. Another was Simon Stanford, a documentary filmmaker I had recently been in contact with. He was the person who convinced me to finally take the plunge and get on a plane.

***

"Nicholas, do you want to go to South Africa with me?" I said. "Simon Stanford and I are going at the beginning of December. We have a month to prepare."

The *New Yorker*'s editor was hard to convince, but in the end Nicholas Schmidle succeeded in selling an article about how I was using Stieg Larsson's research to delve further into the Palme assassination. The condition was that Nicholas had to go through the entire story himself and meet the relevant people, which I hoped might mean his traveling to relevant locations.

"Who's Simon Stanford?" Nicholas asked.

"A South African documentary filmmaker who's lived in Sweden for a long time," I said. "And hard-boiled enough to handle the South Africans."

"Does he know anything about South Africa's possible role in the Palme assassination?"

"Oh yeah. He's been interested in this for a long time. Back in 1996, he had a ticket to travel with Peter Casselton to Cyprus to meet Bertil Wedin, but Casselton couldn't go. He had been crushed against a wall by a truck that he was repairing at the home of another agent."

"Deal," Nicholas said.

***

We had just gotten settled in at the hotel in Sandton, Johannesburg, and gotten one decent night of sleep when it was time for our first visit. Nicholas had succeeded in reaching an agreement with Vic McPherson that we could go to his home for an interview. McPherson was one of Craig Williamson's closest coworkers in the South African civilian security service, until Williamson switched to the military security service in the middle of 1985, so we expected he would be able to describe their working methods.

It took just under an hour on the highway to drive from Johannesburg to Pretoria through hilly countryside. Nicholas Schmidle, Simon Stanford, and I zigzagged our way through the Pretoria suburbs until we managed to find one of the larger streets that was included on our not-very-detailed map. We were in the right part of town at least, which consisted mostly of single-family homes, interspersed every once in a while with a gas station or store with a parking lot out front.

We turned off the main road and traveled slowly through the prosperous neighborhood. The homes here were not surrounded by high walls with broken glass or barbed wire on top, as we had seen in Johannesburg. The few people we saw here were all white. The area and the buildings felt like they could be in Europe, maybe a small city in England.

Finally we found the right street and house number. It was a relatively modest one-story home with a saddle roof, built sometime in the 1970s or '80s, with a well-tended yard in front that continued around and behind the house. We parked in the driveway and checked the name on the door. "McPherson." We were in the right place.

We had spent the previous evening reading about the alleged crimes that Vic McPherson had participated in and had taken the time to carefully prepare our questions. Although I knew that we would be sitting with a person who had contributed to the deaths of many people and had killed people himself, I did not know how I would react to such a man. We waited quietly for quite some time, the tension thick, before the door finally opened.

McPherson looked strong in all the photos I'd seen, generally with a dark mustache and a hardened look, often in uniform. Ten or twenty years and at least one serious illness later, Vic McPherson was a physically broken man. He was barely taller than five foot five and skinny as a rail, and he had a lot of trouble walking as he showed us around to the back. On the other hand, his good friend Karel Gerber, who would be present during the interview as well, was big and strong, with his gray hair up in a ponytail. Karel helped Vic by holding his arm as we walked around the house.

There were snacks and a pitcher of refreshing iced tea laid out in the backyard. Vic's wife came and made sure we had everything we needed before she went back into the house.

"Hospitality is important for us South Africans. When someone visits us, we go all out to make sure they're happy."

Vic's voice was just as weak and frail as his body. The last glimmer of the vitality that must have been in him during all those years in the South African civilian security service was evident in those narrowed eyes. We told him a little about ourselves and why we had traveled so far to meet him.

"Tell me about when you set off the bomb in London."

Vic looked happy to get to talk about his violent past, almost rapturous.

"In 1982, we were assigned to blow up the African National Congress (ANC) offices in London. It was part of Prime Minister P. W. Botha's reaction to what he called 'the total onslaught,' which we South Africans felt we were being subjected to. That necessitated 'the total strategy,' which meant that for the first time it was possible to carry out attacks outside of southern Africa. That required our best agents, who were encouraged to do black ops, black ops to hurt the enemy."

Vic caught his breath and took a drink of iced tea. I resisted my impulse to interrupt with a question. He needed no further nudging—he was more than willing to admit his role in these infamous international crimes.

"We were at Daisy Farm for a week, which had been financed with Swedish money via Craig Williamson's infiltration of the IUEF. We planned the mission there before we flew to London. For two weeks we did reconnaissance on the target for the bombing and on several alternative routes to get out of the country once we were done. One problem in the beginning was that Eugene de Kock and his colleague were stopped by the border patrol because of how they looked. Eugene's rough look and their sunburned skin after months in the bush made it possible to see from a long way away that they were pros. The British security service questioned them."

Vic had to stop, breathing heavily, before he could continue.

"Craig Williamson led the operation. The rest of us on the team were divided into groups of two or three and kept apart. We slept in different places. Each group had its own information and only received the information necessary to carry out their part. Craig sat in a hotel room in London and led the operation. It was standard procedure. Different cells, individual tasks, and information on a need-to-know basis."

"But who was involved?" I asked.

"Most of them were flown in from South Africa. We flew in on different airlines via different routes. It was Eugene de Kock, Jimmy Taylor, John Adam, Jerry Raven, and me. Peter Casselton, who was based in London, was part of it, too."

"How did you communicate?"

"Craig took care of all communications. He knew how to contact us. We couldn't contact anyone apart from Craig. We were summoned to a movie theater by Leicester Square a couple of times and sat in the same audience without showing that we knew each other. That was one way to test that we could hold up under pressure."

As Vic told it, it was an exciting, yet deeply disturbing, story. It was far too easy to forget that in the name of the apartheid regime, these men were carrying out a bombing that could have cost many people in central London their lives. Instead he made it into a spy novel where you ended up identifying with the protagonists, regardless of whether they were good or bad.

"Were you ever almost found out?" I asked.

"Eugene's team reported to Craig that they were being watched, probably by MI5. That continued for a few days. Their team was supposed to place the bomb and every day they announced that they couldn't carry out their mission because of the surveillance. But the third or fourth day, I think it was, they said that the coast was clear, so Craig gave the order for them to place the explosive charge. The rest of us had handled the logistics and made sure that everything was prepared. They placed the bomb and then we waited. When the first news reports came and we realized that we had succeeded, we immediately left the country. We met up in the airport in Amsterdam. Only then did we learn that it was our own guys who had been following de Kock's team on Craig's orders, to make sure they were on their toes. Eugene did not look very happy, but Craig was even more pleased. We were in high spirits, almost euphoric. We were having a few beers and a couple of drinks when we suddenly heard something that got our attention. The loudspeaker asked for Mr. Joseph Slovo to please come to the transfer desk."

That name sounded familiar, but Vic could tell that I wasn't sure who that was.

"He was a white South African and a Communist. We considered people like that traitors. Since he was also a Communist leader, he came in first place."

"First place?"

"Joe Slovo was at the top of our kill list. And now he was in the same airport with some of South Africa's most highly skilled security agents. Eugene immediately said we ought to get him. Craig was more hesitant. Eugene pulled out this orange Bic pen with a blue lid. 'If you lure him into the bathroom, I'll get him with this. I'll just push it up into his solar plexus at an angle and puncture his heart.' In theory that was a good idea, but in the end everyone realized it was too risky and convinced Eugene not to do it. We flew home and were awarded a medal. We got Joe Slovo a few months later. Well, actually we got his wife, Ruth First, with a parcel bomb Craig gave the orders for."

Vic mentioned the murder of this woman in passing, as if it was just another day at the office. This particular woman, Ruth First, had been a personal friend of Olof Palme, and Stieg mentioned her murder in his Bertil Wedin memo. But I wanted to know more about the kill list.

"Was there a kill list? You mean a list of names of people you wanted to kill? Who was on it? Olof Palme?"

"We had a list like that, but they were people in the Communist Party, the ANC, and other opposition movements. Palme wasn't a South African citizen, plus he was the prime minister of another country. I never saw any list with his name or any similar names on it."

"Was there maybe another list that you never saw? Maybe the military kept its own list?"

Vic narrowed his eyes again.

"No, there was only *one* list of people that we wanted to get rid of."

Despite Vic's willingness to talk about the violent crimes the South African regime had actively carried out on foreign soil, he had effectively shot down the possibility that Olof Palme was a target for the South African security services, either civilian or military. Karel Gerber poured Vic some more iced tea. Karel hadn't said a word during the conversation, but I sensed that he didn't agree with his friend.

"You mentioned black ops," I said. "What were those?"

"We had white ops and black ops," Vic said. "The white ops mostly involved gathering information that was sensitive to the enemy. Then we would publish it."

"And the black ops?"

"I can give you an example. Frank Chikane was a pastor who was causing us a lot of trouble. One time on his way to the US, he had a layover in Namibia and had to spend the night. Our men went into his hotel room and rubbed poison into his clothes while he was out. It was a powder from an African plant that they put in all the places where a person sweats, under the arms and in his underwear. He caught his next flight and became really ill halfway to the US. There wasn't anything they could do. When he arrived, he was basically dead. If he had been going anywhere other than the US, he would have died, but the Americans managed to save him in the end. Although they never figured out what the poison was."

"You mentioned that you know of black ops that were never disclosed."

"Yes, there are things I know or that I've heard, but I'm not going to talk about them."

The silence that followed was awkward, and I used the trick of counting silently to ten to wait him out. Vic laughed and shook his head and was quiet for a few more seconds before he gave up.

"Alright. One of the agents in the military secret service got a job. Jonathan Leabua was prime minister of Lesotho, which is an independent enclave within South Africa. Even though Leabua depended on South Africa, he supported the ANC and was on our kill list. And our agent was supposed to take care of that."

Vic picked up his glass of iced tea with a shaky hand and took a sip to clear his throat before saying something he said he had never shared before.

"First he made an attempt with a parcel bomb that he placed along the road where Leabua's motorcade was going to travel. When the prime minister's car passed by, he hit a remote control. He had to press several times before the bomb went off. By then the motorcade had passed, including Leabua's car. The agent had failed, but he didn't give up."

Vic was obviously amused by the scene with the bomb, which could have been part of a Pink Panther movie with Peter Sellers if it hadn't been a near tragedy from real life.

"A while later, we had done our homework. Leabua was going to give a speech to the people in the same place where he usually did. Our guys measured the metal railing that he was going to stand in front of and had an identical railing made with explosives inside it. When the bomb went off, it would explode like a pipe bomb at right about the height of Leabua's stomach and split him in half. This time our man was going to transport the railing there by car, but before he entered Lesotho, he was stopped at a road stop. Not in Lesotho, but at one of our own South African police road stops. They found the railing with the explosives and arrested him. Then they called me and asked me to fix it."

"But you were working for the police, and this agent was in the military security service, wasn't he?"

"When there was a problem, they called me. I was the *cleaner*. I got the name of the prosecutor and called him up and made him understand the problem, but he didn't see a way out, so I also made it clear to him. 'Bright and early tomorrow, the first thing that happens will be that our man will be in court, where he will confess that he is guilty of possessing explosives, an Ak 4, a pistol, and ammunition. He is prepared to pay ten or twenty thousand rand. It will be handled quickly, and he will be out of there before the media or anyone else has a chance to react.'"

Vic chuckled in satisfaction and drank some tea.

"The prosecutor must have had a chance to talk to the judge because the verdict was announced a couple minutes after they entered the courtroom. By 8:02 a.m., the agent was a free man, but Leabua got away yet again."

Vic McPherson had just casually described two attempts at assassinating a country's prime minister, which just a moment earlier he had said was something the apartheid regime had never done. If they were prepared to assassinate one head of state—Leabua of Lesotho—why not Olof Palme of Sweden?

"So that was a black op that didn't succeed," I said. "I want to hear about some that succeeded."

"We stick together. We don't talk about things that we or other people have done. If someone does that, he needs to be ready to be killed. That's how dangerous it is. I'm not going to tell you any more."

"Was the plane crash on October 19, 1986, when Mozambique's president Samora Machel died, a sabotage by the South African security services?"

Vic shook his head and responded without hesitation.

"No, it wasn't. One of my colleagues reached the scene of the accident early and saw that there were vodka bottles by the Russian pilots' feet. They had been drinking and apparently had been flying toward Matsapha in Swaziland when they thought they were flying to Maputo. By the time they touched the treetops, it was too late."

"But isn't that strange? That the South African security services was the first on the scene even though the accident was in the middle of the jungle more than three hundred miles from Johannesburg?"

"Yeah, when you put it that way. The first thing I thought was that it was a black op. But anyway it wasn't, according to the people who would supposedly have done it. But do you know who else was at the scene of the accident early on? Pik Botha, our foreign minister."

Yet again Vic looked pleased, as if he had spread out a jigsaw puzzle so we could see the whole picture. But when we used our imagination to fill in the rest, he mixed up the pieces again and said that it actually depicted something else. I was surprised how easily he discussed people's violent deaths in such a superficial way, which only made sense if you remembered that he was a security agent and had been trained to kill.

"What's your opinion of Craig Williamson?"

"He's the best spy South Africa had," Vic said. He had a hard time finding the words he was looking for next. "He's the best . . . quite simply the best."

"Do you think Craig Williamson was behind the assassination of Olof Palme?"

"I worked with him until the middle of 1985 when he went to the military security service, and up until then I knew everything. After that I don't know anything. I've asked him many times and he denies it. I don't know why they keep bugging him with that same question over and over again. I don't think it was Craig."

But there was one other death that was almost as interesting as Olof Palme's.

"Were you there when the agent Peter Casselton died?"

"I was there. Casselton lived with some Portuguese friends a few hours' drive from here," Vic said just as smoothly as before. "I was at the veterinarian with the Portuguese guys' dogs and Casselton was working on a truck in a narrow driveway. There was a black guy behind the wheel who had the truck in first gear by mistake. Casselton happened to short-circuit the starter, and that was enough to make the truck move forward. He jumped aside, but was between the truck and the wall on the side," Vic said, gesturing with his hands to show where the truck was. "His abdomen was crushed, and he couldn't breathe. I told them that we needed to move the truck, but we couldn't because it was stuck, too. The only option was to knock down the wall but then they started nagging about getting permission from the neighbor. Nagging, nagging, nagging. That whole time Casselton was hanging there without oxygen. In the end they took the wall down and he . . . Casselton just died. They managed to get his heart started with electroshock, and I went with him in the ambulance. They were able to keep him alive, but at the hospital they verified that his pupils were unresponsive. He was brain dead."

Nicholas and I took turns interviewing Vic for two more hours. Simon listened to the stories, which he recognized from a totally different perspective. By the time the sun set, everyone was tired. Vic said goodbye and went into the house through the back while his friend Karel walked us around to our car out front. He had let Vic do the talking all the way through the interview.

"What Vic said about there only being one kill list . . ." Karel began.

"Yes?" I said.

"That's not true. There were clearly two. The military had more power, and they had their own list."

"Are you sure? Do you have a copy of it?" I asked.

Karel laughed, shook his head, and opened my car door for me.

"Have a safe ride back to Joburg!"

***

On the drive back toward Johannesburg, I was forced to concentrate on driving on the left side of the road on an unfamiliar continent in the dark. We all sat in silence as our minds raced.

The bombing in London in 1982 was carried out in cells on a need-to-know basis.

The illustration in the *GT* from 1987 described a scenario with cells just like that for the Palme assassination.

Foreign Minister Pik Botha was among the first upon the scene of Samora Machel's accident, as if he had known the plane was going to crash.

An agent had been tasked with killing a foreign prime minister, even though the South African security services supposedly didn't perform those types of operations.

Vic didn't know anything about what Craig Williamson did after he went into the military security service in the middle of 1985.

When we got back to the hotel, I was the only one who had three fingers of whiskey without ice at the bar. I needed it.

The Heart of Darkness

We had been in South Africa for a good week. Nicholas had arranged several interviews and meetings for us, but my own attempts had been fruitless. Plus, the information was starting to become fuzzy. Who had ratted on whom? Who could be trusted? Who might have been involved in the Palme assassination and who wasn't?

One of Craig Williamson's victims was Fritz Schoon, who described how at the age of three, he survived a parcel bomb sent on Craig Williamson's orders, but it killed his mother, Jeannette Schoon, and his six-year-old sister Katryn.

Barry Gilder had been one of the most important intelligence officers in the armed wing of the ANC, Umkhonto we Sizwe, and he described the fight against the apartheid regime and how he had worked as an intelligence officer both before and after the fall of apartheid.

At the South African History Archive (SAHA), we found traces of documents about the Palme assassination from the Truth and Reconciliation Commission's work and afterward. We were able to see some of them, but others were still marked confidential. And I had failed in my attempts to set up meetings with the three people mentioned in the Review Commission's report whom I wanted to contact.

Riaan Stander, who worked with Craig Williamson in 1986, had fingered him as the organizer of Olof Palme's assassination. Stander was one of Boris Ersson's most important sources for the memo that I had brought with me to South Africa. Stander was described by many people as unreliable and was disliked by basically all the former security agents, but he was also the one who had provided the most detailed information about how Craig Williamson and his colleagues supposedly organized the assassination of Olof Palme. Once I finally found the right phone number, Stander made short work of things: he definitely did not want to meet or talk. Nicholas also tried a few days later—with the same results.

Another person I looked for was Nigel Barnett, a.k.a. Henry Bacon, a.k.a. Leon van der Westhuizen, a.k.a. Nicho Esslin. He was an agent in the South African military security service and one of the people who came up frequently in connection with the Palme assassination. He was also mentioned as one of the members of the murder group that was sent to Sweden. Barnett had been adopted by a Swedish missionary and had lived in Sweden for a while.

When the Swedish police officer Jan-Åke Kjellberg, who worked for the Truth and Reconciliation Commission, received permission to open Barnett's safe-deposit box, there was, among other things, a Smith & Wesson Magnum .357 in there. A shooting test showed that it wasn't the murder weapon, but there were other striking circumstances surrounding Barnett. But my attempts to track him down were fruitless. I managed to find his brother, Olof Bacon, but even he didn't know where his brother was.

Heine Hüman was the third person I wanted to get ahold of. He was South African and lived in Björklinge, fifty miles north of Stockholm, at the time of the assassination. Hüman had contacted the Palme investigation team on several occasions and, among other things, said that he was contacted anonymously six days before the assassination and asked to arrange lodging for a South African citizen. A memo from Säpo concluded that Hüman was probably an "information swindler," which was a term that came up over and over again whenever the Palme investigation set someone's information aside. But I wanted to hear his own account. I found one Heine Hüman in South Africa, and he was a good enough match in terms of his age and appearance, but when I called him, he claimed that he had never been to Sweden, let alone been asked to arrange lodging for South African agents.

During the long hours and days we waited for someone to call back or to conduct an interview, our travel companion Simon Stanford, the documentary filmmaker, told us about his earlier life in South Africa.

***

Simon was a rough-hewn man in his fifties, who occasionally broke into a warm belly laugh. Just under five foot nine with a stern face and an intimidating physique, he certainly helped me and Nicholas feel safe. Simon kept to the background since his role here was primarily to document the interviews and keep track of our safety. But when he started talking about his own life in South Africa and how he had avoided death several times, it was just as exciting as any of the stories we heard from the other people we'd met.

Eventually Simon had decided to trade his precarious existence in South Africa for something significantly calmer in Sweden with his wife, Marika Griehsel, and they hadn't regretted it. If things got too quiet at home, they could always go back to South Africa or Namibia or some other more exciting country in southern Africa, which they did several times a year.

In 1996, Simon had contacted Bertil Wedin's agent colleague Peter Casselton. That was when several South African agents started leaking information about Craig Williamson and Bertil Wedin having been involved in Olof Palme's assassination. Simon was able to tell us about Peter Casselton's activities during the period before his death.

Peter Casselton was the helicopter pilot from the former Rhodesia who had been unswervingly loyal to his colleagues in the South African security services. Casselton was the only one on the team behind the ANC office bombing in London in 1982 who had not been awarded a medal by the South African government, since he was going to keep working in London as a secret agent after the deed. Later that same year he was arrested for breaking into the opposition movement's office and served some time in an English jail, where he was regularly assaulted by a black fellow prisoner who saw his chance to get back at a representative of the racist regime. But Casselton kept quiet, despite hard-core interrogation by Scotland Yard's anti-terrorist division. When he was released he discovered that the capital in his and Craig Williamson's joint venture had been spent, and he didn't have any money. Even so, Casselton continued to keep quiet about the deeds he had helped carry out. But when Craig Williamson himself and a number of others started talking in connection with the deliberations of the Truth and Reconciliation Commission, Casselton started talking, too.

In an interview on South African TV in 1994, Casselton accused his former boss, Craig Williamson, of having asked Eugene de Kock to murder him. Two years later, when more agents fingered Williamson as the organizer of Palme's assassination, Simon managed to get a budget from Sveriges Television to make a documentary. Right away, he contacted Casselton.

"My strategy was to win him over to my side," Simon told me. "I knew that Casselton knew a lot more than what he had said to other people, so I pretended to be South African myself, pretended that I felt quite at home in those circles, to win his trust."

In January 1996, Casselton was in touch with multiple people who were interested in what he knew about Olof Palme's assassination. One of them was Jan-Åke Kjellberg, the Swedish police officer who was on loan in South Africa to assist the Truth and Reconciliation Commission's work. The fact that Kjellberg was there at all was proof of Sweden's historically active role in the liberation process in South Africa, a great deal of which took place at the direction of Olof Palme. An American or British police officer would never have been trusted with the tasks he performed. Casselton and Kjellberg decided to meet a week later. Around this time, Casselton also met Simon on several occasions. On one occasion, Simon tagged along with Casselton to buy Eugene de Kock's favorite dish, oxtail ragout, at a restaurant, which they then delivered to him in jail.

"Casselton was convinced that Bertil Wedin could shed some light on the Palme assassination, that he had played a role as a middleman and helped with logistics, as in so many other operations, and that he could at least lead us to the people who were directly involved," Simon said. "Casselton and I agreed to travel to Cyprus, and I booked plane tickets for us."

The trip was set for a few days after the meeting with Jan-Åke Kjellberg was to take place and a couple of weeks before Casselton was scheduled to testify before the Truth and Reconciliation Commission.

"I called and wanted to see him before the trip. 'No, we can't meet. I'm going to my Portuguese friends' farm. I'll see you at the airport.' And that was the last time I spoke to him," Simon said. "The next thing I heard was when someone called me up and said, 'Buy the paper and see what happened to Casselton.' There was a very brief article about how he had died in an accident."

Peter Casselton's planned meeting with Jan-Åke Kjellberg never took place. He didn't fly to Cyprus with Simon to meet Bertil Wedin. And he never testified before the Truth and Reconciliation Commission. His information about the Palme assassination died with him.

When I interviewed Vic McPherson, he had left out the fact that he himself was a suspect in the South African police's murder investigation into Peter Casselton's death. But soon, the investigation was shut down and the incident declared an accident.

***

Nicholas eventually managed to get a meeting with Craig Williamson, but on the condition that I didn't come. After all those years of accusations, he did not care for Swedish journalists. When Nicholas came back from his meeting, however, he had managed to open a small door. Craig hadn't immediately said no when asked if he was prepared to meet me, but before it could happen, Nicholas was going to meet with him alone one more time.

Time was running out. We had been in South Africa for ten days, and I had only had four interviews. I was booked on a plane back to Stockholm in two more days, and I didn't intend to change my reservation. Both my budget and my patience were beginning to run out. That night Nicholas returned from having met Craig.

"He consents to meet you. No cameras, no tape recorders, no phones, *no nothing*. Those are his terms," Nicholas said.

***

We set the meeting with Craig Williamson at a café near Kyalami Racing Circuit in a Johannesburg suburb. This was where Ronnie Peterson, Sweden's most successful race car driver of all time, won the Formula One event in March 1978. Six months later, he lost his life after a violent crash at Monza race track in Italy. The Kyalami Racing Circuit was forced to discontinue competitions a few years later because of international sanctions against the apartheid regime.

The place we were meeting straddled the divide between a café and a restaurant. On the surface it appeared cozy, but it could have been located anywhere on the planet, furnished with brand-new décor items such as baseballs and wagon wheels sold from catalogs and shipped any-where in the world. The menu included all the familiar Italian café spe-cialties: Caesar salad, various types of hamburgers, and so on. Everyone satisfied, no one surprised.

We had been waiting for fifteen minutes when a shiny black Range Rover parked outside, the driver's door opened, and Craig stepped out. He wasn't as heavy as in the pictures I had seen, but he had aged and looked like the sixty-something-year-old man he was.

Nicholas, Simon, and I lined up, almost at attention, to greet him. Craig noticed my stack of papers and the notepad with the pen on top. He nodded to them and told Nicholas, "That is not what we agreed to."

Apparently he thought the papers on the table went against the "no nothing" terms they had agreed to. For a second, it seemed as if he would turn on his heels and go back to his car, but in the end, he sat down.

"One hundred sixty-five pounds, that's how much I lost," Craig said. "Gastric bypass."

He had already answered the first of the questions I wanted to ask.

Nicholas had already talked to Craig about everything he was inter-ested in during their previous meetings, so he graciously left it up to me to guide the conversation. I proceeded with caution, skirting around my key question. Besides, Craig knew what I was after anyway.

"I'm writing a book about things I found in the author Stieg Larsson's archive, and you were included in some of the materials that were in there."

"OK, we can certainly discuss that. As long as it doesn't mean that I was supposedly involved in the Olof Palme assassination."

His point was clear.

"We were at Vic McPherson's place a few days ago," I said. "He said you were South Africa's best spy of all time. Can we start from there?"

If Craig appreciated that slightly too obvious flattery, he didn't show it in the slightest, but he began to talk anyway.

"We can talk about anything I told the Truth and Reconciliation Commission. I was in charge of all the operations we carried out under orders. It was during the Cold War, and I was a soldier on the side of the West. There and then, we were convinced that we were on the moral high ground."

Craig paused for a moment and then said something I had read before: "I carried out my government's dirty work and my government did that dirty work for the governments of the Western world."

"So the murders of Ruth First and Jeannette Schoon and her daughter were done in the name of apartheid?"

"As I said, it was war. We had orders to kill Ruth First's husband, Joe Slovo, and Jeannette Schoon's husband, Marius Schoon. Those weren't murders, they were war fatalities. Unfortunately, they became collateral damage."

"We met Fritz Schoon the other day," I said. It was a long shot, but I thought I would see if I could surprise him. Craig didn't bat an eye. "He described how his first memory was being carried out of a room with flames behind him. Where his mother and sister died."

Still nothing.

"Was it just random chance that the wives were the ones who died in both parcel bomb cases?"

"The parcels were addressed to Joe Slovo and Marius Schoon. If their wives decided to open them, that was their choice."

The conversation never got any more concrete than that. South Africa's master spy was every bit as clever as he would have needed to be to escape punishment and revenge for decades, despite everything he had been involved in. At the end of our conversation, I was still forced to ask the question I had traveled all the way from Sweden to get answered.

"Were you involved in Olof Palme's assassination?"

Craig looked me straight in the eye.

"I've been accused of so many things. People have said I was behind the assassination of Olof Palme, Samora Machel's plane crash, and the Lockerbie bombing. It's all just nonsense. I wasn't involved in the assassination of Olof Palme."

He had answered but he was not getting up to go, so I thought I would try a different approach.

"I got ahold of Riaan Stander the other day . . . ," I began.

"Riaan Stander," Craig interrupted, "he's dead."

"No, he's not," I said. "He said no to a meeting when I called him a few days ago and gave Nicholas the same answer a few days after that."

That was the only time Craig actually looked surprised.

"I'm going to have to look into that. Riaan Stander is a cockroach."

Nicholas and I exchanged concerned glances. We hoped we hadn't mucked things up for Mr. Stander.

Shortly thereafter, we wrapped up our conversation with Craig Williamson without hitting any more sore spots. We shook hands and departed, my notepad still empty.

***

The plane took off from Johannesburg's O. R. Tambo International Airport. I had done what I had set out to do without anything serious happening to me. I had met victims and perpetrators. Opposition men, agents, and killers. I had met Craig Williamson, the person Stieg and many others had claimed organized Olof Palme's assassination. I had overcome my fear, but it still felt like I had nothing to show for my trip. I had hoped that I would pull off what so many people had previously tried to and failed, but Craig had only said things that were already on the record. Not a word, not a blink, not a look that revealed that he had anything to do with the assassination. To the contrary, his denial had been convincing.

There were still things to do on the other lines of inquiry, but I decided I should set the South Africa line aside for now. The only way to get further along that path was if Craig suddenly felt like saying something. But that didn't seem very likely.

The Wig

When I walked into the simply furnished interrogation room at the police station on Kungsholmen, there was a big sign on the door: Questioning in Progress. I was conscious of the fact that I had been the one to request the meeting, not them, but still, I felt a shiver of fear pass through me as I sat down. Detective Inspector Karin Johansson, who greeted me, was friendly and welcoming, but even so, the sign created a touch of unease within me.

Karin had an overfilled binder on the white laminate table, and I could see the label on the spine. It said "Jakob Thedelin." Soon thereafter, her colleague Criminal Inspector Sven-Åke Blombergsson also entered the room, shutting the door behind him. They informed me that they were going to record our conversation, and it dawned on me that I was, in fact, about to be questioned. On the phone I had asked what they had done with the memo I sent them a little more than six months earlier, then I had promised that I would tell them about my meeting with Craig Williamson. If I gave them something, then maybe I could get something in return.

Blombergsson read the obligatory introductory statement for the questioning session and placed a digital recorder on the table between us. We didn't move for almost two hours. It seemed as if they were genuinely interested in the South Africa line of inquiry and Craig Williamson. I thought maybe that was because Deputy Prosecutor-General Kerstin Skarp had said that she was going to hand over responsibility for the Palme investigation. Since she had started working on the Palme investigation in 1987, Skarp had more or less shown that she believed Christer Pettersson was the gunman, but now the new investigators seemed to be taking the opportunity to consider other lines of inquiry. Or it could have just been the result of a hard-earned lesson that the police would do well to take journalists seriously to avoid negative publicity.

As I told them about my South Africa trip, I had the chance to ask them a couple of questions as well. Karin Johansson flipped through the binder as I asked my questions about Jakob Thedelin.

As expected, they hadn't taken any action after I sent in my memo about him, but now they told me that he was questioned twice in 1987, just over a year after the assassination. Up until the time he was first questioned in May 1987, Jakob was under surveillance by Säpo. The reason for that was that at the end of 1986, he contacted an external Säpo contractor, under a false name and wearing a wig, to talk about Olof Palme's assassination. Then, at the beginning of 1988, he was, for some reason, moved *ad acta*, to the files "without activity." She couldn't find any justification for that.

After another fifteen minutes, I extracted a promise that they would give me any tips that Stieg Larsson had submitted to the police, but when it came to Jakob Thedelin, things weren't so easy. As usual they cited the ongoing investigation and the need to protect an individual's privacy. At the same time, they gave me a glimmer of hope when they said that I could make my request in writing and see if they saw it differently then.

I had already submitted the memo, and now I had also physically gone to the police to tell them what I knew about Jakob. But the police made it clear that they needed something concrete if they were going to take action—like a tip about where the missing murder weapon was located, for example.

I made a note of that.

The Italian Version

When the *New Yorker* calls, people tend to answer. In February, Nicholas Schmidle came to Sweden to meet a number of people who could tell him about the Palme assassination from an angle other than mine. Many people I knew to be hard to get ahold of were willing to help out on short notice and at inconvenient times, and were prepared to travel long distances now that the *New Yorker* was calling. Among them was Hans-Gunnar Axberger, who put together the Review Commission's report, crime guru Leif G. W. Persson, Olof Palme's sons, and a long list of others. The only one who didn't want to be interviewed by Nicholas was Lisbeth Palme. The murdered man's wife had decided to remain a mystery.

The last task on Nicholas's trip to Sweden would take two days, and he and I were going to do it together. We got into my Volvo and drove toward Falköping to find Jakob Thedelin. A week earlier, I emailed him and requested an interview, but he said no. Plan B was to pay him an impromptu visit in Falköping without announcing ourselves in advance.

In addition to Nicholas and myself, my friend Johan was joining us. He was going to help out if anything unexpected should occur, although we hadn't specified what that help might entail. We piled into my car, and when Nicholas asked about the car's design, I was happy to expound.

"It's a 1990 Volvo 780, a two-door coupe by the Italian design firm Bertone. Only nine thousand of them of were made, in Italy. The most expensive Volvo ever made."

We admired the caramel colored leather interior, the dark-red body, the curly birch panels, and the stereo from the 1980s with a tape player and blinking equalizer. A boxy Volvo, but a beauty.

"Unfortunately, they allowed themselves to be inspired by Italian quality," I said, "so it's probably also the worst Volvo that was ever made. But it's a good car."

After a five-hour journey without any difficulties, we were there.

***

Falköping sat between two small mountains in a forgotten part of Västra Götaland County. The countryside was hilly and alternated between forest and farmland. The two mountains, Mösseberg and Ålleberg, were unusual in Sweden since they were flat-topped mesas, which among other things, made Falköping into a gliding hub in the first half of the twentieth century. Using a strong bungee cord and about ten men on either side, the glider was launched from a ramp out over the Västgöta plains and could fly for hours on the thermals along the mesas. In the early 1900s, one of Sweden's finest health resorts was built at the foot of Mösseberg.

At around the same time as interest in gliders and health spas started to decline, the textile industry was also shut down, and the residents of Falköping started commuting to other cities for work and entertainment. By the beginning of the twenty-first century, Falköping had turned into yet another in a string of sleepy little Swedish towns. The primary tourist attractions were a glider museum, a motorcycle museum, and—true to the spirit of the departed residents and aging population—a funeral museum.

Hotel Falköping was perched on a hill downtown and was built in the 1950s. The lavish architecture evoked the days before the factory closures and mass exodus forced the hotel to rent out rooms for less than $150 a night. We checked in and explored the surroundings. Jakob lived only a few hundred yards from the hotel in a modest two-story apartment building. His blinds were closed and there was no sign that anyone was home.

***

"My name is Nicholas Schmidle. I'm a writer with the *New Yorker* magazine."

"Yeah, right?" Jakob said.

After mature consideration, we decided that we wouldn't frighten Jakob by knocking on the door, and that there was a better chance he would talk if Nicholas called.

"I'm contacting you because I'm writing an article about a journalist named Jan Stocklassa."

"I'm not interested in any kind of interview," Jakob replied in fluent English with a slight accent. "I repeat—I don't want to give any interviews."

Despite Jakob's protests, their conversation lasted for twenty-five minutes. Johan and I sat next to him and were impressed by how Nicholas managed to keep Jakob on the phone each time he tried to hang up. In the end Nicholas succeeded in asking all the important questions, including reading Jakob's and Bertil Wedin's emails from 2009 in both Swedish and English.

"Bertil writes, 'Please tell me about the musical activities in Västra Frölunda,' and you respond, 'Bertil! In Västra Frölunda we have no musical life to speak about, but an IDF spokesman can report that thunder and crashes in a bunker, with other sounds that are heard after the bombs fall, remind of rockets that never come again.'"

Jakob had a strong reaction immediately.

"I never wrote anything like that. That's a fabrication. And I want to remind you, sir, that breaking in and stealing an email exchange is punishable with imprisonment according to Swedish law."

Finally Nicholas succeeded in asking why Bertil Wedin had broken off his acquaintance with Jakob for a while after he found out about the dialogue concerning the Palme assassination with Lída Komárková. Jakob said that he couldn't remember that incident and repeated that someone had obtained those emails illegally.

When the phone call was done, we were excited about what we had learned. None of the emails were faked, and it was unlikely that Jakob had forgotten Bertil Wedin's anger over his discussing the Palme assassination with Lída. When Jakob was pressed, he did not tell the truth. We had discovered a little more about Jakob Thedelin and his possible involvement in the Palme assassination, but at the same time, the door to getting to meet him had been slammed shut. An unnecessary hamburger at O'Leary's and an unnecessary night in Falköping remained.

***

One of Sweden's most dangerous traffic interchanges is located in Jönköping. We were driving on the E4 highway and looking to exit to find a place for lunch so that Nicholas could try some real Swedish meatballs. A big rig was in the lane to our right on the highway. In order to make it over to the right lane by the exit ramp, I floored it, pulled in right in front of the big rig, and managed to negotiate the hairpin turn that continued almost all the way around in a circle. We avoided crashing into the big rig with our hearts in our throats. Nicholas was the calmest about it.

"We're lucky we have the Italian version," he said.

Patsy

A surprise email from an admitted government-trained spy and assassin is guaranteed to get a person's attention. It had been four months since I came home from South Africa, and the memories of my three weeks in that other world had started to fade.

Sure, I had given Craig Williamson my business card when we met, but I never expected that he would use it. Let alone did I think that he would remember where he kept it and make the effort to write to me four months after I left South Africa.

But now I did have an email from Craig in my inbox. *It must contain something important,* I thought.

The email had no subject line and contained no text, just a link to an article about Africa from the Dutch magazine *ZAM* entitled: "Dulcie, Hani, Lubowski—A Story That Could Not Be Told."

The article by the Dutch journalist Evelyn Groenink described three murders that on the surface appeared to have been carried out for political reasons to defend apartheid, but that actually had financial motives. Another common denominator was that there were scapegoats in each of the killings—people who could take the blame and who made it easier for the actual perpetrators to get away.

On March 29, 1988, ANC representative Dulcie September was shot to death on the open street near her office in Paris. She was a relatively insignificant person in the South African liberation organization, but in the months leading up to her death, she demanded the attention of ANC leaders, asking for personal meetings with people including Abdul Minty, who was in charge of weapons sanctions at the ANC. She said that she had information about illegal arms deals. Unfortunately, whatever information she had come across was lost when she died.

On September 12, 1989, the activist Anton Lubowski was shot to death in the Namibian capital of Windhoek, less than one year after the South African government agreed to give up control of the country. He had been active in the Namibian independence organization SWAPO, which took over governing the country. According to Groenink's article, the motives behind his murder included oil, diamond, and casino rights. One informant said that Lubowski had interfered with a South African minister's financial interests.

On April 10, 1993, the South African Communist Party's general secretary, Chris Hani, was gunned down outside his house in Boksburg, fifteen miles outside Johannesburg, South Africa. Janusz Waluś, a confused right-wing extremist who opposed the ongoing transition from apartheid to democracy, was arrested at the scene. He had borrowed the gun from Clive Derby-Lewis, a member of the South African parliament. Both were sentenced to death, but the sentences were later reduced to life in prison. Before his death, Chris Hani was an impediment to South Africa's biggest arms deal of all time, which, according to Groenink, was the actual motive for the murder. There were people with ties to arms dealing behind the disturbed right-wing extremist Waluś. But three witnesses saw another person at the scene who could have been the actual killer.

After reading the article, I got in touch with Evelyn Groenink. She told me that she had been threatened by both former foreign minister Pik Botha and French businessman Jean-Yves Ollivier. Her book, which the article was based on, was published only in Dutch, and a threat against the publisher stopped them from releasing it in English in South Africa.

Craig's email was obviously intended to pique my curiosity, but I gave it a few days before I called him.

"Yes?"

"Am I speaking with Craig? This is Jan Stocklassa."

"Hi, Jan."

"You sent me an email with a link to an article," I said. "Why did you send it?"

He let me wait for a bit before he answered.

"Well, it's about the thing you're interested in, isn't it?"

His tone suggested that I ought to understand what it was about.

"I'm interested in the Palme assassination. Is it about that?"

"I only said that it's about the thing you're interested in."

"Do you mean that it's about a killing that everyone thought had to do with the fight against apartheid, but actually there was a financial motive? And that's relevant to the assassination of Olof Palme?"

"I just thought you would find the article interesting given what you're interested in."

I mulled this over. Craig Williamson wanted to communicate something important to me with the article he sent, but he didn't want to say it straight out. This trend continued for some time. In the months that followed, Craig sent me several more emails. One contained documents that showed that he was responsible for an official American delegation in South Africa that arrived on March 1, 1986, which would have made it impossible for him to participate in the assassination in Stockholm. Another email contained a tip about a new book, *Apartheid Guns and Money: A Tale of Profit*. Craig's review was gushing: "Highly recommended. Unbelievable research that dug up a bunch of stuff that most people thought would continue to be speculation."

I answered some of his emails, but not all. The continuing interaction bewildered me. I was one of the people he disliked so much, a Swedish journalist who was interested in him because of his potential involvement in the assassination of Olof Palme. Why was he talking to someone like me? What did he want to tell me?

The bit about Chris Hani in Groenink's article reminded me of something I had seen somewhere else, though I couldn't quite remember where. Soon I started digging back through my papers. It was about time to buy a new filing cabinet, since my own materials were stacked in teetering piles and would soon fill my entire desk, whose weak IKEA construction was beginning to sag under the weight. Nevertheless, I soon found one of the documents I had read before I went to South Africa. It was Swedish journalist Boris Ersson's 1994 memo to the Swedish police about South Africa's involvement in Palme's assassination—the one the police didn't seem to pay much attention to at the time, because they were so focused on finding evidence against Christer Pettersson. In rereading it, I found some information that suddenly took on more weight.

The memo was largely written using Boris's own words, but quotes had been carefully noted in some places. One of his primary sources was Riaan Stander, who eight years earlier, in 1986, was a colleague of Craig Williamson. According to Stander, one of the people who was sent to Sweden was Anthony White, an agent of the military secret service. Boris asked Stander whether the killing was done by White himself or if someone else fired the actual shot, and the answer was: "Do you remember the murder of Chris Hani in 1993? Do you really think that a weird, lone foreigner could have done that all by himself? No, this was standard procedure: You find a suitable person and use him to press the trigger. Or you put him there, make sure that he's there when the attempt is carried out. It's often done in a very subtle way. Many times the person who carries out the actual murder or is arrested at the scene doesn't know who he is actually working for."

Stander's statement about the murder of Chris Hani confirmed Evelyn Groenink's theory that South African security services carried out murders in which they had a scapegoat handy. And because Craig sent Evelyn's article to me, he had indirectly lent support to Riaan "the Cockroach" Stander's 1994 statement.

I pulled out the CIA's assassination manual and compared the scapegoat setup described in those pages with the Chris Hani setup Stander described. Stander's statements fit the "lost" scenario, where the killer was a scapegoat intended to be apprehended or even killed. In such a setup, according to the manual, the assassin would be a fanatic of some kind and wouldn't know the identities of the other members of the organization, which, according to Evelyn Groenink, was the case with the Polish right-wing extremist Janusz Waluś, the man who was convicted of killing Chris Hani. If the fanatic succeeded, there was no link back to the murder plot's originators and it didn't matter if he was caught. If he failed, there was a backup who would complete the mission, leaving the scapegoat at the scene to be arrested or shot.

The result was a professionally organized killing that looked like it was carried out by a lone madman.

After being arrested for the assassination of John F. Kennedy, Lee Harvey Oswald said, "I'm just a patsy." If he was part of a conspiracy, then that statement would fit with the "lost" arrangement. It would also explain why he was shot two days after the assassination by nightclub owner Jack Ruby, before Oswald had a chance to reveal anything about who he'd met with before the assassination. In October 2017, 61 percent of the American public still believed that there was a conspiracy behind Kennedy's assassination, even though the official account was that it was the act of lone gunman and extremist Lee Harvey Oswald.

I went back to Boris's memo. Riaan Stander continued talking about the assassination of Olof Palme. He discussed his close work with Craig Williamson in the Long Reach company, which had been tasked with performing various missions around the world—gathering information, splintering solidarity groups, carrying out attacks and murders if necessary.

According to the memo, the code word for the assignment to assassinate Olof Palme was "Hammer." The planning for the mission supposedly happened in Johannesburg and at multiple locations in Europe, including Sweden. Some Swedish people, "Swedish security agents," cooperated with the South Africans by mapping Olof Palme's movement patterns and habits during the weeks leading up to the attack. According to Stander, these agents worked in a department with a female boss. The work wasn't done with the department per se, but with the individuals. After the assassination, the phone numbers were changed at the department. The person who was responsible for the assassination on-site in Stockholm—who "received the green light to kill Olof Palme"—was the same South African agent who had been tasked with the assassination attempt on the Lesotho head of state.

Surprised, I read and reread this ambiguous quote, one that seemingly implied that White had killed Olof Palme himself, but might just as well have meant that he would ensure it happened by someone else's hand. Regardless, I had to bear in mind that it was only an allegation made by a security agent. Another person who Stander mentioned as being involved in the assassination of Olof Palme was named Paul Asmussen, a South African of Scandinavian origin. There were, according to this document, supposedly two motives for the assassination:

1. To neutralize Sweden's support for the fight against South Africa in the 1980s. Olof Palme was the dominant statesman behind the support of the anti-apartheid regime. He loudly censured South Africa in Sweden, in the UN, and in other international arenas. He had to go, just like the new generation of black leaders in South Africa who were

being methodically imprisoned, tortured, and murdered during the hard years at the end of the 1970s and beginning of the 1980s.

2. Another, more private, motive. There was apparently a personal conflict between Craig Williamson and Olof Palme. The conflict was significant and had to do with money that had gone astray in connection with IUEF. Stander hinted that Craig Williamson may have had some kind of hold on Olof Palme in connection with this conflict.

Riaan Stander was known as a braggart and a swindler and was unpopular with almost all his colleagues within the security service. Some of the information in the memo sounded strange, like his assertion that Craig Williamson supposedly had a private motive to kill Palme. But perhaps that was second-hand information that Stander had reinterpreted.

But what he said about Swedish assistance and using scapegoats matched a number of pieces of information with regard to the South Africa line of inquiry that had come out in 1996. It also matched nicely with the contents of the article that Craig had sent me. And it supported Stieg's theory about South Africa, with Wedin as the middleman, using Swedish right-wing extremists for logistical assistance.

But was there really a designated scapegoat in Palme's assassination? If so, was it Jakob Thedelin, someone else, or even several people? And who were the Swedish security agents with the female boss?

One other possible motive for assassinating Olof Palme was one Stieg mentioned when he wrote to Gerry Gable twenty days after the murder. I took out that letter again.

Deep State

"Speculations would include the possibility that South African interest was behind the murder. The Palme Commission—of which Palme himself was a crucial figure—had begun a campaign against arms dealers selling to RSA."

Stieg wrote that line less than three weeks after the assassination. Thirty years later, Craig Williamson recommended further reading to me about South African arms dealing during the apartheid era. Craig, who knew how interested I was in the Palme assassination, apparently thought I should do more research into South Africa's role in the international arms trade.

It was in the very nature of arms dealing to cause death, and it was not always limited to those who died in war. Some of the world's biggest export contracts applied to weapons, and if anyone stood in the way of these deals or threatened to reveal secrets that could harm the bottom line, then a human life was a low price for being able to complete the highly lucrative and often shadowy deals.

The book Craig recommended to me, *Apartheid Guns and Money—A Tale of Profit* by Hennie van Vuuren, was a brick, a good six hundred pages long, plus a number of illustrations to show how, when, and from whom South Africa bought weapons and oil—despite official sanctions. As I flipped through the pages, I got a glimmer of a motive that was far more concrete and actionable than the vague notion that Palme was among the foremost of apartheid's countless enemies.

I had received yet another not-so-subtle nudge from Craig Williamson.

***

In the middle of the 1980s, the biggest armed conflict in the world was the war between Iran and Iraq. Olof Palme himself was a mediator in the war between 1980 and 1982, which turned out to be an impossible assignment, and the war continued all the way until 1988. Another strategically important conflict was the one between Nicaragua's socialist government and the Contra guerillas supported by the United States. A third was the war in southern Africa, where the most significant fighting was between the apartheid regime and the black resistance movements headed by the ANC.

The new book about apartheid arms dealing that Craig tipped me off about reinforced and fleshed out the picture that was described in another book that had been recommended to me. Stieg's partner, Eva Gabrielsson, had suggested I read a book from 1988: *Arms Smugglers* (*Vapensmugglarna*) by Bo G. Andersson and Bjarne Stenqvist, which focused on explosives smuggling and illegal arms trading.

One important piece of the puzzle that was covered in van Vuuren's book was that South Africa had played a role in one of the biggest and most complicated conspiracies of the twentieth century, the Iran-Contra Affair, the very scandal that had almost cost Ronald Reagan the presidency.

Despite an explicit ban by the US Congress, the CIA decided to support the counterrevolutionary Contra guerillas in Nicaragua by providing them with weapons. At the same time, people realized that Iran's Islamist regime was there to stay and that it was desirable to start reestablishing ties with Iran by selling them weapons. Congress forbade this as well, but CIA director William Casey, one of Ronald Reagan's personal appointees, designed a complex plan to avoid unnecessary interference by the United States' democratic institutions. Thus, the CIA facilitated arms sales to Iran with a markup good enough to finance providing arms to the Contras.

On November 3, 1986, eight months after Palme's death, the Iran-Contra Affair was revealed and shook the US for the entirety of 1987. An important part of the arrangement, which didn't receive very much attention but was described in detail in van Vuuren's book, was the export of oil from Iran to South Africa. Because of international sanctions, South Africa sometimes found itself only a few weeks away from running out of oil reserves. Through the arrangement, Iran received revenue as well as assistance in meeting its enormous need for weapons, and South Africa received the oil that they couldn't buy on the open market. The deals were carried out with the help of the CIA, which received part of the profits and was able to finance arms for the Contras in Nicaragua and other anti-Communist resistance movements.

CIA director William Casey visited South Africa several times to draw up the deals and met the highest-ranking political leaders, including Pik Botha. According to the *Boston Globe*'s sources in Congress, William Casey made a secret visit to South Africa on March 8, 1986, to meet President P. W. Botha, only eight days after the assassination of Olof Palme.

Craig Williamson confirmed to me that he had met Casey on two occasions, but not in March 1986.

In order to carry out the deals that had been agreed to, a fair amount of logistical help was required, and the so-called sanctions busters played an important role. These sanctions busters were usually businessmen who were happy to disregard the legal details in order to close big deals and earn a lot of money. Two prominent sanctions busters were the Italian Giovanni Mario Ricci and the Swede Karl-Erik Schmitz.

***

Giovanni Mario Ricci had established himself as a force to be reckoned with in the Seychelles, with close ties to South Africa, President France-Albert René of the Seychelles, and the Italian Mafia. The Seychelles were key to South Africa's frequent efforts to evade sanctions in order to deal in arms and oil. For his company GMR—named from Ricci's initials—Ricci found a business partner who was well connected in the top circles of South African politics. That partner's name was Craig Williamson.

Williamson and Ricci worked together busting sanctions in 1986 and 1987 by, among other things, supplying the apartheid regime with oil from Iran. The deals through the Seychelles most likely happened with the knowledge of CIA director William Casey. In an interview published by the Association for Diplomatic Studies and Training with the headline "The Seychelles—Gangsta's Paradise," the CIA chief of station at the US embassy in the Seychelles said he had been given an unusual order by Casey: "You are hereby instructed never to report, never to use any assets or any resources to pursue anything regarding international fraudulent banking operations in the Seychelles."

One possible victim of these deals was the Seychelles opposition leader Gérard Hoarau. On November 29, 1985, two months before the assassination of Olof Palme, he was shot to death on a street in London after threatening to go public with information about a financial scandal involving Giovanni Mario Ricci and President René.

According to Craig Williamson, the operation within GMR was just a "cog in the wheel." But it was a big enough cog for Giovanni

Mario Ricci to become a billionaire by the time he moved to South
Africa at the end of the 1980s.

***

Swedish businessman Karl-Erik Schmitz, nicknamed Bobbo, was relatively new to arms dealing. His family had owned companies in South
Africa for a long time, and he signed his first munitions contract in the
country in 1983 for a delivery of 4,500 tons of South African gunpowder
and charges to Iran, intended for American guns. Bobbo—who according to his business colleagues was a charming risk-taker who had been
financially ruined five times over and had become terrifically rich just
as many times—succeeded, after a fair number of practical difficulties,
in carrying out the delivery to the Iranians' satisfaction.

During the days between Christmas and New Year's in 1983, he
signed seventy new contracts in Tehran for a total of 2.7 billion kronor
($291 million) in today's money. Managing the deliveries of those enor-
mous volumes of gunpowder and explosives required the production
capacity of a large number of European producers in what was called
the gunpowder cartel. Bobbo handled the physical shipments by leas-
ing several Danish vessels, arranging false end-user certificates from
Kenya and other places, and creating routes through various countries
including East Germany, Yugoslavia, and Pakistan to avoid attracting
suspicion.

By then Mats Lundberg, the marketing director of the Swedish
arms manufacturer Bofors, had heard of Bobbo's large-scale deals and
contacted him so that the Swedish manufacturer could also get a piece
of the cake.

On January 2, 1985, Bobbo met Mats Lundberg and offered him the
whole war matériel package he had signed for the week before. Bofors
and its subsidiary, Nobelkrut, would inherit the orders for 5,000 tons
of howitzer gunpowder, 1,100 tons of explosives, 400,000 shell casings,

and 1,000,000 mortar charges. The result of that meeting was a close collaboration between the two, which in the end would put them both at risk of spending many years in jail.

On February 8, 1985, Bofors applied to Carl-Fredrik Algernon, the head of the National Swedish War Materials Inspectorate (KMI), for an export permit to Pakistan for a portion of the orders. In March 1985, Bobbo received help from the Bofors corporation's principal owner, Erik Penser, in contacting the bank Arbuthnot Latham, which agreed to act as an intermediary for payments from Iran to Bobbo's business account and onward to Bofors and other producers.

In March, April, and May 1985, Swedish customs officials raided Bofors and its subsidiary Nobelkrut.

In the middle of May 1985, marketing director Mats Lundberg met Nobelkrut's CEO, Hans Sivertsson, and canceled confirmed orders that would have required illegal smuggling of the equivalent of 370 million kronor ($40 million).

On June 5, 1985, *Dagens Nyheter* revealed that Bofors was suspected of smuggling gunpowder to Iran.

On June 13, 1985, Sweden's foreign trade minister Mats Hellström put a stop to the planned smuggling of war matériel across Pakistan to Iran. Bobbo remained in a precarious situation. In one fell swoop, he lost his main supplier of war matériel and also had problems delivering a long series of civilian products under a total of 204 contracts with Iran, mostly intended for building an ammunition factory in Isfahan. Bobbo realized that it was only a matter of time before customs came knocking on his door and he would be forced to hastily reorganize his smuggling operation, as well as look for new suppliers.

On July 25, a plane landed in Mehrabad outside Tehran. Twenty-two tons of Bobbo's gunpowder deliveries were unloaded from the plane, one he had leased as an emergency solution to fulfill his contract and temporarily remedy Iran's acute shortage of explosives. The plane was a Boeing 707 that Bobbo had rented from Santa Lucia Airways, which was indirectly owned by the CIA. A month later, Bobbo rented yet another Boeing 707 from the same company for deliveries to Iran. Three months later, Lieutenant Colonel Oliver North started using the same airline company and the same type of plane to deliver Hawk and TOW missiles to Iran. Santa Lucia Airways and their Boeing 707s were also used for arms deliveries to the UNITA guerilla group in Angola, which was supported by both the US and South Africa.

At the end of August 1985, the first of several raids was conducted at Bobbo's company, Scandinavian Commodities in Malmö. His arms deals were gradually exposed over the course of that autumn, and even though he made a show of cooperating with the Swedish authorities, Bobbo still managed to continue the deliveries all the way up until midway through 1987, although with producers and dedicated companies outside Sweden. Bobbo described the Swedish customs folk as the "elephants in a china shop" who broke a high-functioning international network of smuggling companies in the explosives sector.

In the fall of 1985, both Swedish and foreign media wrote about the startling extent of these arms deals, but interest quickly waned when Olof Palme was assassinated on February 28, 1986. Parallel to this, Bobbo continued his gunpowder deliveries to Iran via multiple producers, without the Swedish authorities or the media knowing about it.

In June 1986, *Dagens Nyheter* published a series of articles that showed that Bobbo's dealings affected most of the countries in western Europe, some in eastern Europe, and Israel.

On November 19, 1986, the Swedish customs criminal investigation police informed Bobbo that he was suspected of criminally breaking the sales ban, just a couple of months before the head of the National Swedish War Materials Inspectorate, Carl-Fredrik Algernon, died under mysterious circumstances when he was hit by a subway train in Stockholm.

In May 1987, the Swedish government, via minister Anita Gradin, reached the conclusion that Bobbo had not broken the sales ban but rather the law on "trading in explosive products," a law that was often used in connection with sales of dynamite and firecrackers to private individuals, and which fell under police jurisdiction. In this way, the Swedish government was able to avoid being directly responsible for his case. Immediately thereafter, the prosecutor felt forced to write off the suspicions against Karl-Erik "Bobbo" Schmitz. No further actions were taken.

***

Information on South African involvement in the assassination of Olof Palme started coming to the Swedish police immediately after the murder; it came from multiple sources, and it continued to come through the years. In all, almost forty pages of the 1999 Review Commission's report on the police investigation were dedicated to the South Africa line of inquiry. In the days following the assassination, multiple tips were received that pointed to South Africa.

One of them came from the chairman of the Swedish Civil Defense Association, Karl-Gunnar Bäck; on the Monday or Tuesday after the murder, he was contacted by an acquaintance of several years who was a British citizen. This man came urgently to Stockholm the next day and explained how the foreign section of the British intelligence service MI6 had received information that the assassin should be sought among South African contacts and that there was a connection to South African arms dealing. Furthermore, a Swedish police officer or police source at Säpo was supposedly involved. More concretely, the information said someone who received kickbacks during the Bofors scandal played a big role in the assassination.

After Bäck received this information, his information officer gave it to a personal contact at the local department of Säpo in Uppsala. Säpo thus received this highly sensitive information the week after the murder. However, for inexplicable reasons, the tip was not passed on to the

Palme investigation team, which did not hear about it until eight years later, and at that point, the tip came from a journalist.

Only then did the Palme investigation team look into where the first tip ended up. No one had heard of it, so they came to the simple conclusion that the tip had never been submitted. No actions were taken to look into the actual substance of the tip or how it had gotten lost.

The handling of the tip from Karl-Gunnar Bäck was just another example of the curious circumstances and coincidences that led to the possibility of South African involvement in the assassination never being properly investigated in three decades.

***

The quote from Stieg's letter from twenty days after the assassination talked about a campaign that had begun—and in which Palme was supposedly participating—against arms dealers who did business with the apartheid regime. With the help of *Apartheid Guns and Money*, which Craig Williamson had recommended, and *Arms Smugglers*, which Eva Gabrielsson had recommended, it was easy to find a handful of names that had significant financial interests in stopping an anti-smuggling campaign of that type. But for some reason, the Swedish police effectively avoided getting to the bottom of that for more than thirty years.

The only time investigators visited South Africa was in 1996, ten years after the assassination. And at that time, the head of the investigative team, Hans Ölvebro, and Jan Danielsson went on a trip that was a combination of work and vacation travel, half-convinced that the trip was not necessary, since they were sure they had found the guilty party already: Christer Pettersson, the alcoholic. Inexplicably, the Swedish police had simply not been all that interested in what the apartheid regime might have gained from assassinating Olof Palme. The decision was always "No action taken."

Luckily, there was nothing to stop me from taking a closer look.

Cui bono?

Stockholm, April 2016

The articles in *Svenska Dagbladet* from 1987 that were in Stieg's archive were written by Mari Sandström and her colleague. They contained information from an anonymous source, a man who had done sanctions-busting work in South Africa. I met with Mari several times, and we often came back to one sentence from the source: "The murder of Griffiths Mxenge was just the first rung on the ladder."

My thought was that if there was a motive behind Olof Palme's assassination that was related to arms trading, then there would be similar motives behind other murders from that same period of time—and more than just the three murders that Evelyn Groenink described in her article. If that were true, then there must be one or more persons in South Africa who had received an advantage by making people disappear from the face of the earth. *Cui bono?* Who stands to gain?

I put together a list of important deaths and events in which South Africa and their business partners stood to gain something from an assassination or other dark deed being carried out. I included many events that were known to have been carried out by South African security services—for example, the murders of Griffiths Mxenge, Ruth

First, and Jeannette Schoon. Other deaths had been investigated, but the South African authorities had decided they were accidents—for example, Samora Machel, Franz Esser, and Peter Casselton. Some events were not directly linked to South Africa, such as Olof Palme's assassination, but did further their goals. Finally there were deaths that were not directly tied to South Africa and were considered accidents by the police, such as those of Swedish journalist Cats Falck and Carl-Fredrik Algernon of the National Swedish War Materials Inspectorate.

I could see three different motives, which sometimes blended together, for the incidents on my list. The first acts, from the years 1981 to 1984, primarily seemed to have involved eliminating opposition against apartheid. In subsequent years, arms trading and other sanctions-busting activities were important motives; the final motive was preventing information about the shady deals and crimes tied to them from spreading.

Many of the deeds I read about would have been complicated to implement and would have required at least one or, more likely, two to three months of preparation. Some took place in South Africa, others in neighboring countries, and a few in Europe. A small group of possible perpetrators came up over and over again in connection with the events. It was obvious that there were relatively few people in the South African military and civilian security services that had the ability to carry out this type of job. In the article by Evelyn Groenink that Craig Williamson sent me, she wrote that "carrying out such a murder needs skill and experience of a kind that an average South African policeman simply did not possess."

The chronology was interesting. The dates of the events were relatively spread out, usually about six months apart, long enough for a small group of agents to have time to debrief, take a well-earned break, then plan the next operation.

My list was long. First came the murders that journalist Mari Sandström's source said everything began with.

November 19, 1981 Durban, South Africa	Griffiths Mxenge Human rights lawyer	Stabbed to death with a knife, stabbed forty-five times, and hit with a hammer. Three South African members of a death squad later received amnesty for this deed from the Truth and Reconciliation Commission.
March 14, 1982 London, England	ANC office	Bombing organized by Craig Williamson, who, along with several others, received amnesty for this deed from the Truth and Reconciliation Commission. Other participants included Vic McPherson, Eugene de Kock, and Peter Casselton.
August 17, 1982 Maputo, Mozambique	Ruth First	Parcel bomb sent on Craig Williamson's orders. He later received amnesty for this crime.
June 28, 1984 Lubango, Angola	Jeannette Schoon and her daughter, Katryn	Parcel bomb sent on Craig Williamson's orders. He later received amnesty for this crime.
November 1984 Stockholm, Sweden	Cats Falck Swedish journalist	Died along with a female friend after their car drove into the water in Stockholm. She was said to have been working on a scoop about arms dealing through East Germany. Officially an accident.

August 1, 1985 Durban, South Africa	Victoria Mxenge Human rights activist	Shot to death in front of her children on the orders of the South African security services. Had pushed for human rights issues and continued the activities of the law firm of her deceased husband, Griffiths.
November 29, 1985 London, England	Gérard Hoarau Seychelles opposition leader	Shot to death with a machine gun in London. Was going public with accusations of arms smuggling against Craig Williamson's business partner Giovanni Mario Ricci, who was doing business with countries including South Africa and Iran. Unresolved.
February 28, 1986 Stockholm, Sweden	Olof Palme Prime Minister of Sweden	Shot to death on an open street in Stockholm. According to Stieg's information he was starting a campaign against arms dealings with South Africa. Unresolved.
September 8, 1986 Stockholm, Sweden	ANC office	Bombing in Stockholm. South African security services suspected but the preliminary investigation was shut down. Unresolved.
October 19, 1986 Mbuzini, South Africa	Samora Machel President of Mozambique	Died in a plane crash. South African security services suspected of sabotage, but no conclusion reached. Officially an accident.

January 15, 1987 Stockholm, Sweden	Carl-Fredrik Algernon National Swedish War Materials Inspectorate (KMI)	Died in the subway at a sensitive stage of the investigation into arms trading. Officially an accident.
September 19, 1987 Geneva, Switzerland	Olav Dørum Norwegian ambassador and activist	Hit and killed by a representative of the Namibian liberation organization SWAPO, who was driving drunk. His life was threatened before his death. Officially an accident.
March 29, 1988 Paris, France	Dulcie September ANC representative	Shot to death outside the ANC's office in Paris, France. Was in the process of informing the ANC leadership about arms deals. Unresolved.
December 21, 1988 Lockerbie, Scotland	Bernt Carlsson Assistant secretary general of the UN and United Nations commissioner for Namibia	Died when Pan Am Flight 103 was blown up. Had begun to fight the plundering of natural resources in Namibia. No investigation into whether Carlsson was a specific target.
May 1, 1989 Johannesburg, South Africa	David Webster Anti-apartheid activist	Shot to death outside his home by the South African security services.
September 12, 1989 Windhoek, Namibia	Anton Lubowski Anti-apartheid activist	Shot to death after interacting with French arms traders who worked with South Africa. Unresolved.

January 9, 1990 South Africa	Franz Esser and his family German car dealer	Died in a head-on collision with a truck. Had contacts at the highest level in South Africa and was said to have arranged the cars for the assassination of Olof Palme. Officially an accident.
April 10, 1993 Boksburg, South Africa	Chris Hani General secretary of the South African Communist Party	According to Evelyn Groenink's article, Hani got in the way of a big arms deal. Shot to death outside his home by Polish right-wing extremist Janusz Waluś.
January 1997 Outside Pretoria, South Africa	Peter Casselton South African security services agent	Crushed to death by a truck that he was repairing. He was supposed to testify before the Truth and Reconciliation Commission and had named Craig Williamson and Bertil Wedin as having been involved in the assassination of Olof Palme. Officially an accident.

***

When I read the list that I made, I could see a pattern and a number of deviations. The timing of Griffiths Mxenge's murder was interesting, of course. "The first rung on the ladder," as Mari Sandström's source said. Craig Williamson's infiltration of the Swedish-led organization IUEF in Geneva concluded in January 1980, and Griffiths Mxenge's murder was committed barely two years later.

In the beginning, the assassinations were carried out at regular intervals, but the gap in 1983 was a departure. Either they had taken a break or I had missed one or more operations. From August 1984, the deeds occurred relatively regularly again up until Franz Esser's car crash in January 1990. Then it was a long time before the deaths of Chris Hani and Peter Casselton.

I saw another exception. The bombing of the Stockholm ANC office took place only six weeks before Samora Machel's plane crashed. Maybe a bombing in Stockholm could have been carried out by the civilian security service—the same way the bombing in London a few years earlier had been—while an operation involving a head of state as the victim involved complicated logistics and would need to be carried out by the military security service.

Craig Williamson had often said in interviews that when the Berlin Wall fell in 1989 and the Cold War ended, the Western powers didn't need the apartheid regime in South Africa any longer. Sure enough, after Nelson Mandela was released and Prime Minister F. W. de Klerk lifted the state of emergency on June 7, 1990, the number of operations dropped dramatically.

Both Franz Esser and Peter Casselton had threatened to talk about previous operations, which was a sufficient motive to get rid of them— as Vic McPherson said applied in general to the agents. Officially, though, their deaths were still considered accidents.

My list was a compilation that showed that white South Africa had benefited in various ways from a long string of people's deaths, whether they were considered murders or accidents, or were unresolved. In my view, the list increased the possibility that South Africa was involved in the assassination of Olof Palme, but it was far from something that would hold up in court.

If I wanted to find any concrete evidence, the odds were significantly higher if I put my energy into the area where I had actually found new information—Alf Enerström and Jakob Thedelin.

M 000057 RIKSPOLISSTYRELSEN
           Säkerhetsavdelningen   Bilaga 1
           STOCKHOLM   1986-11-21
           Sekretariatet
           Pint T Forsberg   Ex £(2)

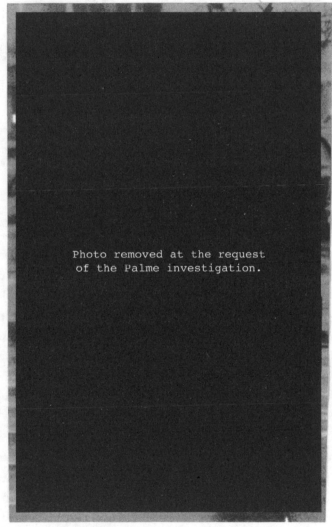

Photo removed at the request
of the Palme investigation.

Säpo's surveillance image of Jakob Thedelin from November 1986.

Interrogated

It was December in Sweden—the temperature was just above freezing and the damp air penetrated my quilted jacket, right into the marrow of my bones. The darkness was even worse. The sun rose at nine o'clock in the morning and set just after three in the afternoon, but people didn't really notice anyway. It was dark all the time thanks to the clouds.

At least I had plenty of time to sit at Nyberg's Café and drink my five cups of coffee and eat a sandwich with egg and smoked fish roe or liverwurst with gherkins. They had started making the popular saffron buns on Saint Lucia's Day. I ate one every day, like a bear getting ready to hibernate.

It had been a few months since I had finally decided to write to the police and request some materials. Most of my request was denied, but in the end, the police gave me a couple of items. The envelope had just arrived. The material wasn't as comprehensive as I'd hoped, but a reconnaissance photo of Jakob and transcripts of his interrogations showed that they had in fact been interested in him. And that interest had already begun just a few months after the assassination.

I smoothed out the reconnaissance photo on the table in front of me. It had been taken with a telephoto lens and showed Jakob crossing the street at a crosswalk with a black briefcase in his left hand. Two cars typical of the era could be seen in the background, a dark-blue Saab 95 and a Volvo 245 with light-blue metallic paint. He was wearing black pants, chunky street shoes, and a gray jacket that came down to his waist. His glasses were big with steel rims, the lenses lightly tinted, maybe photoreactive. He was wearing a curly wig, which seemed to be of low quality and wasn't put on very well; it almost looked like a cap that had been pulled down over his head.

I did a quick check with the witness statements from the scene of the murder. About half of them said the man was bareheaded and the other half said that he was wearing something on his head. Some of them also changed their minds by the next time they were questioned.

Above the photo it said: "Appendix 1, Stockholm 11/21/1986, Säpo, Secretariat, Pint Tore Forsberg."

In 1986, Tore Forsberg was the head of counterespionage, so the surveillance had been handled by a relatively high-level Säpo employee, which must have meant that it was high priority. This was the same Tore Forsberg that I thought might be the model for the character Evert Gullberg in Stieg's third novel. At the beginning, the photo had been an attachment to another document, but there were no clues as to what the main document might have been.

The first interrogation with Jakob took place on Thursday, June 4, 1987, between eight forty-five and eleven thirty in the morning. Jakob was picked up at his home earlier that morning without prior notice. Police Superintendent Tore Forsberg from Säpo and the interrogating officer Alf Andersson and Detective Inspector Stig Kjelson, both from the National Criminal Investigation Department, were present for the questioning. Jakob was picked up for the questioning session fifteen months after the assassination, having been under Säpo surveillance

for six months. The document was fifty pages long and had been transcribed verbatim from a tape recording.

Interrogating officer (IO): Where were you at the
time of the assassination?
Jakob: I was sleeping.
IO: It was a Friday night. It was the twenty-eighth.
Were you at home in Täby?
Jakob: No, I was woken up by a lodger.
IO: Whose place were you at?
Jakob: Seppo H. and uh . . . in the morning then . . .
IO: What did you do in the evening?
Jakob: Yeah, that . . . I remember in the morning,
them coming in and waking me up and saying
that . . .
IO: Did he come in and wake you up?
Jakob: Yes, he woke me up and said that they shot
Olof Palme. Then what I did the night before. Yes, I
almost ought to have my schedule to know exactly.
And whether I worked that evening or had it off,
those are about the two alternatives there are, huh.
IO: What do you usually do in the evenings? Are
you maybe tired? Were you at home and asleep that
night?
Jakob: Yes, I might have been doing that. I don't
actually dare answer that really.
IO: You didn't see Alf on those days?
Jakob: Afterward I saw him. I called him, of course.
IO: At the time?
Jakob: Yes, after.

IO: You mean in the morning when Seppo H. said that they had shot Palme? What did you do then?

Jakob: Yes, then I went out. I called from a phone booth, called up Alf Enerström and asked if I could come up.

IO: Straight away that morning?

Jakob: Yes, I suppose I ate a little something then and later I went out.

IO: So he was home then?

Jakob: Yes, he was home. For how long, I don't know. But he was home when I called and also when I went there.

IO: What time in the morning was that?

Jakob: It could have been a few days later, I don't know.

IO: It hit you right away then: I have to get in touch with Alf Enerström now?

Jakob: Well, well . . . but it was, well . . . like, I knew it, of course, when he had told me before. And then I thought, oh my God, what now . . . how is it going now with the political solutions?

IO: Yes, so anyway you spoke with Enerström the day after?

Jakob: Yes, or something like that.

IO: Who was at his house then?

Jakob: The people who could . . . ?

IO: Yes, the ones who were at his house when you got there?

Jakob: There was no one at all, it was only Gio and me and Alf and the kids. If they were sleeping or eating breakfast or something.

IO: You didn't see him before the assassination then?

Jakob: Yeaaah . . .

IO: Some day before the assassination? That week?

Jakob: The problem is that I'm often bad with dates and things like this and maybe I saw him. Sometimes, you know, you call, it's impossible to say so long after the fact.

Jakob apparently had trouble remembering both what he did on the night of the assassination and the day after. He changed his mind several times when the interrogating officer, Alf Andersson, asked a follow-up question.

Then they got into Jakob's views on Palme, Enerström's opinions, and who he and Enerström had been in contact with before and after the assassination. Even though the interrogation had taken place thirty years earlier, their views were the same as the ones that came up again in Jakob's emails to Bertil Wedin and in his Facebook messages with Lída. Olof Palme was a Soviet spy who was selling Sweden out to the Russians. The people that Jakob said he and Enerström had seen were representatives of the EAP and the military, who also apparently recognized Olof Palme's betrayal. Enerström's organization, the Social Democratic Opposition, purportedly had fifty thousand members and that was why Palme made sure that someone stole money from Enerström's account and arranged to have his son Ulf taken from him. I recognized these convoluted narratives from my meetings with Enerström. Names and organizations from Stieg's research came up all the time.

After a while, Alf Andersson returned to the questions about where Jakob had been around the time of the assassination.

IO: Yes, but you said that you visited the scene of the assassination.

Jakob: After the assassination.

IO: The same day?

Jakob: Well, I guess it was a few days later. I don't dare answer . . . Or if a person walks by there sometimes. Looks to see what it says on the pieces of paper people write. It makes me sick that people kind of don't see what I've seen.

IO: Alf Enerström then, when you saw him, what did he say then? Where had he been when the assassination happened?

Jakob: I don't remember, probably at home in Sölje.

IO: You said earlier that you saw him.

Jakob: I saw him a few days or a day later.

IO: You said the address then. Norr Mälarstrand.

Jakob: I think he was in Stockholm or if maybe he was down in . . . or came from Stockholm . . . Came to Stockholm from Sölje . . . It's too long ago for me to remember stuff like this in detail. But I don't think he did that.

Alf Andersson did not ask any follow-up questions to Jakob about why he didn't think Enerström had assassinated Palme. Nor did he ask why Jakob thought that one year was a long time to remember what he had been doing when Palme was assassinated, given that it was one of the most important events to ever happen in Sweden.

IO: So you never met Palme?

Jakob: Never. I saw him from about fifty yards away.

IO: Do you know where he lived and all?

Jakob: What?

IO: Did you know where he lived?

Jakob: Then?

IO: That he lived in Gamla Stan, you knew that?

Jakob: After the assassination, then I knew that. Before that, it's possible that I had heard that he had an apartment in Gamla Stan, but that it was on Västerlånggatan, that I don't remember. It's possible . . .

IO: How did you manage the contact with your landlord? I mean, there's a guy who could say if you were home that night. Is that so?

Jakob: I don't know if I might have been gone the evening before, but we each went our own way, in different directions. Sometimes we were together, sometimes not.

IO: How did you dress last winter?

Jakob: I had a light-colored parka or something like that. Possibly a dark . . . duffel coat I guess it's called.

IO: Did you have a cap?

Jakob: No. A hood or sometimes nothing and dark pants.

On the other hand, the wig looked warm like a fur hat, I thought. Jakob's stumbling answers should have made the police more interested in Jakob. And sure enough, soon there was another interrogation.

***

On August 21, two and a half months and one long summer after the first interrogation, the police called Jakob back in again. This time they did not send a police car to bring him in. Tore Forsberg began questioning him at Säpo. Then they continued at the Palme investigation team's offices at the National Criminal Investigation Department, where Alf

Andersson took over without Forsberg's assistance. The report was written as a summary, which was only two pages long.

Jakob was asked what he thought of Alf Enerström's opinion that under Palme, Sweden was heading toward Soviet-style Communism. Jakob agreed with Enerström about this. But he had no answer to the question of why, in that case, the Soviet Union would have killed Palme.

In the first interrogation, Jakob hadn't wanted to mention by name which members of the military he had met. In the second questioning session, he mentioned for the first time that he had gotten together with Commander Hans von Hofsten around the time of the Hårsfjärden incident involving a Russian submarine in Swedish waters in 1982. This was the same von Hofsten who was included in Stieg's research, and who led what was called the "naval officers' rebellion" in the fall of 1985. Jakob had met von Hofsten at his home, at his country house, and in the city. According to Jakob, von Hofsten maintained that Palme lied about the submarine incident and that a Russian submarine escaped. Jakob said that von Hofsten was very upset at Palme's actions.

No one questioned why Jakob went to see von Hofsten, but it must have also struck the investigators how small and tight the network of Palme haters was. Under his false name of "Rickard," Jakob had been to see a long list of the people that Stieg had looked into in his research. And he had met them both before *and* after the assassination.

***

Compared with the overfilled binder about Jakob Thedelin that I saw in Karin Johansson's hands at police headquarters on Kungsholmen, very little of the material was shared with me. They didn't give me the other documents that Karin had mentioned, not the one-hundred-and-fifty-page report that Säpo wrote after their surveillance of him or the questioning sessions with the people acquainted with Jakob. And to fill that binder to the bursting point, there must have been significantly more documents of interest.

But what I was able to grasp was that more uncertainties about Jakob remained. He had stumbled over answers, hesitated, changed his testimony, and said he had forgotten things that he should have been able to remember a year after the assassination. He couldn't remember what he was doing the night before the assassination, whether he was working, whether he went to see Alf Enerström the next morning, whether he knew where Palme lived, or whether he visited the scene of the assassination the day after. Of course, he could have been nervous or wanted to avoid answering. Or the most likely option—he had something to hide.

The best idea I could come up with was to ask Alf Enerström when Jakob Thedelin had contacted him after the assassination. At the same time, I would be sure to ask some hard questions that had come up ever since Gio rescinded Alf's alibi and told me that he owned a Smith & Wesson revolver.

The Person Who Saved Sweden

Stockholm, December 2016

Alf Enerström and his friend Bo were punctual, arriving exactly at the prearranged time. Alf was somewhat less worn out this time, and it was clear that someone had made sure he had clean clothes, probably someone at the psychiatric-care nursing home he had moved into. He wore a little hat that covered the wound on his head that I had seen last time, and it made him look like an elderly hipster. But he still had on five Dressmann-brand shirts worn in layers; apparently no one had been able to talk him out of those. I showed the two men into the office where we were going to sit. Our conversation began as easily as it had the last time we saw each other, but after some idle chitchat, I was ready to get down to business.

"Gio says that you went out on the night of the assassination, after the nine o'clock news," I said.

"She does?" Alf said. "We were together the whole evening."

"And then she said you had a Smith & Wesson revolver."

Alf thought for a bit.

"I don't remember that. I had a bunch of guns."

Alf started telling a story about how he had seen two police officers he knew on Sveavägen late on the night of the assassination. Later on he realized that they were the ones who had assassinated Palme.

"Can you describe the police officers?" I asked.

"Yes, I can. But I won't."

Alf snorted and put both hands over his mouth to show that his lips were sealed.

"Why not?"

"Well, because if I do that, then they sentence those police officers because of my testimony."

"But wouldn't it be right for them to be sentenced for an assassination? They committed one of the worst crimes there is, right?" I said.

"There are things that must be done, things that have nothing to do with the law. Because the legislators haven't considered . . . Do you understand what I mean? The individual person who finds himself in this . . . Well, he doesn't follow the law then. If that leads to the ruination of the country."

"So you think they did the right thing in shooting Palme?"

"They didn't do the right thing in shooting Olof Palme," Alf said. "He should have done as I said and stepped down the day before . . . I mean, after it was done. Then it would be like they have to serve a life sentence, even though they saved Sweden."

"And you didn't want that?" I said.

"I think that if a person has saved Sweden, then he should have all the commendations there are. Shouldn't we think that's good, to save ten million people? Or what do you think? Ten million people, regular workers, toiling away at their jobs. Because if Olof Palme had been allowed to continue, then Sweden would have been Greece. It was the best country once, the cradle of democracy. But now it's the worst country. And Sweden would have been even worse."

Alf had chuckled throughout his description, but now he grew serious.

"It's happening all over the world, you know. Why was Kennedy murdered? Think on that. The very best we had in the whole world, he was killed, you know. And death is used wrongly and it's called assassination. And assassination is something one shouldn't engage in. Who decided that? Who coined the term 'assassination'? Do you know him or her? No, but life is so . . ."

Alf grew quiet and I let him be for a few seconds. He had denied Gio's version of what they had done that night, and he didn't know anything about the revolver that Gio said he owned for twenty years. I had his answers, even though Gio had been more convincing when she spoke.

"How do you know Bertil Wedin?" I asked.

"I don't know who that is," Alf said.

I looked at Bo in surprise, but he showed with a shake of his head that he didn't know who Wedin was either.

"And Jakob Thedelin?" I asked.

"Who is that?"

"Your assistant or trainee, who lived with you sometimes."

"I don't remember that," Alf said.

Bo seemed to draw just as much of a blank at Jakob's name. I was at a loss for what to say, so I asked the question again, in vain. I knew from the email conversation between Jakob Thedelin and Bertil Wedin that both Alf and Bo knew both Jakob and Bertil. But they flatly denied it. I had some questions left and went through those before they left the office a while later.

***

A couple of days later, Alf and Bo wanted to get together again for a cup of coffee. Their recollections had cleared up, and now they knew who

Wedin and Thedelin were. But Bertil Wedin was only someone they had spoken to on the phone a couple of times. And Jakob Thedelin was an acquaintance of Gio's—not Alf's, they told me. I was quite certain that was not true. First, Alf and Bo hadn't wanted it to be known that they had had contact with Bertil Wedin and Jakob Thedelin. Now they were trying to minimize their importance.

Each time I tried working on a new portion of Stieg's theory, I kept coming to a dead end. But I also learned something new each time, which made it worth trying again. I had met Bertil Wedin, Craig Williamson, and Alf Enerström. Anders Larsson, the right-wing extremist, and Carl-Gustav Östling, the police officer, were dead. Jakob Thedelin remained, but the only way to find out more about what Jakob had done that night and whether he was involved in the assassination would be to ask him all the hard questions directly. But even if he agreed to an interview, it was unlikely that he would actually tell me anything.

Creative use of Facebook and a deus ex machina email delivery had helped get us this far, but it was going to take more than that to get Jakob to talk. That wasn't going to happen without making a bunch of tough decisions. In fact, there were logistical issues and ethical complexities to consider.

The Decision

Stockholm, March 2017

The idea itself was simple, but the decision and execution rather more difficult. Lída's questions to Jakob via Facebook and the emails she provided had been painless. I had asked Lída for help and she had interpreted on her own what needed to be done and how to do it. Some of her friends probably helped with some form of digital sleuthing, and both the Facebook dialogue and emails had arrived without my needing to ask myself if what I was doing was right.

Several years had passed since I first contacted Lída, and I had discovered a series of things that strengthened Stieg's theory, along with my addendum that Jakob Thedelin had been involved in Palme's assassination. But even though I submitted to them a thorough memo and published articles in *Svenska Dagbladet*, the police had not taken any new action against him.

It felt hopeless and I only saw two options. One alternative was to wrap up my research without publishing it, either as articles or a book. I could quite simply give up, which some days felt like a rather appealing option.

The other alternative was to make use of the only journalistic method that Stieg Larsson had used that I had yet to try: undercover journalism or infiltration. An undercover reporter meets one or more people to obtain evidence that cannot be acquired in any other way, in order to confirm the information that one already has. But the project needed to be of significant interest to the public in order to motivate me to use such a drastic method.

Jakob Thedelin and his potential involvement in the Palme assassination met all those criteria. A bigger dilemma was that, while he had extremist views and was suspected of playing a role in the Palme assassination, he was also a vulnerable person in many ways. He had apparently retired early, after some difficulty getting along in his various workplaces, and he appeared to have a very small network of friends. His personal difficulties needed to be weighed against the potential positives of an undercover operation.

For a couple of months, I weighed the pros and cons of diving even deeper into this investigation. At some point during that time, Nicholas Schmidle also called and said that he had met with his editor at the *New Yorker*. The editor really liked the first half of his article. The problem was the second half, which was supposed to tie everything together. It just hadn't coalesced and if there was no new concrete information, it would be hard to publish it at all. I listened and took in what Nicholas was saying, but chose not to tell him about my own dilemma.

In the end, I made my decision. Giving up really wasn't an option. Undercover work was a long shot but certainly worth a try.

I made a phone call to Prague and explained my idea to the enigmatic Lída Komárková.

Jakob and Lída

Landvetter Airport, Göteborg, July 2017

Lída emerged from the terminal. She had her cigarette lit before we reached my Volvo.

"I just need to water down the fresh air a little," she said in English as we walked to my car, which was parked in the short-term lot.

"So, this is Göteborg?" she asked. "Pretty much like any other rainy airport."

She got into the passenger's seat and waited while I put her luggage in the trunk. I could tell she was central European from how she just assumed that I would deal with her bag, but at least she had put out her cigarette before getting in my car.

"Jakob moved from Borås to Falköping, an isolated little town surrounded by a few small mountains, fields, and a lot of forest," I explained as I sat down behind the wheel. "It'll take a little over an hour to drive there."

"Göteborg, Borås, Falköping. Same, same but different," Lída said, then fell asleep with her face leaning against her seat belt.

The forest roads off Highway 40 were winding, and Lída protested a bit in her sleep when the turns were too tight.

It had been three years since Lída interrogated Jakob over Facebook and sent me his and Bertil Wedin's emails. We'd lost touch after that. Lída had looked in Prague for her next exciting project, and I thought we were done since I assumed the police would respond to my memo on Jakob. And yet they never did.

But timing was everything. When I finally realized that I wanted to go through with the infiltration, I knew I needed Lída's help. I happened to get in touch just as she was returning from two years in the US and a romantic breakup, and for some reason, she accepted my offer to fly her to Sweden to meet Jakob. It was hard for me to understand her as a person. For one thing, I myself would never have agreed to meet a possible murderer, especially when asked to do it by a person that I hardly knew. But Lída was another story. She seemed to have lived her whole life seeking out risky situations and exciting adventures. This time around, it was just a bit riskier and a bit more adventurous.

"Why did you agree to come when I asked?" I said.

"I always say yes when I think something sounds exciting," she said. "I've always felt comfortable with whoever or wherever I've been in the world but have never succeeded in creating something long term," she continued. "This project feels like the kind of thing I've been waiting for. If I succeed in getting at the truth, then that would be something that a lot of people have wanted to know for thirty years."

Lída had addressed what I'd been wondering about in a very straightforward way. Why she had decided to come to Sweden and meet Jakob Thedelin, even though it could be dangerous. But the truth is rarely so simple, and I still wondered why she didn't want to tell me her real name. I couldn't understand how it was that she knew people who could get access to a stranger's email account. Maybe I would never get answers to those questions, but still, somehow I trusted her. Together we might be able to do something similar to what Stieg and Gerry Gable had done in the 1990s.

We reached Falköping by midnight. I had booked two rooms at the same hotel as the last time, Hotel Falköping, and made sure that the reservation could be extended for as long as necessary.

Before Lída went to her room, she handed me a plastic bag full of equipment that she had bought based on a list I'd sent her. The plan we had devised was divided into three distinct parts: technology, logistics, and risk scenarios. I laid out the items on the white laminate desk by the window in my hotel room. A solitary streetlamp lit up the large parking lot outside with a handful of cars in it. For safety's sake, I closed the burgundy-red curtains so no one could see in. The plastic bag labeled "Spy Shop CZ" contained some small cardboard boxes that I opened. For less than ten thousand kronor ($1,250), I had obtained gadgets that Stieg would have found many uses for. Another person who would have been thrilled was Palme's and Holmér's old friend Ebbe Carlsson, not just about the technology per se but also about importing it. Of course, this kind of equipment was now completely legal and easily obtainable twenty years after the scandal that bore the fitting name of the Ebbe Carlsson affair.

I went through the items one by one, from left to right. There was a pen with a microphone that was activated when you slid the clip up. If you had it in a pocket, all you would need to do is push it down a bit farther to activate the microphone. The next pen combined video recording with sound and was turned on by pressing the top. There was a fake car key fob that could film in 4K with high-quality sound.

The eyeglasses had been the hardest to choose, according to Lída. The frames were not all that modern and you could see the camera lens on some of them, but the ones she ended up choosing were completely acceptable, a unisex model with a camera that wasn't visible. The price for that was a battery life that was limited to twenty minutes. Even though we had three cameras, I had already realized that if it were to be a longer encounter, we would be forced to supplement with a smartphone that could record for several hours and maybe with a couple of GoPro cameras that I had brought from Stockholm.

The last piece of equipment had no recording functionality but was no less important. It was a GPS tracker in a box slightly bigger than a matchbox. It was made of a dull, dark-green plastic and had only two buttons and a red diode. I opened the bottom and inserted a SIM card and two AA batteries I had brought with me. Calling the device ten times in a row programmed it to react to my specific phone. Then I sent it a text message and a few seconds later I got a text back. The text contained GPS coordinates and a link. When I clicked on it, a map covering a square kilometer around the hotel opened up with a geotag in the location where the little tracker unit was located. One of the buttons was an on-off button; the other was marked SOS, and when I pushed it, another text message came to my phone with coordinates and a map. It was a plain little box that couldn't do very much, but it might mean the difference between life and death.

I reviewed all the important instructions about how to control the various gadgets. This took a fair amount of time since there were generally only one or two buttons to control all the features, including activating the device, turning it off, recording, and transferring data. It was three o'clock in the morning by the time I finished, so I lay down on the narrow bed to get a few hours of sleep.

***

My friend Staffan's train arrived from near Göteborg just after ten the next morning. He was a cool-as-a-cucumber guy who had just turned fifty and lived a quiet life in Copenhagen, waiting for an exciting job to pop up. When I called to ask if he wanted to come to Falköping and act as backup when Lída met Jakob, he said yes right away.

Staffan and I were going to be ready in case anything unexpected should occur. Hopefully, we could resolve an unpleasant or threatening situation just by showing up quickly at the right place. And if Lída pressed the SOS button on the GPS tracker, we would know right away where that right time and place were.

Staffan settled into my hotel room by tossing a big bag on the floor and lying down on the bed with his shoes on. Lída came over a little while later, and we ran through the plan and the equipment. We were starting to realize that our spy equipment was cheap for a reason. It recorded at a relatively high quality, but the handling, battery life, and reliability were terrible. We gave Lída a crash course on how to use the various devices and mostly succeeded, but we had no idea how it would go when the situation was more tense.

Lída and I had intentionally chosen a Friday, since the Sabbath began at sunset and the odds were good that Jakob would stay home. Suddenly a problem occurred to me that I should have considered ages ago.

"Wait! Sweden is so far north that it never really gets dark here at the beginning of July. How can the Sabbath begin in the land of the midnight sun?"

"Chill out, Jan," said Lída, who always seemed to grow calmer the more stressful the situation became. "I checked. The Sabbath starts at nine forty-five even though the sun hasn't set."

Lída logged into her Facebook account and checked Jakob's status. As one of the preparatory steps, Lída had been using her Facebook profile to check when Jakob was online, but without contacting him. Just as he had a couple of years earlier during their dialogue, he stuck to the library's hours, which suggested that he was still using the computers there.

"He's online," she confirmed. "Could Staffan walk down and check to see if he's sitting in the library?"

Our plan was that Lída would show up as a surprise, thus making it harder for him to say no. A pretty woman on his doorstep was significantly harder to turn away than a journalist calling him or sending an email.

He was online right now. Here was our chance to check and confirm if he was in Falköping, so suddenly we were in a rush to get going. Staffan was going to look and see if he was in the library, because Jakob might have been able to recognize me from my byline photo in *Svenska Dagbladet* and we wanted to wait before Lída made her entrance.

As we walked to the library, I showed them the few pictures I had of Jakob on my phone and tried to describe him to Staffan. Lída and I sat down on a bench by a small pond with a fountain. City hall was to our left, and across the pond we had an unobstructed view of the front of the library. Both buildings were two stories tall, made of brick, and lavishly outfitted with 1960s details that showed they had been built during Falköping's heyday. It took only a few minutes before Staffan emerged from the library and gave us a subtle thumbs-up at waist height.

We got up and followed him, walking about twenty yards behind him. As we rounded a corner, he showed us two blurry pictures of a man at a computer. It was enough for me to be able to identify Jakob. He was in Falköping, as we'd hoped.

We walked along the bicycle path to Saint Olofsgatan and found Restaurant Alfred. Lída and I ordered the day's lunch special, a pork loin with gravy and boiled potatoes. Staffan ordered a Sydney pizza with extra everything, which came with French fries and shaved kebab meat on top. A half hour later, we were stuffed and left the last of our overly strong coffees behind. Then we walked back to the hotel to wait in the room until the library closed at five o'clock.

***

Staffan's and my adrenaline levels were starting to rise, but the person who was going to be exposed the most was once again the calmest. We had to knock hard on Lída's door to wake her up from a nap. She opened it drowsily then started getting ready. I had taken the time to do one last equipment check and charge all the batteries.

I positioned the smartphone crosswise in the front pocket of the overalls I had instructed her to buy. The phone was held in place with adhesive Velcro strips so it could film through a hole I had cut in the fabric. After a few attempts, the hole was big enough to capture the entire picture, but the lens was visible if you looked closely. It was too late to do anything about that, so we were going to risk it. Lída put on the eyeglasses and ran through how to turn the camera on.

We decided to drive to the building Jakob lived in, even though it was less than half a mile away. But before we got to the car, Lída turned left into the lobby and walked over to the bar. She downed a double vodka then nodded to us that she was ready.

We crept past the little yellow two-story building, quite confident that my old Volvo was nondescript enough that it wouldn't attract attention. There was no sign from the windows that Jakob was home. The blinds were drawn and his balcony doors were closed. We slowly turned at the corner and I stopped the car. Lída got out. She was on her own now.

Staffan and I drove quietly around Falköping without any particular goal. After fifteen minutes, we risked driving past the building again. I kept my eyes on the road because Staffan could look over at me like we were talking and, at the same time, see what was going on outside.

"She's sitting out in front of the building with a man, drinking beer," Staffan said. "It could be Jakob, but I don't think so."

I wanted to do a U-turn and drive back to look for myself, but I realized that that would be too risky. There was basically no traffic in town, and Lída and the man who might be Jakob were sitting facing the street—it wasn't worth getting caught. Reluctantly we drove back to the hotel to wait.

***

When Lída arrived at the building's front door, it was locked. She gave the door one more tug, but that didn't help. She peeked in through the glass with her hand against the pane to see better and suddenly felt a hand on her shoulder.

"What are you looking for?" someone asked in Swedish.

The language surprised her a little, and she quickly looked over her shoulder. The man was significantly shorter than Jakob's five foot nine, barely taller than she was. When she responded in English, it was the man's turn to be surprised.

"I'm looking for Jakob. Is he here?"

The man hesitated and took a step back before he responded in halting English with a thick Swedish accent.

"No, I don't think so. He went out a while ago, and I don't know when he's coming back."

"Oh, could you let me in so I can ring his doorbell?"

"But he's not there . . ."

As soon as the man turned his key in the door, Lída ducked in and darted up the stairs. Jakob's last name was on his door, and she quickly rang the bell several times. The man had followed her and stood on the stairs looking up at her.

"I said he wasn't home, didn't I? Do you know Jakob?"

Lída swore at herself for not coming straight here when the library closed. What if Jakob had gone away for the weekend. She decided all she could do was wait nearby, in which case this man could help her do that.

"Hi, I'm Lída. I'm a friend of Jakob's. I've come all the way from Prague to see him. Who are you?"

"I'm Håkan, Jakob's upstairs neighbor. Maybe he'll be back soon."

"Yeah, maybe," Lída said in a significantly gentler tone than before. "Is it OK if I wait here?"

She gestured that she could sit on the stairs, but Håkan shook his head.

"Come have a beer with me. It's nice out and I'm not opposed to a little company."

"OK," Lída said with her biggest smile.

Håkan was a harmless guy who had just been drinking beer on the lawn in front of his apartment building in quiet Falköping in the middle of July. Lída couldn't really decide if that was normal Swedish behavior, but she did see that this was a perfect opportunity to wait for Jakob. Håkan pulled out another white plastic chair and hurried upstairs to get another beer.

"So, do you like Falköping?" Håkan asked as he poured Lída's beer into a glass.

"Yes, very much. Do you?"

"Yeah, Falköping is the best."

The conversation flowed very slowly. Lída caught Håkan staring at her a couple of times as she drank her beer. He looked like he'd just won the lottery.

"My ex-wife lives over there. And my mom lives there. And my daughter lives over there."

Håkan pointed to three different nearby buildings and Lída realized that if you lived in Falköping, the world could be quite small. Time passed. If Jakob didn't come home, she supposed she would wait in this strangely deserted town until the next day.

"There he is."

Håkan's statement was neutral, but Lída felt a rush of adrenaline. She turned her head and there was Jakob. He looked taller than his five foot nine, maybe because he was so skinny. His eyeglasses were darker than in the pictures she had seen, but they didn't look like sunglasses. They probably reacted to the sunlight.

"Hi, Jakob! How are you?"

Jakob stood frozen for a few seconds that felt like an eternity. She tried again.

"Hi, Jakob! It's me, Lída from Prague. I have a different picture on Facebook, so maybe you don't recognize me."

This was a crucial moment to convince Jakob that she was the woman he had gotten so close to through their dialogue on Facebook. He stared blankly for another couple of seconds.

"Aha, Lída! But that must have been three years ago," he finally said in good English.

She decided not to hug him, instead holding out the little plastic bag of presents until he was forced to take it. He looked surprised, but also happy.

"It's a porcelain kiddush cup. And a bottle of kosher wine," Lída said.

He looked down into the bag, obviously pleased by the presents. He would have a hard time worming his way out of this situation.

"Thank you so much! But what are you doing in Sweden?" he finally said.

"Boyfriend problems. I'm getting away from him for a few days. So I came here on a whim. Do you have time for a little visit?"

"Yeah, I have time. The Sabbath doesn't start for a couple hours."

"Maybe we could get a beer or a glass of wine somewhere," Lída suggested. "Håkan recommended a place called O'Leary's."

Jakob was starting to relax now and seemed to like the suggestion.

"Let me just take this bag up and grab a different jacket."

He opened the front door but made no attempt to let her in, which was just as well since she knew she shouldn't go up to his apartment before she could decide if that was safe. She spent that time sending a text to the guys at Hotel Falköping: *"Ahoj Mami, mám kontakt, vše ok. Jdeme do O'Leary's na pivo. Pac a pusu Lída."* (Hi Mom, I got in touch, everything's OK. We're going to O'Leary's for a beer. Hugs and kisses, Lída.)

Right as she hit send, the front door opened and there was Jakob. Instead of the shorts he had been wearing, he now had on a pair of black slacks that looked like they were from an old-style suit. They started walking to the restaurant.

***

There was a beep that roused me from my drowsiness. Staffan was actually asleep, but I shook him awake. I showed him the text.

"We're obviously going over there!" he said when he saw that I was on the fence.

"Sure," I said, even though I wasn't as sure.

"Take my cap and pull it down over your eyes. Then he won't recognize you."

It was only a five-minute walk from the hotel to O'Leary's. Everything was close in Falköping. When we walked in, a young woman greeted us in her thick Västra Götaland dialect and showed us to a table close to the bar. But out of the corner of our eyes, both Staffan and I noticed that Jakob and Lída were sitting at the other end of the restaurant, behind a panel of frosted glass. There was one free table behind the glass panel, and Staffan and I both asked at the same time if we could sit there. The woman looked a bit surprised, but shrugged and led us over to it.

Now we were literally sitting an arm's length from Jakob and Lída and could hear their voices, although not what they were saying due to the music and the noise in the restaurant. It was obvious that the situation was not critical and that they hadn't noticed us. After a while, I signaled to Staffan that we should leave Jakob and Lída. We would have access to Lída's recordings soon and didn't need to risk having Jakob discover us.

***

We waited a good hour in the hotel room, and I sent a text to the GPS tracker a few times to check if they were still at O'Leary's. Then a text arrived from Lída: "We're going to his place."

My pulse sped up and I showed Staffan the message. In her usual succinct way, she'd left no room for discussion. It didn't make any sense to try to stop her.

Staffan and I put on our shoes, jogged down to Jakob's apartment, and just managed to catch a glimpse of Lída and Jakob before they walked in the front door of the building. We turned back toward the hotel to continue waiting. Suddenly it hit me.

"What if Jakob wants Lída to spend the night? And what if she agrees?"

Staffan let that thought sink in and his eyes widened.

"Well, surely she can do what she wants?"

"I mean, we didn't agree on anything aside from being cautious until we knew if it was safe . . ."

". . . and it was safe, so now she's going back to his place," Staffan completed the thought.

"The fact that she's here at all, meeting Jakob in person, is because she's not risk averse and now she thinks she has the go-ahead," I said. "Nothing's going to stop her."

Staffan and I looked at each other. Neither of us knew how to handle a situation where someone was inside a locked apartment with someone we suspected of murder. I sent a text to the GPS tracker. No response.

Jakob—First Day

Falköping, July 2017

When he opened the door to his apartment, it was like entering another world. Jakob was hard up, but what little he had, he had put into his apartment. Even if it was only a one-bedroom place with a kitchen, it was evident that he had chosen his furnishings and décor carefully. The little hallway had yellow wallpaper with pink vines on it, dark-blue furniture in the entryway, and a little oil painting in a dark wood frame. To the left, there was a simple kitchen with white laminate cupboards and the bedroom where Lída could just see dark-green wallpaper through the door that was ajar. They walked into the living room, which felt like an old-fashioned parlor. There was burgundy-red medallion wallpaper, a baroque revival cabinet with glass doors filled with glassware and porcelain, an upholstered sofa set with ornate wooden details, and a dining table with a lace tablecloth and a seven-branch menorah made of gold.

Lída sensed the change in Jakob as soon as they sat down on the sofa. They were in his home now and he felt safe here. He relaxed and started talking more freely. They opened the bottle of wine Lída had brought, and she enticed him to drink often. By the time Lída poured the second glass, he was a little tipsy and was talking more openly, but she also sensed a hardness that she hadn't seen at the restaurant. She remembered how easy he had been to lead in their Facebook dialogue and thought maybe she could get him to continue where they had left off three years earlier. Perhaps this time, she could finally get him to tell her everything, but that would take time, and it surely would come at a cost.

"Tell me where you got all these nice things from," Lída said.

"I inherited a couple of the paintings and some of the furniture. But I was forced to buy most of it."

"Inherited? Are your parents dead?"

"Yes. My mom died back in 1994. I got practically nothing then. Then when my father died last year, I hoped I would get some of the things I had pointed out. But he gave me a lot less than I had thought. I don't know where his money went, but I did get a little anyway, so I was able to rent this apartment."

"Were your parents nice to you when you were little?"

"I don't really know," Jakob said. "I was an only child, and I remember that they sometimes left me alone so I got scared. Sometimes my grandmother, my mother's mother, would watch me. She was the one who showed me Jewish Seders, even though she wasn't Jewish. But I wasn't allowed to tell my mom. Then when my grandmother moved in with us, she said we couldn't keep it up. But that's how I ended up wanting to convert."

Jakob talked about how his small family had moved around to various places in Sweden due to his father's job as a Pentecostal pastor. His parents had been distant in their relationship with Jakob, and he had a hard time making friends. By the time he made a friend in a new place, it was time for their next move.

"My childhood in rural Czechoslovakia was happy until my father lost everything during privatization," Lída said. "Then my life was hell."

Lída saw that Jakob had noticed her use of the word "hell."

"My dad suffered, and we felt bad for him," Lída continued. "But he didn't do anything to move on from that. Finally he had ruined his own life and ours. That's my biggest secret."

"I can understand your being ashamed in the presence of other people if your father was so dejected," Jakob said.

"No, that's not what my secret is," Lída said. "My father's death was my fault. Maybe I'll tell you when we get to know each other better."

"I'd like that," Jakob said.

"But then I want to hear your secrets, too," Lída said.

She looked provocatively into his eyes until he looked away. She made it clear that she wanted him to tell her everything.

"When my dad died, I finally made some friends," Lída said. "They could come to my place and I could laugh with them. Life got better again."

"Friends are important," Jakob said thoughtfully. "I don't have that many, but that has to do with the life I chose. When I was little, maybe five or six, I used to pray that I wouldn't have a usual life. That came true."

"And when did your life become unusual?" Lída asked.

"I was slightly more than twenty when I went to Stockholm and went to see Dr. Enerström and Gio Petré. That was in the early 1980s. I had followed their work for several years and decided to go look them up."

"That was a big decision! But how did you find them?"

"I went to Stockholm on speculation. Once I was there, I went to a phone booth. There were still phone books on the shelf in the phone booths back then. So I looked under *E* for Alf Enerström and there was the address: 24 Norr Mälarstrand. I got there in under half an hour, on foot."

"So gutsy to just do it without calling first," Lída said.

"The front door of the building was locked, which I had never encountered before, but as I was wondering what to do, not knowing where to go, someone came out and held the door open. Swedes were polite back then."

"So you went in?"

"To the fourth floor. It was a grand building with high ceilings and an elegant old elevator, but I took the stairs. It said 'Enerström Petré' on the door. When I rang the bell, Gio opened the door, and she was as beautiful as ever."

"But weren't you scared to just show up there?"

"Not me, but my mom was. Before I left, I told her. She was very scared."

"So what did you do?"

"I calmed her down by telling her that I would wear a wig and go by a fake name. I became Rickard."

"Wow! Like a spy?"

"You could call it that. I started helping Alf with his political work very soon after that."

"So then later you didn't need to wear the wig and call yourself Rickard?"

"Oh, yes, I wore the wig for many years, when I needed to."

"That sounds really exciting."

"Yes, it was exciting at times. Dr. Enerström was my role model and we did great things together. Unfortunately, he went too far in recent years."

Lída suggested that they eat something, and Jakob walked into the kitchen. She was not drinking that fast, but the wine had affected Jakob so much that he was having a hard time completing his thoughts and almost looked like he was falling asleep. They went into the kitchen and cut up a little fruit, and Jakob seemed somewhat reinvigorated. When they returned to the living room, Lída sat down closer to Jakob on the sofa.

"Tell me what happened with the doctor," Lída said.

"Many years later, when Palme's successor saw to it that Dr. Enerström was confined to a mental hospital for the first time, he should have realized that he couldn't win the fight against the enemy."

"What happened?" Lída asked.

"When Alf got out of the hospital the first time, things eventually went so far that the police had to evict him from his apartment on Norr Mälarstrand. It was absurd. Alf had a bunch of money in a secret account in Luxembourg, but according to the police he hadn't paid his rent. When they entered the apartment to remove him, he shot the pistol out of a female officer's hand without injuring her. But that didn't matter. He was arrested and locked up again."

"How awful."

"Yes. And I blamed myself. It should have been me."

"What do you mean?"

"It would have been better if I shot the cop. Then Alf could have carried on with his fight."

Jakob grew quiet and appeared to be brooding about the situation, the sense that he had let Alf down. Lída asked about Dr. Enerström, but after a while Jakob was too tired to stay on topic, so she decided to save those questions for the next day. Lída gave Jakob a kiss on the cheek and pretended to stifle a yawn. That was enough to get Jakob yawning, too, which gave Lída the opportunity to pull her hand out of his.

"It's time for me to head back to the hotel, Jakob."

"Yes, I understand. I'll walk you there."

Jakob obediently accepted that Lída was leaving, which helped her feel safer. Before they stood up, Jakob raised his wine glass and indicated that Lída should raise hers.

"Cheers to the death of the traitor, Olof Palme!"

Lída repeated Jakob's words and they drank.

***

We met in Staffan's and my room to debrief about the evening.

"The GPS tracker stopped working," I said. "We had no idea where you were!"

"Yes, I shut it off," Lída said.

Staffan had poured everyone an extra-strong gin and tonic, and Lída sipped hers calmly.

"What do you mean, you shut it off?" I said. "Then we don't have any idea where you are!"

"No, but it was beeping, so I had to. Plus, I don't know what you guys were planning to do if I was caught in the apartment."

I searched for a good response, but both Staffan and I realized that she was right. We wouldn't have known what to do either. I started checking the rest of the equipment that Lída had left on the table.

The eyeglass-mounted camera had died after just an hour, but there was some valuable information, including when Jakob looked Lída in the eye and said, "We need to be careful. There can be cameras all over the place." The battery in the phone she wore in the chest pocket of her overalls had lasted the whole evening, but the hole had been too small after all, so you mostly saw frayed fabric bits on the recorded video. The sound had worked better than expected, though, and since we had three redundant recordings, we could pretty much hear every single word of Jakob and Lída's conversation the whole evening.

Even though I'd been researching Jakob for many years, this was the first time I could see and hear him. His voice was clear and a little strained, but firmer than I expected. His English was significantly better than anticipated, and even though the things he talked about might stick out as odd—it was mostly about the Cold War and the fight against Olof Palme in one way or another—he expressed himself well.

Lída started yawning. She had certainly earned the right to go to bed. The situation had been stressful for Staffan and me, but she was the one who had been in Jakob Thedelin's apartment for several hours. When Lída got up to go back to her room, she took me by the arm.

"He'll talk tomorrow."

Jakob—Second Day

Lída talked to herself a little on the walk from the hotel to Jakob's apartment. She was warming up her voice, knowing that everything she said was being recorded. The cell phone in her overalls was filming through a slightly bigger hole than the previous evening, and the pen, which was clipped to the suspender strap, was filming, too. The other pen on the outside of her purse was recording sound. And the eyeglasses would record for as long as their battery lasted. Plus, we had agreed that the GPS tracker would stay on, since I had figured out how to turn off the problematic beeping.

Lída was going to approach the issue more directly today. Jakob had bought fish and they were going to make lunch together. Lída had observed that Jakob wasn't that used to alcohol and brought two bottles of wine with her today. They were working together in the little kitchen when she brought up the topic.

"In what way was Olof Palme a traitor to the country? Was he a spy?"

"He was selling our country out to the Russians," Jakob said. "We were so incredibly close to becoming a dictatorship."

"Really? Betraying one's own country . . . I thought only Communists did that kind of thing. And you managed to reveal that?"

"In a way. In 1984, I met a commander from the Swedish navy. His name was Hans von Hofsten and we met several times. He described how Palme had released Soviet submarines that regarded the Stockholm archipelago as their own. And just over a month after the assassination, Palme was supposed to travel to Moscow. They were going to agree there on Sweden becoming a new Soviet republic."

"So Palme died just in time?" Lída said.

"He died way too late. I wish I had killed him when I was thirteen, when I planned to shoot him with my friend's father's flintlock pistols."

"Wow. That would have been amazing, a thirteen-year-old hero," Lída said. "But then who did end up doing it?"

"Palme was being revealed. The KGB killed their own spy to keep him from talking. And as a warning to others."

Lída leaned back, crossing her arms.

"Would they really take such a risk? Assassinating their own spy, a prime minister?"

"Yes. That's how it was," Jakob said. "My friend Bertil Wedin has evidence of that. A person named Anders Larsson knew about the assassination and turned in a warning before it happened. The clues lead from Anders Larsson directly to the KGB."

Jakob was speaking freely about who he had met during the period around the assassination, and he had also mentioned Bertil Wedin, which was a good sign. He was feeling comfortable talking with her.

"So you think the KGB would have killed their own spy and that another KGB spy provided advanced warning that the KGB was going to do that? Is that really what Bertil Wedin says?"

Jakob hesitated, seeming to realize that his theory didn't sound rational.

"Yeah, obviously it could have happened some other way, too," Jakob said after a brief pause.

Lída noted that Jakob had related Bertil Wedin's version of how the Palme assassination happened. That meant that if Wedin and Jakob themselves had been involved, then Jakob was prepared to lie to her, even though he had sworn to tell her the full truth. This was not surprising at all, given that they would have had to have met many similar challenges to have kept the secret for more than three decades, if they were in fact involved.

Lída pondered Jakob's behavior. At times he was hard as stone in his opinions, and it seemed that nothing could move him. He spoke with a firm voice and had no problem leading even complicated reasonings to an end, albeit with conclusions that quite often seemed as if they'd been borrowed from someone else. The next moment he showed a complete naivety, as when he had accepted her standing at his door after years of zero communication. He seemed easily led and happy to let anybody close to him make decisions on his behalf. Despite a bit of dyslexia, he was good at languages, but his mathematical skills were almost nonexistent. If Lída had to guess, she suspected Jakob might be somewhere on the autism spectrum.

They prepared their meal together, which consisted of breaded cod, boiled potatoes, and salad. Jakob had set the table, so when the food was ready, they sat down at the table in the living room. The porcelain looked English, with a green floral pattern. The silverware was heavy electroplated nickel silver with a classic design. The pieces of furniture weren't actual antiques, but the overall impression as they sat at the table was that they were sitting in an apartment somewhere in England, definitely not in Falköping.

After a few minutes of companionable silence, Lída saw that Jakob was ready to say something.

"They questioned me, too," Jakob said.

"What? About the Palme assassination?"

"It was about a year after the assassination. I had been under surveillance for a couple of months. They came and picked me up early in the morning. There was a knock on the door at seven o'clock and it was the police. One of them, Alf Andersson his name was, wanted to search my apartment and started picking things up. But Tore Forsberg from Säpo, who I started working for later, stopped him and said that wasn't necessary."

"Wow . . ."

"Then they brought me to police headquarters and questioned me. But I didn't tell them anything important."

"Was that it, then?" Lída asked. "Did they leave you alone after that?"

"They questioned me again a few months later, but that time I went there on my own."

Lída didn't say anything, just took a sip of her wine and looked serious.

"I've been betrayed horribly," Lída said.

"Betrayed by a man?" Jakob asked.

"Yes, by my great love. He lied to me for several years. Sometimes he held things back. Sometimes he flat out lied."

"So awful," Jakob said. "I'll never do that."

"So you're telling the truth now and you always will? Do you promise on your honor and conscience?"

"Yes, I do," Jakob said.

He hesitated for a second.

"But what do you do if you promised someone else you would never tell about a certain thing?"

Lída looked deep into Jakob's eyes until he looked away. She decided to make him feel even safer with her. They talked for several hours about things other than the Palme assassination until once again it was evening and Jakob yet again walked her to the hotel. They hugged goodbye.

"Next time I come to Sweden, I want to feel like you're telling me everything, that you're not holding anything back."

"I promise. When will that be?" Jakob asked.

Lída gave him a quick kiss on the lips and walked in the front door of hotel without answering. Jakob hadn't told her today either, but it was the right call. She needed more time with him.

∗∗∗

In the hotel room, the procedure from the day before played out once again. Staffan and Lída drank gin and tonics that were too strong, while I emptied the memory card and checked the equipment.

"He's hiding something and it has to do with the assassination," Lída said. "But he promised someone he wouldn't tell. Alf and Bertil, I'm guessing. There's going to have to be another trip."

I was disappointed. Twenty-four hours earlier, Lída had been sure that Jakob would tell her everything. I wouldn't have dared to do what Lída did, but even so, I had hoped for more. We all needed more time with Jakob Thedelin.

The Grave

Following the advice I found on an internet forum for investigative journalists on undercover operations and infiltrations, we waited two weeks before Lída even sent another message. Jakob had sent her one almost every day. When she did write, it was brief:

> Hi Jakob,
> I come Stockholm. Want to see you. First August is ok? 11 o'clock at railway station?
> Love,
> Lída

Ten minutes later, she had a response back from Jakob confirming the time and location. He also wrote about what he wanted to show her in Stockholm: the House of Nobility (Riddarhuset), the Royal Armoury, the Royal Palace, and the spot where Olof Palme was assassinated. And if she stayed another day, they could go to Falköping again together.

Lída and I made all the necessary preparations. The GPS tracker had stopped working, but if they were going to be moving around in public in Stockholm, we decided that she would be safer than she had been at Jakob's place. Lída would be sure to send a text when she went to the bathroom, so I could show up and follow them for a while to assess whether everything seemed safe. But mostly she would be on her own with Jakob.

***

It was a typical Stockholm summer day. The temperature was supposed to get up to seventy degrees once the sun had a chance to do its thing. Big cumulous clouds floated across the deep blue sky.

Lída got to the meeting place almost half an hour late, so she wouldn't need to wait for Jakob. Sure enough, he was standing there, but his clothing surprised her and she didn't immediately fling her arms around his neck as she had planned. She cringed inwardly at the attention they would attract as they walked around in Stockholm.

"Hi, Jakob," she said. "So . . . you wore a kilt today."

"It's a MacTire clan tartan for festive occasions, which today is, since I get to visit the House of Nobility and the armory with you. Shall we go?"

Lída gave him a big hug, while at the same time making sure not to press too tight lest he feel the phone in her chest pocket. In addition to the equipment from Falköping, she wore a loose-fitting cap with a GoPro camera mounted so that it was filming to the side through a little hole we'd cut. Her cap, overalls, and chunky camera-glasses along with Jakob in a kilt made them an odd sight as they moved through the city.

"First I'll take you to Sweden's House of Nobility, Riddarhuset. I always go there when I'm in Stockholm."

"Exciting. Is it far?"

They went up onto a pedestrian and bicycle bridge and Jakob pointed in the direction they were headed.

"Do you see that roof over there? That's Riddarhuset. Right by Gamla Stan."

"Gamla Stan? Isn't that where Olof Palme lived?"

"Yes, that's right," Jakob said.

"Do you know where?"

Jakob stopped by the railing and started fiddling with something.

"If we're going to talk about Palme's assassination, then I just want to take the battery out of my phone. So that no one can listen in."

"Do you think someone's listening?"

"No, I don't think so," Jakob said.

"Oh, good," Lída said, hoping the recording caught that.

"Someone pointed out to me where Olof Palme lived," Jakob said. "So, yeah, I know."

***

The guide at Riddarhuset answered Jakob's questions politely, but Lída noticed the expression on the woman's face looking increasingly puzzled the more detailed his questions became and the more time that went by. After almost two hours, they moved on, walking toward the palace and the armory. Jakob showed her the outfit Gustav III was wearing at the masquerade ball when he was shot to death, a series of uniforms, and finally the Swedish crown jewels. He was obviously very interested in the symbolism of royalty and nobility. And Lída was starting to feel like it was time for something to happen.

"Can we go to where the assassination took place?" she asked.

"We're already on our way," Jakob said. "And to the cemetery."

As they strolled back toward the city, Jakob pointed out 24 Norr Mälarstrand across the water on the other side of Riddarfjärden.

"That's where Dr. Enerström and Gio lived."

The walk to the scene of the assassination took just under half an hour. The street corner where Palme was assassinated didn't really look like it had in the pictures Lída had seen. Instead of an art supply shop, there was a grocery store and a trendy restaurant. They'd put an entrance door right into the corner of the building so it was hard to avoid stepping on the plaque in the sidewalk that read "Olof Palme, the prime minister of Sweden, was assassinated here on February 28, 1986."

"Should we buy something to eat here?" Lída asked. It was almost seven in the evening and they hadn't eaten anything.

"Sure," Jakob said. "We can sit up on Brunkeberg Ridge by the church. Don't forget to ask for utensils."

Jakob took it for granted that she was going to pay, even though she was the guest. She bought two salads and some sort of greenish drink. After she paid, she made sure to send a text message to say they were at the assassination site.

When she came out of the store, Jakob was standing nonchalantly with one foot on the plaque, almost as if to show that he was alive and Olof Palme was dead. They walked toward the stairs up onto Brunkeberg Ridge while Jakob described how the assassination had played out. It sounded like any other description that Lída had read. If he had been involved, he wasn't letting on at all.

They each went up their own staircase to begin with—one to the left of the tunnel and one to the right—and met on the first landing. Jakob told her that the assassin had fled this way. After they climbed all eighty-nine steps, Jakob turned left on Malmskillnadsgatan, toward Saint John's Church. They walked into the cemetery, then suddenly he took Lída by the hand and started running all the way until they were around the corner of the church. There was a bench there behind some bushes, out of sight and not lit. Guaranteed to be undisturbed and unsafe for Lída.

"Now we've shaken anyone that might be following us. I'm famished," Jakob said.

***

After I received Lída's text message, I hurried to the corner where the assassination took place. I got there in time to see Jakob and Lída heading up the stairs. After waiting a couple of minutes, I followed them. When I got up to the top, I was really out of breath. I looked around in all directions, but there was no sign of them. I walked around the area at random but had no idea where they'd gone.

***

They ate their salads and drank the smoothie, which tasted like grass, definitely more good for you than plain good. Jakob told her things about the assassination that were public knowledge, and which Lída already knew. When they finished eating, they walked for a while in the neighborhood on top of the hill, then down the stairs on the other side toward Birger Jarlsgatan and then up again. After that, they started walking toward the cemetery where Olof Palme was buried.

"I wish I had a time machine," Jakob suddenly said. "Then I would shoot Palme and you could wait up on the ridge in a car, so I knew where I should go."

"That would be amazing!" Lída said. "Then I would make sure that you made it to a safe place. But tell me, what did you do on the day of the assassination?"

"I was on Sveavägen. My plan was to go to the movies, but the movie they were showing at the Grand didn't interest me."

"So you went to the movies on the day of the assassination?"

Jakob gave Lída a look. Had she been too direct? Suddenly he wasn't so sure about what he had done.

"I don't know. Maybe it was earlier that week. But I didn't want to see the movie the Palmes went to. The next morning, I woke up because my landlord woke me up and told me Palme was dead."

"But you were on Sveavägen that day?"

"Maybe. I don't know."

Lída stopped pressing him. Jakob sounded confused and didn't seem to be able to keep what he was saying straight. By now they had crossed Sveavägen and walked into the Adolf Fredrik Church cemetery. There, Jakob grew calmer. They walked toward an irregularly cut tombstone about a yard high with an engraved stone slab in the ground in front of it. Jakob again made a point of standing on Olof Palme's plaque. He cleared his throat.

"Are you going to spit on it?" Lída asked.

"Bloody spy," Jakob said.

The instant the glob of spit left his mouth, two elderly women stepped up to the grave. Jakob turned to them and said in Swedish:

"Olof Palme was a Soviet spy. He was recruited in 1962. So that's why I'm spitting on his gravestone. I've opposed him my whole adult life."

Lída watched one woman walk on without stopping. The other woman put her hands on her hips and stared perplexedly at the man in the kilt, before she decided not to comment and walked off after her friend.

"She agreed with me," Jakob said. "It's important to tell people about all the evil things Olof Palme did."

"Truly," Lída said. "Truly."

"I have a plan I usually think about."

"A plan? How exciting!" Lída said.

"One dark night, maybe in November, I'm going to come here. Maybe I'll wear a vest that says City of Stockholm or something like that. And I'll have rented an excavator. It doesn't need to be a very big one. And I'll dig up that traitor Olof Palme, spit on him and destroy his body. Traitor!"

Lída didn't understand how someone could even come up with such a thought, let alone what the point would be. If Jakob had shot

Palme, then he should have been satisfied. Killing the object of your hatred ought to be enough without desecrating his body, too. Maybe that was a sign that Jakob hadn't shot Olof Palme after all?

"That's an amazing plan, Jakob."

She hugged him and gave him a kiss. For the first time, she felt how he responded to her advances. It would be safest to cut the evening short.

"It's late and we're going to go to Falköping tomorrow, right?" Lída said. "We could walk to the subway station together. And then I'll meet you in the morning before the train leaves."

"Sounds good," Jakob said.

The young woman in overalls and the man in the kilt strolled away from Adolf Fredrik Church down toward Vasagatan and wrapped up their evening with one more hug.

***

Lída and I met at Belgobar just off Vasagatan. I had managed to find and follow Lída and Jakob each time she sent a text message, apart from when they had suddenly started running by Saint John's Church. A half hour later, I once again caught sight of them as they walked down the stairs toward Tunnelgatan and Sveavägen. That half hour had been an anxious one, and Lída and I were both reminded that she was very much on her own with Jakob. And soon, she would be spending another day at his place in Falköping.

Back to the Scene of the Crime

They met in the same place outside Stockholm's central station at eleven the next morning. To Lída's relief, Jakob did not wear a kilt this time. The train was late and they each drank a Guinness at Stockholm's own O'Leary's outpost. Jakob forgot about the time and Lída had to remind him. They wandered over to the tracks and took their seats just as the train began to pull away.

As they crossed the central bridge, Jakob already had his arm around Lída, but she knew the biggest risk wasn't that Jakob would make a pass at her, it was that he would start to suspect something. He was easily led, but when he mentioned that he had talked about her with Bertil Wedin and with another person, she felt uneasy. In all likelihood, they had better judgment than Jakob and could help him uncover the ruse. She had caught him lying or withholding things that she knew about on a couple of occasions. That probably meant that he was on his guard.

"Are you going to keep your promise to me?" Lída said.

"Which promise?" Jakob asked. She only needed to look up at him for him to continue. "Oh, yeah. Tonight when there's no one around us, I'll tell you something I've never told anyone."

"You make me feel safe," Lída said.

She slid down so that her head rested on his shoulder. After four long hours of chatting about nothing, they reached Falköping.

As they walked from the station to Jakob's apartment, Lída looked around discreetly to see if the burgundy-red Volvo was parked anywhere. She had been on her own with Jakob on the train, but she had felt safe with other people around. But now that she was going to sit alone with him in his apartment again, she wanted to know that someone she trusted was nearby.

When they reached Jakob's building and were about to walk into the yard, Lída spotted a dark-red Volvo driving down the street. *Good timing,* she thought.

***

Jakob took the ingredients for a salad out of the fridge and a bag of frozen fish fillets out of the freezer. He had thought through what they would have for dinner in advance. He had also acquired three bottles of white wine, which were in the fridge, and he opened the first one straightaway.

"A toast to the traitor's death," Lída said.

"Cheers," Jakob said without repeating her words.

Lída noticed that something was different about Jakob. He was nervous and burned the fish. When the rest was ready, he realized he had forgotten to put on the potatoes. Lída left him in the kitchen and popped out to the living room.

"Do you recall me mentioning two hostile journalists?" Jakob said.

"Sort of. Remind me," Lída said.

"One's name is Nicholas Schmidle and he works for the *New Yorker*. He called me a while ago and I said no to an interview."

"But why? That would be super exciting!"

"He started asking a bunch of questions. I lied to him."

"You did? What about?"

"Eh, something about Palestine and Israel. But then I wrapped up the conversation."

Lída remembered Jakob's conversation with Nicholas quite well and the only thing Jakob could have lied about was the email about the rockets in the bunker that would never come again. Palestine hadn't come up at all. So now Jakob had gotten confused and lied to her, too.

"But you mentioned two journalists," Lída said. "Who's the other one?"

"His name is Jan Stocklassa. This is my file on him. Probably KGB. That's what his modus operandi suggests."

"Can I see? Wow, you keep files on your enemies."

The stove sizzled as the potatoes boiled over, and Jakob ran out into the kitchen again. When he came back into the room, he was still troubled. Even after they sat down on the sofa, each with a glass of wine, he didn't calm down.

"I want to tell you something," he began, but immediately went silent.

Lída struggled not to jump in and cut him off. He was having a hard time getting to the point and she felt impatient, but she succeeded in keeping quiet. Then Jakob's tone changed.

"When you said that your father's death was your fault, I thought that was an unbelievable coincidence."

Lída waited.

"I was involved in something, and because of that I feel responsible for my mother's death," Jakob continued then paused. It was a long time before he started speaking again. "My Jewish friend in America, who knew what I did, told me that it was possible that it was the reason my mom died so young. And since I had sinned, then I didn't get my inheritance. My dad inherited everything from my mom. When he sold his house, he got SEK 750,000 (equal to around $81,000 in 2017), but when he died, I only got SEK 50,000 (less than $6,000 in 2017). King Solomon told me that God would intervene. And I realized that my involvement was the reason. I think he was too harsh."

It was close now. Jakob had been involved in doing something wrong and that caused him to be disinherited. He was about to tell her now. Lída didn't understand what the Biblical reference had to do with this, but she badly wanted him to continue. What followed seemed like Jakob was rambling, but at the same time Jakob seemed more focused than ever.

"And what were you involved in, Jakob?"

"It was during the Second Temple era, two thousand years ago. I had the chance to be part of history, but this angel . . . The angel told me too late to go down. And I thought, maybe time works differently here? But I was supposed to do something that took time, so I became so upset that I refused to go down. And it caused a bunch of stuff. Things went wrong."

"And what happened?"

"I tried to put things right. The prophet Paul said that he was Yeshua, but that wasn't true. It went quite far."

"What happened?"

"I went into the archive and saw that there was nothing on Paul, but I did my research and put together the pieces and realized he was a Roman spy. So I tried to assassinate him, but I didn't succeed."

It was hard for Lída to make any sense out of what Jakob was saying. His talk about trying to assassinate a traitor could allude to Olof Palme. The research he did could also match what he did concerning the Palme assassination. But everything was set around the time of Jesus's birth and Paul being a traitor against Judaism because he spread Christianity. She couldn't exclude that he was simply incoherent or insane, but then again she could still communicate with him. When she asked a question, he did answer in a consistent way. In the end, she came to the conclusion that the most likely explanation for what seemed like ramblings was that it was a way for Jakob to tell Lída everything while at the same time keeping his promise to someone else that he would never tell.

If what Jakob said had to do with the Palme assassination, then he was involved. He was given the order to shoot, but seemed not to have succeeded. And in that case, he wasn't the one who shot Olof Palme. She would need to try to find out more about the actual night of the assassination.

"There's one thing I'm wondering about," Lída said. "Yesterday you said that you were on Sveavägen on the day of the assassination. But later you said that you weren't there. That's confusing to me."

Jakob's answer came surprisingly fast.

"Ah, you're thinking about that. What I said was that I crossed Sveavägen that day. I wasn't at the scene of the murder when the murder happened."

"Yes, but you must understand that it's very hard for me to understand."

"Yeah, yeah, I understand. You should have asked me when it happened."

"But you say one thing and then you change the story, and then I think you're lying to me. It's so important that you tell the truth."

"I wasn't there when it happened. I crossed Sveavägen at around five o'clock. Maybe I walked over toward the Grand movie theater, but I don't remember."

"But then why did you say that you weren't there that day at all?"

"There's an English word for that: I 'misspoke.' But I'll say this about that incident. If I did it . . . If I had done it, then I wouldn't talk to a soul. Even if a person couldn't be prosecuted because they already prosecuted Christer Pettersson and sentenced him in the first trial. Then it would be hard to prosecute another person. But if I did do it . . . if I had done it . . . I would probably . . . I don't know, but maybe . . . probably I would have told you and made sure that we didn't have any phones or any witnesses. Because just one witness statement, even if you should tell someone by mistake, shouldn't hurt. If I did it . . . if I had done it. I wouldn't have been able to do it, because my face would have been recognized. I was an assistant of Dr. Enerström's, and it would have been completely crazy if I tried to do something like that. I would have been recognized."

Lída was sure that later on, they would listen to the recording of this exposition many times. He had gotten himself tangled up in a hypothetical discussion where he was constantly misspeaking, to the point that it sounded like he had done it. And his best argument for why he couldn't have done it was that someone would have recognized him. But that was during the period when he often wore a wig and called himself Rickard. No one knew who he was and he was well aware of it.

"I have to believe you," Lída said.

Jakob continued to affirm several times that he probably would have told her if he had done it, but something was different. The mood between them had changed since the day before. Once again Lída had the sense that Jakob had been affected by having discussed their meetings with someone. The last time something like this happened, Bertil Wedin had temporarily broken off his friendship with Jakob after Lída and Jakob's Facebook dialogue. He had mentioned that he had talked to Wedin and one other person, but regardless of who it was, that could explain the change in Jakob's behavior. He had been so close to saying something but had clammed up after telling that convoluted story about Paul and the angels.

"I have a fantasy," Jakob said. "If someone invented time travel, then I have an idea. I'll go back in time and kill Palme. But it would be safe! We can do it together. You can wait up there with the car. And since we know the situation, then it will be safe for us."

Lída was already familiar with this fantasy from the day before in Stockholm. They laughed together.

"Should we eat now?" Lída said.

"Yes, the potatoes are definitely done now," Jakob said.

After dinner, Lída was careful not to get too close to Jakob, and that was enough to keep the situation from becoming too intimate. Jakob cleared the dishes to the kitchen, and she timed it so that she yawned just as he came back in.

"I think it's time for me to go to the hotel," she said.

"If you think so," Jakob said.

In his way, he looked disappointed, but was there an element of relief as well? If he had started to suspect that she was someone other than who she said she was, that would explain his expression. Jakob walked her to the entrance of the hotel lobby. The kiss was brief. She was leaving early the next morning, but they made plans for their next meeting. Maybe in Falköping. Maybe in Prague.

Lost

Jakob Thedelin had disappeared. No answer by text. No answer in Messenger. No answer to emails. Hadn't logged into Facebook since a couple of days after the visit to Falköping. Cell phone turned off. Landline no longer in service.

While Lída was trying to get ahold of Jakob, I listened to the recordings of their last night together several times. When I heard Jakob, I came to the same conclusion Lída had. These were *not* the ramblings of a crazy person. It was a well-prepared story that he told her for a reason; he had promised to tell her everything, but couldn't break his promise to another person not to tell. By placing his actions in biblical times, he had told without telling. We had come so close, then he had started to suspect something and now he had disappeared.

Finally I looked up his neighbor Håkan's telephone number, and Lída called to ask if he could keep an eye out for Jakob. A couple of days later, Håkan called back and said that he had seen Jakob, who told him that he was going to the mountains for a month to go hiking. Obviously Jakob was lying, which just confirmed our suspicion. Jakob had somehow realized that Lída wasn't who she claimed to be. And he was convinced enough to break off contact and go underground. He was a ghost.

***

I had gone as far as Stieg would have. I had tried the methods he used, including getting access to emails and running an undercover operation. Jakob was gone and Lída's cover was blown. We had come pretty far, but just as Stieg had set his research aside so many years earlier, I too decided that enough was enough. It was time to let Lída know.

I sent Lída an email and she called me not long after. Now was not the time to tiptoe around the matter, both because I had already decided and because I knew that Lída hated it when I didn't get to the point.

"We're canceling the project," I said. "We got as far as we could with Jakob. We got pretty far."

"But it won't take us long to find out where he's gone. When he travels, he leaves more digital traces than when he's at home."

"No, Lída. It's time to give up."

In Lída's voice, I sensed a tinge of desperation that I hadn't heard before.

"But this feels like I've failed. This was for real. I could turn my weaknesses into strengths and coax the truth out of him. I think I just overestimated how hard I should go at it. I shouldn't have pushed so hard that last night. But it'll be better next time. I promise!"

"No," I said. "I've listened to the recordings and you didn't make any mistakes. No one could have done it better. You were perfect."

Lída didn't say anything. Finally the silence grew so long that I thought we might have been disconnected.

"So you're a quitter?" she finally said. "If I'd known that, I would have never started working with you."

"Hey, I've been working on this for seven years and you've put in, what, maybe a couple of months total? Obviously I get to decide when I can't do it anymore."

"All the more reason not to give up," Lída said. "You've done everything and met everyone and now, when you might have someone who was involved, now you're going to give up?"

I really wanted to be done with this conversation, and I made that clear.

"Look, if you think that it's so damn easy, why don't you find out where in the world Jakob is?"

I realized too late that this was just the encouragement Lída was waiting for.

Aliyah

It had been almost two weeks since I had last spoken with Lída, and I was starting to think that that was the end of things. It was five o'clock in the morning when my cell phone buzzed. I reached for my phone and saw through sleep-dazed eyes that it was Lída calling. She left a message, clearly expecting me to call her right back. I sat up in bed and tried a few words to make sure my voice box worked before I dialed her number.

"He's going to request aliyah."

I had no idea what she was talking about.

"My contact who helped with the emails before has been out fishing and picked up some new information," she continued. "I have his most recent emails and some other things. He's in Israel."

Lída didn't wait for me to respond.

"A few weeks after Jakob and I said goodbye to each other, he went to Göteborg. But that week he had time to figure out what I had been up to, and he emailed Bertil Wedin that he wanted to go to Cyprus. Wedin gave him a direct order not to go there, despite a previous invitation."

I started waking up, but let her continue.

"My contact found quite a few more or less relevant messages. I used Google Translate to translate a couple of the more interesting-seeming ones from Swedish. Among other things, he wrote to Wedin about his enemies. For him that includes you, me, and some other journalists he thinks work for the KGB."

I was sitting on the edge of the bed, my sheet twisted up like a rope after a restless night's sleep, but suddenly I was wide awake.

"OK," I said. "Will you send me everything you received from your contact?"

"Of course," Lída said. "Keep an eye on your email. And then come to Prague as fast as you can."

I hung up and went over to my desk where I shoved aside a stack of papers so that I could set my computer down. First I googled "aliyah" and read about every Jew's right to move to Israel and obtain a residence permit and citizenship. Jakob's trip to Israel wasn't just a vacation or an attempt to lie low for a while—he was planning to stay.

I checked my email and Lída had sent a ZIP file with the striking name "takeout," which I expanded. There was a PST file, a bunch of JPEGs, and a TXT file. I imported the PST file into my email program and started searching.

There were several interesting messages including the ones Lída had mentioned, in which Wedin insisted that Jakob not go to Cyprus, and one in which Jakob wrote that he had instead gone to Israel to make aliyah. The only time I had seen a similar sharpness from Wedin toward Jakob was when he broke off their relationship over Jakob's Facebook dialogue with Lída. Now he had shown for the second time that he was prepared to sacrifice his friendship with Jakob if he risked being pulled into anything pertaining to the Palme assassination.

Quite a lot of the Facebook messages went to a Sara who seemed to help Jakob with practical arrangements and moral support in connection with his move to Israel. Jakob wrote repeatedly of his financial problems, wondering how he was going to be able to pay his bills. In addition to his rent, he also had a monthly electric bill of SEK 600 and a phone bill of SEK 350. At the end of the year SEK 1,500 was also going to be automatically deducted for his safe-deposit box.

In one of the most recent private Facebook messages, which was only a couple of days old, an American named Adrian wrote that he had set Jakob's laundry on the bed in his room. When I checked Adrian's profile, his most recent check-in was at the Aliyah Return Center near the Sea of Galilee, where new arrivals who were planning to apply for aliyah could live when they first came to Israel. If Jakob's laundry was there, then he was probably staying there, too. Now I knew where Jakob was.

The JPEG files were screenshots that showed where Jakob had logged in to his Gmail account. The last time he had been in Falköping was at the beginning of September. After that he had logged in twice in Göteborg and, even more importantly, one failed and one successful login in Tel Aviv, which established without a doubt that he was in Israel.

The last attachment was the TXT file. When I opened it, there was only one long chunk of text that filled four densely printed A4-size pages. There were no headers or anything else to reveal what kind of document it was, but as I scanned through it a couple of times looking for key words like "Jakob," "Wedin," "Gmail," and "Facebook," I decided it was a file of all his keystrokes including typos and deletions. I also found a message in that sea of text that had been started but never sent, to Lída. A message in which he tried to take back what he had told her that last night in Falköping about how he had caused his mother's death because he had done something that was wrong. But he hadn't come up with any good explanation and the message was never sent. That showed just how important what he had told her was. And now he was on the run.

When Bertil turned down Jakob's request to go see him in Cyprus, Jakob hadn't known what to do. At first he went underground in Sweden for two weeks and then he moved to Israel to settle there permanently.

I didn't know what we should do to go further with Jakob, but Lída asked me to go see her, so I packed a bag and bought myself a ticket to Prague.

"M"

Prague, October 2017

On the plane I ordered a little bottle of bad airplane wine and contemplated how I was going to confront Jakob. The most obvious approach would be to travel to Israel, look him up, and request to ask him some questions about what I had found out. It was highly unlikely that he would respond and even less likely that he would tell the truth. I dismissed that option.

The only other possibility that I could come up with was doing another undercover operation where we could get Jakob to share more. That would entail a huge number of complications and risk factors, but it was the only option that made it likely that Jakob would talk.

As the glass of wine slowed down my pulse, I listed the various components that would be necessary to accomplish that: design, setup, logistical planning, buying props, checking legalities, finding a local partner. The whole operation would take place in Israel, and although I had been there several times, I had no idea how I would manage to carry out something like this. I moved the last item to the top of the list: find a local partner, someone to help me with all the other items. The only problem was that I didn't know anyone in Israel.

Jan Stocklassa

***

I checked into the Hotel Pyramida in Prague 6, a mile from Prague Castle. I dropped off my luggage in a rectangular single room with a lot of beech veneer, then went out again. Streetcar line twenty-two went all the way downtown, and I got off at Národní Třída. Lída and I had arranged to meet at Café Louvre, which was one floor up. This place was one of Prague's biggest cafés, which gave us the sense of anonymity we were looking for. We sat way in the back—by five unused pool tables—and each ordered a *vinný střik* with white wine and soda.

"We need a local partner," said Lída as if she had read my mind. "There's a bunch of stuff that has to be arranged locally, and for the setup to be believable, it'll have to be an Israeli who contacts Jakob."

"Exactly," I said. "Someone who's daring, trustworthy, and used to these types of confrontations. I thought about it on the plane down here, but I can't think of anyone. Maybe I could ask some other Swedish journalists if they have any contacts, but that'll take time and it's iffy."

"But I have someone who can help: Schmuel, whom I met in France many years ago. He's in Israel right now. I talked to him and he says he can arrange what we need. He's awaiting your call in exactly . . ."

Lída glanced at her watch.

". . . three minutes."

She looked pleased. I was impressed, but also felt a little like a paratrooper suddenly dropped out of a plane. I had to call an unknown journalist without having time to find out any more about him or prepare questions. I quickly jotted down a few points that I couldn't forget before Lída called Schmuel on Viber and passed her cell phone to me.

"Hi, I'm a friend of Lída's and need some help on a project," I said.

"Yes, so she said."

"So maybe you know what this is about?"

"You want to get someone to talk."

"Yes, that's right. We want him to answer a number of questions," I said.

"OK. I think we can help you," Schmuel said. "I'm sitting here with a person who freelances for *M*, if you know what I mean. He specializes in getting people to talk."

"Hmm," I said, and quickly googled a list of Israeli newspapers and found *Maariv*, which was a smaller newspaper, under the letter *M*.

"That sounds good. A freelancer makes it easier, of course. Then there won't be any competition over the story," I said.

"He does a lot of projects in Africa."

"Really? Well, this one is in Israel, but obviously it's good if he has international experience."

"Where's the target?" Schmuel asked.

"The target?" I repeated, thinking that was an unusual turn of phrase for a journalist. "He's at an aliyah center near the Sea of Galilee."

"Good. We can have him here in twenty-four hours."

"Awesome!" I said.

"And we can get a confession from him within forty-eight hours."

"Wow, that's great," I said.

"Whether he did it or not."

"Unbelieva—" I stopped in the midst of my excitement. It didn't sound like we were talking about the same thing anymore. I was talking about a journalistic undercover operation. The man on the other end of the call seemed to be referring more to some type of interrogation, an interrogation session with a foregone conclusion. That sounded more like something suited for an intelligence agency. A freelancer for an intelligence agency. A freelancer for an intelligence agency that started with *M*. I asked for a little time to think about it and wrapped up the conversation as quickly as I could.

Lída had put me in touch with someone who claimed that he did contract work for Mossad, the Israeli intelligence agency. Someone who wanted to earn a little on the side by interrogating someone and coercing a confession. Or maybe someone who had totally different aims. How could I know? I quickly realized that I hadn't been quite clear enough when I talked to Lída and agreed to do an undercover operation. I had been picturing something like what we'd done in Falköping. She had been thinking of something quite a bit more assertive than that.

***

This sign was so strong that I couldn't help but take it seriously. Up until this point I had been able to justify my investigative journalistic methods, but only just. On a couple of occasions, I had been forced to decide if it was ethical to proceed. When we did the infiltration on Jakob with Lída, we were close to the line, but I made the decision, and we succeeded in confirming most of what we wanted.

But coercing a confession was far beyond the realm of what was acceptable. I had allowed myself to be drawn into the excitement of being close to solving the Palme assassination and was even considering traveling to the Middle East to conduct an undercover operation. What was I thinking? Was my obsession with the assassination and Stieg's investigation of it getting out of control?

I closed my computer and set it aside on the café table. Then I ordered another glass of wine for Lída and myself, without the soda this time. I looked her in the eye.

"We have to stop now," I told her.

She took it hard but understood the decision. We had reached the end of the road. I had reached the end of the road.

Revolver

Prague, November 2017

I was in no hurry to get home to Sweden, so I decided to stay in Prague until I felt like going home, until I got used to not having a project that was always on my mind that I could escape into. To be honest, there was nothing compelling drawing me back to Sweden, so a few days more here wouldn't be an issue.

I realized that I actually felt fine about discontinuing my big project. I had done what I had set my mind to and carried on Stieg Larsson's research into the Palme assassination, but I wasn't getting any further now. It was time to drop the assassination and carry on with my own life.

It remained a mystery to me how Lída happened to have contacts who could do the sort of illicit work I couldn't dream of, even interrogating Jakob in Israel, but I enjoyed her company and we got together when we felt like it and when it was convenient. Today Lída had two tickets to a classical-music concert and she invited me to join her. I didn't attend cultural events anywhere near as often as I wanted to, so I accepted, even found myself looking forward to it.

The concert would be held in the concert hall at the Academy of Performing Arts in Prague, which was part of the slightly-past-its-prime Liechtenstein Palace on Malostranské náměstí. The music had been composed by Geraldine Mucha, the daughter-in-law of art nouveau artist Alphonse Mucha, and was being performed on the hundredth anniversary of her birth. Even though she was Scottish, she had spent the majority of her life in Prague with her husband, Jiří Mucha, before she passed away in 2012.

Lída's and my seats were quite far forward in the hall, and we apologized our way to the middle of the row a couple of minutes before the designated time. The master of ceremonies was the composer's son, John Mucha, who spoke both English and Czech impeccably and discussed his mother's life and work.

The conductor came in the stage door and greeted the audience as he gestured toward the orchestra who had come from the city of Pardubice. I tried to make myself smaller in my seat so that I wouldn't block the views of the people behind me. The program began with an intense piece called "Overture to the Tempest." It was perfect for slipping into a sort of contemplative reverie, and I realized I had two hours ahead of me during which my thoughts could roam free. They soon found their way back to my project of the last seven years.

In Stieg Larsson's story about Olof Palme's assassination, the antagonist had not been the murderer. Instead, Stieg was fighting something much more abstract, which I believed was the incompetence of the Swedish police. Stieg submitted multiple tips, and through a number of mistakes and bad decisions, they were never actually investigated. I did my best to move forward with Stieg's theory and also submitted concrete tips to the police, but more than three decades had elapsed since the assassination, and it seemed as if even a confession wasn't going to be enough to wrap up this investigation.

Piece by piece, I mentally reviewed what I now knew about Palme's assassination, based on Stieg's research and my own investigations. I was able to fill in holes with facts from other published materials, and for the gaps where there was nothing concrete, I added the guesses I personally considered most likely. A possible picture emerged of how the assassination took place. If, that is, Stieg's theory was right.

The music in the background helped me think.

I started with what Stieg wrote to Gerry Gable twenty days after the assassination and what Craig Williamson hinted at in his emails and in the various reading suggestions he made to me: arms dealers doing business with the apartheid regime.

In 1985, the US, South Africa, and Iran did big deals in secret, but after Swedish customs and the National Swedish War Materials Inspectorate stopped the arms and explosives deliveries intended for Iran, the three countries were all in a mess together.

The deals were part of a larger agenda, which came to be called the Iran-Contra Affair. The actual specifics of the transactions would be absolutely explosive if they hit the press. If Olof Palme or someone close to him had made that information public, it would have threatened those who were behind the plot. The architect of the deals was CIA director William Casey, who was very close to President Ronald Reagan. If Reagan were forced to step down, that would have impacted the final years of the Cold War and threatened America's victory.

South Africa's role in the expanded Iran-Contra Affair consisted mostly of buying arms and oil, but also of organizing deals via a number of intermediate countries. One of the countries being used was the Seychelles, where Craig Williamson's business partner Giovanni Mario Ricci lived. Together, the two of them trafficked oil from Iran to South Africa, merely one cog in the massive machinery of global transactions.

After the Swedish Social Democrats won the parliamentary election in 1985, Olof Palme continued as prime minister, and it was clear that Swedish authorities were going to persist in creating problems for these arms dealers. In my theory, based on and supported by information from several sources and documents in South Africa, the decision to have Palme assassinated would have been made after the summer of 1985, even though I hadn't found any conclusive evidence proving as much.

In the unholy alliance between the US, South Africa, and Iran, there weren't that many people capable of carrying out the assassination of a prime minister, and if it could have been tied back to the United States in any way, it would have caused enormous damage. So my best guess was that the CIA couldn't have carried out the assassination itself. Instead, a plausible possibility was that the loyal apartheid regime in South Africa was asked to take on the assignment to give the United States deniability and ensure its continued support for the apartheid regime. Plus, a few South African government ministers and arms dealers wanted to protect the financial advantages that they were getting from the trade.

While I formulated the possible motives for the apartheid regime to engage in something as risky as assassinating a Swedish prime minister, I heard the final tones of the concert's second piece, "Carmina Orcadiana." I had completely missed the song.

As the orchestra dug into Geraldine Mucha's "First String Quartet," I started putting together my theory of exactly how the assassination might have been organized.

I had not found any detailed accounts written by Stieg of how the murder might have been executed. But the newspaper articles in his archive from 1987, from *Svenska Dagbladet*, *Arbetet*, and the *GT*, were based in part on Stieg's information, and together they provided a good picture of how the assassination could have played out. Important details came from journalist Mari Sandström's conversations in 1987 with an anonymous source who was a sanctions buster in South Africa. Other information was added to the *GT* illustration that showed the different parts—the cells—of the assassination organization. The flowchart from the *GT* matched the information that I had found but also described the possible arrangement in even more detail.

Patsy or Scapegoat

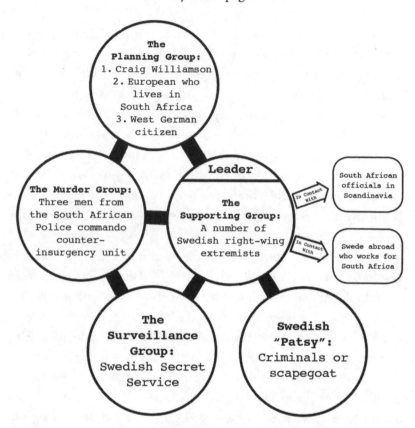

The murder organization according to the GT on May 28, 1987, supplemented with new information on a surveillance group and a Swedish patsy.

In 1986, Craig Williamson was, beyond a doubt, the South African agent who would have been most qualified to carry out an international operation of the kind required to assassinate Olof Palme. Williamson demonstrated that in 1982 with the successful bombing of the ANC office in London, among other things. After his years infiltrating the IUEF organization in Geneva, Williamson would have been acquainted with the Swedish temperament. He was familiar with Stockholm after multiple trips there, and he had even met several of Olof Palme's closest colleagues.

When I asked, Craig Williamson denied that he was the one who organized Olof Palme's assassination, but he said that South African security services agents did "the dirty work for the South African government, which did the dirty work for governments in the Western world." In the theory coming together in my mind, the assassination of Olof Palme could have been part of that "dirty work."

Several witnesses have said that they saw Williamson in Stockholm in the days around the assassination, but Williamson's own documentation contradicted this. There was a real possibility that some other South African agent with skills equivalent to Williamson's may have organized the assassination.

I had come to believe that, like the bombing of the ANC office in London, Olof Palme's assassination was carried out by an arrangement of multiple cells, each with its own limited information, information shared only on a need-to-know basis. There were a couple of collaborators loyal to the apartheid regime in Stockholm—for example, Heine Hüman, who contacted the Swedish police and said that six days before the assassination, he was asked to organize lodging for a South African citizen. But unlike in London, this time more local help would have been required. Palme was a moving target, the Swedish language was unfamiliar to many South Africans, and it was harder for South Africans to fit in in Stockholm than in London, so Swedes would have been needed to carry out certain tasks.

If the illustration in the *GT* article from 1987 was correct, one of the cells, the surveillance cell, could have consisted of Swedish police and security personnel. According to Craig Williamson's former colleague Riaan Stander, the surveillance group—"people from a Swedish intelligence organization"—had been tasked with watching Olof Palme. Police officer Carl-Gustav Östling and several of his colleagues with contacts in South Africa might have been involved in this capacity.

The Swedes would have had a different motive than the South Africans. To them, Olof Palme was a traitor to his country who was about to sell Sweden out in his upcoming trip to the Soviet Union. Most of them presumably didn't know who they were working for or even what was going to happen to Olof Palme. They received their information on a need-to-know basis.

Another cell—the supporting group—might have consisted of Swedes, headed by right-wing extremist Anders Larsson. They were in on what was going to happen, but believed they had been contacted by the CIA. The supporting group's job would have been to find a local assassin and scapegoat—a patsy who would assassinate Palme or at least be near the scene of the killing in order to take the blame for the assassination. If this was how it happened, then it would have been a "lost" job, according to the CIA's assassination manual from Stieg's archive.

According to Stieg's memo, Craig Williamson's agent Bertil Wedin was the likely middleman in the assassination and as such could have helped find the Swedes—the patsy and the supporting group members. The first person asked to carry out the assassination might well have been former mercenary Ivan von Birchan—an acquaintance of Bertil Wedin's from the Democratic Alliance in the 1970s. Von Birchan made contact with a helicopter pilot who called himself Charles Morgan or Peter Brown, whom he knew from the war in Rhodesia, and they met a couple of times in the Sheraton hotel in Stockholm at the end of 1985. Bertil Wedin's agent colleague Peter Casselton had also been a helicopter pilot in Rhodesia, and he or one of his colleagues from that time may have been the person who requested the service.

But von Birchan said no. Instead, he turned in several warnings about the impending assassination to the city council of Stockholm and to Säpo.

The next person pulled into the planning, I thought, would have been Bertil Wedin's acquaintance Anders Larsson, who would have made the perfect scapegoat since he was a profound enemy of some of

Bertil Wedin's other friends. According to the articles from 1987, Bertil Wedin and Anders Larsson were in touch before the assassination. But when I asked Wedin about this, he denied it.

There were multiple theories of how Larsson found out that Palme was going to be assassinated and decided to issue a warning—and he himself changed his story several times before he died in 1991. In the time before the assassination, Larsson hung around with a small group of right-wing extremists, including the first suspect, Victor Gunnarsson— which seemed to form the supporting group that was sketched out in the *GT* article and of which Larsson was the leader.

Anders Larsson most likely realized that he wasn't capable of carrying out the assassination himself and may have asked Alf Enerström for help. Alf had recently published a book in which he said that there was only one penalty for a traitor to his country such as Olof Palme— implying the death penalty. When Anders Larsson asked, Enerström said he knew a guy, Rickard, who would be a perfect fit to assist in the assassination of Olof Palme. Only Enerström knew his actual identity— Jakob Thedelin. Enerström told me that he met Anders Larsson in his apartment on Norr Mälarstrand, and he also mentioned that people came who wanted to see Palme dead. But even if there were no witness statements that Larsson asked the question about assassinating Palme or that Enerström suggested Rickard, this stood out as a likely scenario.

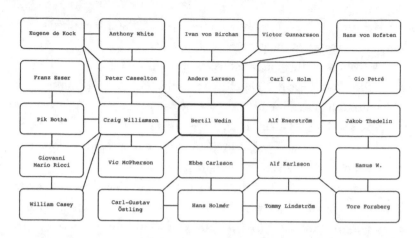

Network of people around the intermediary Bertil Wedin.

During the preparations, Anders Larsson may have begun to realize the risks of participating in the assassination and was scared of being blamed. For safety's sake, he submitted a warning eight days before the shooting, an ace up his sleeve that he could pull out if he ended up becoming a suspect during the investigation.

According to journalist Mari Sandström's source and the *GT* article, a three-agent South African murder squad was sent to Sweden in November 1985. On their way, they picked up cars in Munich from criminal car dealer Franz Esser. Then they drove to Stockholm, where they stayed for a while and enjoyed themselves with women and booze. The source also said that the murder squad received reminders from headquarters in South Africa that they needed to act, not just have fun.

According to Williamson's colleague Riaan Stander, surveillance of the Palmes' residence began a couple of weeks before the assassination. The surveillance would have been done in shifts, involving various people from the entire assassination organization to limit the likelihood of being detected. One of several witnesses was the parliament janitor Henry N., who said he observed the surveillance and that it was carried out by people who spoke a German-like language, which could be Afrikaans. From a photo in the paper, he later identified Craig Williamson as one of the people.

On February 21, 1986, the conspirators missed a chance to strike when Olof Palme gave a speech with the ANC's Oliver Tambo at a conference called the Swedish People's Parliament Against Apartheid at The People's House (Folkets Hus) on Sveavägen.

On February 24, Olof Palme visited the Jämtland region, but after that, he did not plan any long trips for the rest of the week. On Wednesday, two days before the assassination, Alf Enerström suddenly cut short his winter break with his family and traveled from Värmland to Stockholm with Gio Petré—he later said he did this to write a pamphlet. According to the motor vehicle registration office, Alf owned a white Mercedes and a VW Passat, two of the types of cars that were observed by witnesses around the time of the assassination.

One week before the assassination, the Palme couple's home was under intense surveillance, and Lisbeth Palme noticed two men watching the windows of their residence, but she did not call Säpo. Shortly after the assassination, according to Inspector Åke Rimborn who talked with Lisbeth Palme twice on the night of the assassination, she said she thought she saw those same two men at the scene of the crime.

The "Second String Quartet" had already begun as my thoughts circled closer to the night of the assassination. I glanced over at Lída and she had her eyes closed.

In the scenario I envisioned, it was time for Jakob Thedelin to enter the scene. Although there was more guesswork the closer I got to the actual sequence of events on the night of the assassination, there was quite a bit to go on. The Review Commission's report, the published witness statements, Stieg's archive, my own analysis and background material, and last but not least, what Jakob had told Bertil Wedin and Lída.

At his questioning session with the police in 1987, Jakob said he knew where the Palme couple lived, but couldn't remember if he had known that before the assassination. In my idea of what happened, it was likely that he took part in the surveillance.

On the afternoon of the day of the assassination, the surveillance group could have found out that the Palmes were planning to go to the movies—likely from a tap on the phone call between Lisbeth Palme and her son Mårten's girlfriend, Ingrid Klerin, at around five o'clock in the evening, or alternatively, by surveilling the couple on their way to the theater. Together with their son and his girlfriend, Mr. and Mrs. Palme were planning to see *The Mozart Brothers* at the Grand Cinema at nine fifteen.

The other cells would have been informed of this as soon as the Palmes headed out: the planning group directing the operation, the murder group with the South Africans, the surveillance group with Swedish police and security men, the supporting group with Swedish right-wing extremists and Alf Enerström. The latter would have been in touch with the anonymous Rickard in a wig, otherwise known as Jakob Thedelin, who, according to my theory, would have been the patsy chosen to assassinate Olof Palme.

Just after eight thirty in the evening, Mr. and Mrs. Palme left home to catch the subway from Gamla Stan to Rådmansgatan. Multiple witnesses saw them being tailed at a distance by people with walkie-talkies.

Mr. and Mrs. Palme entered the Grand Cinema just after nine, and now the organization knew that Palme would be coming out two hours later, which was enough time for the planning group to instruct the various cells and for additional people to come to the location. Some of the conspirators understood that it was best to stay away—Anders Larsson was at home taking good care to be talking on the phone during that whole critical period. Other people made sure they had an alibi by going to the pub or leaving Stockholm. A few, however, wouldn't have been able to resist the temptation to be in the area—Victor Gunnarsson sat in the restaurant Mon Chéri a few hundred yards from the scene of the murder and talked extensively about Olof Palme with several people in the restaurant. The so-called Skandia Man would have made sure he worked late in the building right by the scene of the crime.

Jakob had already come downtown in the afternoon from Täby, where he rented a room in an apartment. In the evening, Enerström told Gio Petré that he was going out to put money in the parking meter. Instead he would have met up with Jakob. Enerström owned a large number of guns, and they could each have taken one. One of the guns was a Smith & Wesson revolver, which Alf had owned for a long time, according to Gio Petré.

A simple task for Jakob might have been to keep an eye on the entrance to the Grand during the show. But Jakob was an awkward person and would have been too conspicuous. According to multiple witnesses, a man stood in front of the entrance, wearing wire-rimmed glasses of the same type as Rickard's, staring anxiously into the lobby for several minutes. One person described him as a "dorky" man wearing ski clothes that looked like they were from the 1950s, a description that could fit Jakob.

Near the theater, there would have been the group of South African agents and people from the surveillance group. They reported routinely on walkie-talkies to the planning group, who were also sitting nearby.

The most likely path back to Gamla Stan for the Palmes to walk was north up Sveavägen to the Rådmansgatan subway station entrance. When the movie ended, the Palmes stood outside the theater talking to their son Mårten and his girlfriend for a few minutes, then they started walking south down Sveavägen, the opposite direction from what was expected. The planning group would have had to enact an alternate plan, which required more improvisation than the original one. Two unknown men walked down the sidewalk in front of the Palmes and another man—"incredibly big" according to witnesses—walked behind them.

The sequence of events surrounding the assassination itself was filled with conflicting witness statements and information. Thirty years of theories and countertheories had also spread a dark veil of guess-work and lies over the little kernels of fact. When I pictured how the assassination went down, I included what Jakob had told Lída in their Facebook dialogue and in person.

One person in the organization would have been tasked with quickly going to the corner of the Skandia building. Jakob Thedelin's words to Lída about how he tried to murder a spy, placed in biblical times, from their last meeting came to mind: "I went down and tried to assassinate him, because I knew that he was dangerous."

The situation would have become chaotic as multiple people in the organization needed to move in the opposite direction from the one that had been expected. The South African agents were in very close proximity, as well as some of the Swedish surveillance people. Jakob Thedelin and the extremely tall Enerström were on Sveavägen, in my scenario. Everyone had walkie-talkies, some had guns.

During this time, Mr. and Mrs. Palme crossed Sveavägen and continued to head south on the sidewalk across the street alongside the Skandia building. According to witnesses, a man was waiting, standing by the side of the building near the corner at Tunnelgatan. Several people in the organization watched from a distance as Mr. and Mrs. Palme approached the man on the corner. Another man crossed the street and positioned himself a little way away as backup. The organization had been preparing for a long time and would not want to miss this opportunity.

As the Palmes passed the man on the corner, the second man from the organization was seen by Lisbeth Palme, and so would have been very close. The chaotic situation determined which of the two pressed the trigger. I thought again of Jakob's words to Lída about the Roman spy: "I tried to assassinate him, but I didn't succeed." If Jakob was the one waiting on the corner, then maybe he wasn't the one who took the fatal shot.

The one who squeezed the trigger would have cocked the trigger for the first shot and hit Olof Palme in the middle of the back. For the second shot, he used the double-action function and squeezed significantly harder with his finger too far around the trigger, which caused the shot to slant to the right. The bullet cut across Lisbeth Palme's back, even though my best guess was that he was aiming at Olof. In the tumult, Lisbeth fell to her knees beside her husband.

I estimated that it would take a few seconds after the shot before Lisbeth Palme looked up from her husband. Maybe she alternated between looking at Olof and the man, but her impressions were, in any case, understandably fragmentary. More witnesses were noticing what was happening at the scene at that point. They saw Lisbeth kneeling beside her husband and a man standing right by the couple. Lisbeth Palme looked up from Olof and recognized the two men standing a little way apart from each other as the men who were outside her residence the week before—according to Inspector Åke Rimborn's conversation with Lisbeth Palme. The dark-haired man of average height wearing darker clothes was standing closer, and the strikingly tall man was standing a little farther away. The latter quickly started moving south away from the scene; a witness talked about a figure in lighter clothes moving faster than everyone else heading toward Kungsgatan.

The somewhat darker man of average height recovered his wits and moved quickly toward the stairs at the end of Tunnelgatan and ran up. On top of Brunkeberg Ridge, multiple witnesses saw a man in several different places, which I interpreted to mean that he didn't know where to go. I remembered from the recordings of the conversations with Lída how Jakob wished he had a time machine: "Then I would shoot Palme and you could wait up on the ridge in a car, so I knew where I should go."

Fifteen to twenty minutes after the murder, a man was on Smala Gränd and almost crashed into the witness Sarah, whose description of him went on to become the composite photo, the one that strongly resembled Jakob Thedelin, including the facial mark. On Snickarbacken, the man finally came across one of the group's cars, a VW Passat, as described by a witness. He changed his jacket before he got into the car, and it drove away from the scene.

After the assassination, Alf Enerström feared for his life and moved to his estate in Värmland with his entire family and demanded that the children be homeschooled. On several occasions, Enerström ordered Jakob to use his alias, Rickard, and—wearing a wig—to look up people who might know something about the investigation. Among other people, Jakob went to see Ivan von Birchan, who had warned of the assassination, and the first police officer to arrive at the scene of the murder, Gösta Söderström, as Jakob later described to Bertil Wedin in emails.

Victor Gunnarsson was soon apprehended by the police and became the first suspect. The South Africans returned home without complications.

The middleman, Bertil Wedin, through his good contacts, planted the idea of PKK's involvement with Säpo and the Turkish newspaper *Hürriyet*, the theory that very soon became Hans Holmér's main line of inquiry.

When suspicion started to fall on the supporting group of Swedish right-wing extremists, including Anders Larsson and Victor Gunnarsson, they would have realized that they were scapegoats. They might have started to try to cover their tracks. Another of Anders Larsson's friends called the Baltic Committee and asked them in a harried voice to clear out the EAP materials that Larsson and Victor Gunnarsson had copied there, all according to a key source for the articles in Stieg's archive from 1987.

The right-wing extremists worried unnecessarily. It's true, Victor Gunnarsson was a suspect early on, but the attention quickly turned to the Kurdish PKK instead. It wasn't until more than a year after the murder that Anders Larsson was called in for police questioning, but both his and von Birchan's warnings before the assassination were dismissed as make-believe. The supporting group of right-wing extremists splintered, and Anders Larsson was left alone with his confused thoughts. It was probably Anders Larsson who, under a false name, started writing letters to the police describing how the assassination played out. In 1991, he died of a perforated ulcer at the age of fifty-three.

His acquaintance Victor Gunnarsson moved to the US, where he was murdered in December 1993 in North Carolina. Three and a half years later, police officer Lamont C. Underwood was sentenced to life in prison despite his denials of having committed the crime.

Jakob Thedelin continued working for Enerström. Wearing a wig and using his pseudonym of Rickard, he contacted handler Hanus W.—who did contract work for Säpo—and started talking about the Palme assassination. Hanus W. reported on Jakob to Tore Forsberg at Säpo, and via surveillance conducted for more than six months, Säpo succeeded in ascertaining his true identity. Thedelin was brought in for questioning in May and July of 1987. When Hans Ölvebro took over as head of the investigative team at the beginning of 1988, the investigation of Jakob Thedelin was set aside along with most of the other lines of inquiry. One lingering mystery was why Jakob Thedelin, via Hanus W., supplied information to Tore Forsberg at Säpo and, by his own admission, to the CIA.

In 1996, when South African agents accused Craig Williamson and Bertil Wedin of involvement in the Palme assassination, Alf Enerström recognized Wedin's possible role as middleman and contacted him, apparently to discuss the matter. Two years later, Enerström was detained for a violent crime in Värmland. Jakob had received instructions from Enerström to call certain people if something should happen to him. Bertil Wedin was one of them, and this resulted in the first personal contact between Jakob and Bertil. I speculated that sometime during this period, Jakob also received instructions about what to do with Enerström's Smith & Wesson revolver if Enerström was not able to look after it.

Much later, when Enerström was in a psychiatric clinic, Jakob was in charge of the revolver. Jakob and Bertil began communicating regularly. On January 5, 2009, Bertil sent his first email to Jakob and asked about "musical activities in Västra Frölunda," the coded question that both men understood referred to the revolver that was used in the Olof Palme assassination. Jakob responded with a joking description of rockets in a bunker "that never come again," an analogy that was far too close to reality. Wedin informed Jakob by regular mail that he needed to be more careful, but the damage was already done. The email was still there in the cloud. And many years later, I found it.

I realized that this picture of the sequence of events that I created while orchestral music swirled around me fit beautifully with the witness statements from before the assassination, the day of the assassination, and after the assassination. Obviously I filled in holes, prioritized between conflicting pieces of information, and selected the witness statements that I considered to be correct. On some points, where information was lacking, I allowed myself to speculate, but the coherent sequence of events I arrived at corresponded neatly with the existing facts and also explained a number of strange circumstances and conflicting witness statements about the assassination.

Almost all the people I mentioned as part of my theory were included in Stieg's research and his mapping of right-wing extremism in Sweden, with one exception: Jakob Thedelin. But Jakob knew or had met a number of the people that Stieg looked into—for example, Alf Enerström, Hans von Hofsten, Filip Lundberg, Ivan von Birchan, and not least of all Bertil Wedin.

Or to put in another way: Jakob Thedelin was the missing link in Stieg's theory. An outsider without a position or friends, one who could be easily sacrificed, a perfect patsy.

By the time Geraldine Mucha's "En Los Piñares de Jucar," inspired by Spanish girls dancing, started as the last piece in the concert, I had a clear picture of the assassination in my mind. I had also gained an important insight: my doubt had become a conviction that I was close to solving the Palme assassination.

For every stone I had overturned, I had found new facts and new factors. My dejection following the setback of Jakob's escape to Israel and the called-off undercover operation suddenly evaporated. Now I could see all the pieces of the puzzle, all of which had come together since I started to take an interest in Alf Enerström and the Palme assassination. An explanation could be found for the strange circumstances that other theories ignored. I had to keep going!

I would give the Swedish police the new information I had. Nicholas Schmidle, the *New Yorker* reporter, had been waiting for more material. Now he would receive several completely new pieces of information that he couldn't possibly ignore. There were also a number of threads that I could tug on myself.

The CIA's William Casey had fallen ill and passed away very rapidly in 1987, just as he was supposed to be questioned in Congress about the Iran-Contra Affair. But, I thought, there must be information in the CIA documents that regularly became accessible through the Freedom of Information Act.

South Africa's foreign minister Pik Botha had also passed away, but French businessman Jean-Yves Ollivier was still alive and would have much to tell about the deals with Iran and their meetings with politicians from Western powers, including the US, the UK, and France. And there were some more apartheid agents still alive whose names had come up in connection with Palme's assassination.

Bertil Wedin still sat in Cyprus, available to talk about his interactions with South Africa and Swedish right-wing extremists before the assassination.

In Sweden, several of Anders Larsson's and Carl-Gustav Östling's acquaintances among the right-wing extremists from the 1980s were still alive.

A few of Tore Forsberg's colleagues, including handler Hanus W., could discuss the role of Säpo and individual coworkers.

But even if I managed to pull all these remaining strings together, an important piece of the puzzle was still missing. Without concrete evidence, each theory, no matter how well supported it was, could be dismissed. The only thing that would count was hard evidence, and there was only one possibility—I needed to find the revolver.

Through Lída's infiltration, I had been so close to finding out more about what Jakob Thedelin knew about the assassination, but just as he was going to talk, he saw through her and fled to Israel. She wasn't able to find out what he meant by "rockets that never come again." Or where the "bunker" he wrote about was.

It had to be a description of a gun and where he had stashed it. Most likely it was about the revolver that had killed Olof Palme. Otherwise Jakob wouldn't have needed to lie about that email on two separate occasions. And Bertil Wedin wouldn't have broken off his acquaintance with Jakob or, much later on, written that Jakob was incriminating himself by writing such an email. I had thought for several years that that one email was the key to where Jakob hid the revolver, but I was never able to figure out what kind of "bunker" he was referring to.

The music led me to look deeper into the details than usual. Suddenly I thought of Jakob's most recent messages that he had sent from Israel. They were mostly about practical arrangements, about how the flowers needed to be watered and the bills paid, and thus generally uninteresting. But Jakob wrote that one bill was more important than the others. He mentioned it twice and emphasized that there had to be enough money in the account when the bill was due in December. It was a bank bill.

"Yes!"

My exclamation was not so terribly loud, but the first violinist still shook his head in disapproval. Some members of the orchestra looked up from their music, curious to see who had expressed such exaggerated enthusiasm. Many audience members seated in the rows ahead of me turned their heads, as did Lída. I was a little embarrassed, but my other emotions were stronger. I found it! The concert ended right after that, and Lída and I hurried away from the curious gazes during the applause.

Jakob Thedelin had a safe-deposit box. A storage space in a bank vault that only he could open, no one else. In a bank vault that resembled a bunker. A safe-deposit box large enough to hold the revolver that was used in Olof Palme's assassination, but which would never be used again. A place where he could see and touch the trophy that had altered the course of Swedish history. The missing gun—that was what he was referring to, the rockets "that would never come again," in the bunker—Jakob's own safe-deposit box.

I did realize that the revolver may have been moved in the five years that had passed since I got my hands on the mysterious email or the two years since Jakob Thedelin learned that I knew about it. But, I thought, he would hardly get rid of the revolver if he had guarded it carefully for more than three decades. I caught myself once again making plans on how to move forward in my investigation. After eight long years, I was close to a solution that made all the pieces in the puzzle fit, but it was obvious that my quest was far from over.

Lída and I were out in Prague's raw November air, walking on big cobblestones worn smooth, heading for the streetcar stop. I told her my entire theory, and she listened without interrupting. She, too, realized that our work was far from done. Soon I would once again have to restrain Lída from her limitless plans, but this time I was looking forward to what would come out of them.

As we strolled along the city streets, the cool air calming my mind, another thought made me smile to myself. What if Stieg could have been here tonight? I'm quite sure he would have enjoyed the concert, but even more, he would have been elated at the possibility that the murder weapon might be found and the assassination resolved thanks to his tireless work, so many years after his death. It would be like a thriller, perhaps one written by Stieg Larsson.

Epilogue

More than a year has passed since the concert in Prague. I turned in my tip to the Palme investigation team. They have learned that the revolver might be in Jakob Thedelin's possession. The police also know that they have free access to everything in Stieg's archive and in my own research whenever they want it.

A few months ago, Jakob Thedelin was once again taken in for questioning by the police, more than three decades since the last time he was interrogated. The police continue to map his whereabouts and actions that late night of February 28, 1986. They are intensively investigating the possible involvement of the South African security services and its agent Bertil Wedin. Unlike on Ölvebro and Danielsson's infamous trip to South Africa in 1996, their interest is real this time.

I believe the new prosecutor in charge and the leader of the preliminary investigation, Krister Petersson, is right when he says that the Palme assassination will be solved.

In the meantime, like Stieg before me, I continue to tug on the strings that stick out from the ball of yarn that is the Palme assassination. And like Stieg, I am convinced that with enough diligence,

tenaciousness, and imagination, one day soon we will be able to say
what has long been considered impossible: the Palme assassination has
been solved.

Afterword

This book is the result of more than eight years of research. Before I began, I knew as much about the Palme assassination as your average Joe. I trusted the statements from the police and politicians that the investigation had achieved "police closure" and that the perpetrator was named Christer Pettersson. I am now convinced that he is not guilty. I also know a frightening amount more about the world's largest active murder investigation, and yet I have only familiarized myself with a mere fraction of the available research.

Someone estimated that it would take nine years for a person with legal training to read through all the material in the police investigation, which is collected in binders that take up 820 feet of shelf space. The investigation has been ongoing for over thirty years. A total of 10,225 people have been questioned at least once. More than 130 people have claimed responsibility for the assassination. There is also an almost inexhaustible quantity of information beyond the actual investigation—reports, articles, books, online discussion threads, blogs, vlogs, podcasts, and so on.

My book does not claim to provide a comprehensive picture of either the assassination or its investigation. It is primarily limited to the lines of inquiry and theories found in Stieg Larsson's archives and in my own research, although those also happen to be the lines of inquiry that I consider to be most relevant. In that context, it is important to emphasize that I am not presenting any conclusive evidence that anyone in this book is guilty of having shot Olof Palme or being involved in the assassination.

My goal was to write an easily accessible book on a tough subject, where any conclusions would be based on known facts and clearly presented as possible but not proven. If more people come to understand how it is that the Palme assassination can still remain unsolved, how Stieg may have been on the right track, and what one possible solution might look like, then I will have achieved my goal. To get there, I have tried to be consistent in how I approached the material.

As an aid, I have had journalist and author Gunnar Wall investigate the facts in this text, focusing in particular on the parts that deal with Palme's assassination and the police's investigation. I made the final decisions about the text myself and am responsible for the analyses, conclusions, and my own research. For the sake of readability, my Swedish publisher, Erik Johansson at Bokfabriken, and I chose not to use footnotes in the text and not to include a complete list of references.

The first part of the book describes primarily Stieg's research and the various phases of the police investigation that ran parallel to each other. I have consciously chosen to dramatize the chain of events and happenings as I believe Stieg experienced them and did so to bring them to life. The intention is to come closer to reality than if I just quoted directly from documents and interviews. The background material is a long string of interviews, Stieg's own texts, other documents, and the small number of recordings he saved.

All the texts written by Stieg are set in a distinct typeface. The letters to *Searchlight*'s editor in chief, Gerry Gable—which I had access to directly from Gerry—are important for understanding how Stieg was thinking in the months following the assassination. The letters have been reproduced verbatim aside from a couple of occasions when they were shortened to streamline the narrative and avoid repetitions. The essential content has not been changed. Nor have I corrected errors contained therein, in terms of stating times or individual witness statements, since I chose to reproduce the texts as Stieg wrote them. I decided that these small errors didn't affect the conclusions that Stieg and I drew.

Other important documents are the memo about the "middleman" Bertil Wedin and the tip about Victor Gunnarsson and the EAP, as well as Stieg's article in *Searchlight* from 1996. I obtained further information and clarification from a number of conversations and interviews with some of the people who were close to Stieg and who saw his work, especially Eva Gabrielsson and Gerry Gable.

The CIA report *A Study of Assassination*, which was translated from English for the Swedish edition, is printed here in the original English, though shortened and edited to convey the contents to the reader efficiently.

To shape the narrative in part one, I dramatized dialogues based on the material and interviews I had access to, with the ambition of all the essential facts being correct.

It has not been possible to pin down whether Stieg actually met the investigator, Alf Andersson, but it is extremely likely. Both investigated the same people and organizations during the same time period, and Stieg was repeatedly in contact with the police. Alf Andersson was the one driving the line of inquiry involving Swedish right-wing extremists almost completely on his own and usually without support from the investigative team leaders—according to an interview with Alf Andersson by Lars Borgnäs.

I compiled the lists of people, organizations, and addresses in the chapter "Mission: Olof Palme" from relevant documents in Stieg

Larsson's archives. My selection is intended to help readers orient themselves to the enormous quantity of material and provide a point of departure for the rest of the story. Stieg dedicated countless hours of research to all of these people, organizations, and addresses. The network chart of contacts in the same chapter is a copy of a picture that Stieg asked Sven Ove Hansson and Anna-Lena Lodenius about in a letter dated September 29, 1987.

All the names in the book are real with a few important exceptions: the witness Sarah, the girl Sally who was injured in a car accident, Schmuel, who offered to conduct an interrogation for me, Lída Komárková, and Jakob Thedelin. The most important reason to change these names is to protect the individuals' integrity. In some cases, they would also be put at risk for acts of reprisal. The other names are real since the people are all well known and have been widely written about for many years.

Lisbeth Palme's description of two perpetrators at the scene of the assassination, whom she had also seen outside her residence a few weeks earlier, is based on information from Inspector Åke Rimborn. He talked to Lisbeth Palme on two occasions at Sabbatsberg Hospital on the night of the assassination and took notes that support his view. The information was also checked by Deputy Chief Commissioner Gösta Welander and was included in the national all-points bulletin text on the night of the assassination. Later on, Lisbeth Palme herself did not connect the two men at the scene of the assassination with the men outside her residence, but I have chosen to believe Rimborn's description of her witness statement on the night of the assassination.

Part two describes primarily my own investigations, in which I accomplished several things that the police had not. For thirty-two years, for example, those working on the Palme investigation had not managed to meet with Bertil Wedin, and yet I succeeded on my first attempt. I'm convinced that the reason for this is that the Swedish police didn't try as hard as they claim, but we will never hear them admit that.

Car dealer Franz Esser is another person the police had trouble with. According to the Review Commission's report, Säpo had not even been able to confirm that he existed. He was written about in a number of Swedish, German, and South African newspaper articles, and I located and talked to his daughter who survived the car crash that took the lives of the rest of the Esser family. Once again, the Swedish police failed where others succeeded, but as Hanlon's razor says: never attribute to malice that which is adequately explained by stupidity.

The dialogues reproduced in this part of the book were transcribed from recorded conversations, but I have at times shortened and edited them to make the account clearer, without changing the meaning of what was said. There is recorded sound and, in many sections, also video of my meetings with Bertil Wedin and of Lída Komárková's meetings with Jakob Thedelin. One exception is the quotes from Craig Williamson, which are based only on notes and email, since he did not allow any recordings of our meeting to be made.

It is important to bear in mind that Bertil Wedin, Craig Williamson, and Jakob Thedelin deny any involvement whatsoever in the assassination of Olof Palme.

In the second half of the book, I changed the timing of a few of the events, either to simplify or clarify the story or to protect sources. This applies to my first meeting with Lída Komárková, the timing of when I submitted my memo about Jakob Thedelin to the police, which was shifted to protect a source. Also, Lída and Jakob met for a total of six days, not four as described in the text. In the same spirit, I reduced the number of my meetings with Alf Enerström and Gio Petré respectively and didn't mention that Ola Billger from *Svenska Dagbladet* was present for a couple of these meetings. All of these changes were made without substantially affecting the value of the events.

The journalist Boris Ersson's memo to the Palme investigation team is an important document in part two, and several important parts of it are reproduced in the Review Commission's report—for example, the identity of source A—but I have chosen to include some sections that have not been previously published.

The photos in the "Composite Photo" chapter are edited. A ring was added to the composite photo marking the circle placed over the left corner of the mouth when looking at the person head on. The second photo is two pictures that have been overlaid—50 percent the composite photo and 50 percent a photo of Jakob Thedelin at the age of forty-eight. The picture of Jakob Thedelin was edited to remove his eyeglasses, straighten it, make it black and white, and change the size to match that of the composite photo.

There is a lot more to be said about the genesis of this book and the material that serves as the basis for it, and I would love to say more.

List of Characters

Lars Wenander
Journalist from the newspaper *Arbetet* who, along with Håkan
Hermansson, worked with Stieg in 1987 to map out Palme haters.

ACTIVE IN THE PALME INVESTIGATION

Alf Andersson
Police inspector who drove the right-wing-extremist line of inquiry in
the Palme investigation despite the lack of interest from the investigative team.

Ebbe Carlsson
Political fixer who carried on the investigation into the assassination
after his close friend Hans Holmér stepped down as head of the investigative team.

Hans Holmér
Head of the Palme investigation for the first year, and the first person
to lead the police in the wrong direction.

Tommy Lindström
Head of the National Criminal Investigation Department and émi-
nence grise with many roles in the Palme investigation.

Kerstin Skarp
Prosecutor in the Palme investigation from 1997 to 2016.

Hans Ölvebro
Head of the investigative team who led the Christer Pettersson line
of inquiry and was responsible for the Palme investigation from 1988
to 1997.

Suspects and People Interrogated During the Investigation

Alf Enerström
Under the nickname of Sweden's Biggest Palme Hater, he collected money from trade and industry sources for campaigns against Palme.

Victor Gunnarsson
Right-wing extremist who was also called "the 33-year-old" and was the first person to be arrested as a suspect in the Palme assassination.

Hans von Hofsten
Swedish Royal Navy commander who led what has come to be called the "naval officers' rebellion" against Olof Palme.

Anders Larsson
The spider in the web of Swedish right-wing extremists; he turned in a warning eight days before Olof Palme was assassinated.

Gio Petré
Actress who became Enerström's common-law wife and assisted in his campaigns against Olof Palme.

Christer Pettersson
Notorious alcoholic and the only person to be sentenced for Olof Palme's assassination; he was then acquitted.

South Africans or People with Ties to South Africa

Pik Botha
South African foreign minister during the last decade of apartheid.

Bernt Carlsson
Close colleague of Olof Palme and the UN commissioner for Namibia; he died in the Lockerbie bombing.

William Casey
CIA director behind the events that led to the Iran-Contra Affair with contacts at the highest level in South Africa.

Peter Casselton
South African agent who implicated Craig Williamson and Bertil Wedin in Palme's assassination.

Franz Esser
German car dealer with contacts at the highest level in South Africa; he allegedly supplied the murder group with cars.

Eugene de Kock
South African police colonel, nicknamed Prime Evil, who named Craig Williamson as the assassination's organizer.

Vic McPherson
South African police colonel who worked closely with Craig Williamson until the middle of 1985.

Riaan Stander
Colleague of Craig Williamson's who named him as the organizer of the Palme assassination.

Bertil Wedin
Outside contractor for the South African security services and, according to Stieg's memo, the middleman in the Olof Palme assassination.

Craig Williamson
South African security services master spy who, along with several of his colleagues, was singled out as the organizer of the Palme assassination.

Thank You!

This book would not have happened without the support and efforts of a long list of people. Some have been with me for a bit of the journey, others for the entire road to publication.

Erik Johansson at Bokfabriken and Jacob Søndergaard at Rosinante were my first two publishers. They dared to put their faith in me and my ability to write the book in only ten months. It turned into eleven, but if they hadn't counted on me, the book would have remained a dream. Then my agent, Judith Toth, did some sleight of hand and sold the unwritten book to publishers in twenty-five languages in fifty countries. I couldn't have even dreamed that up.

As if this weren't enough, a dream team from the US seemed to just appear. My publisher at Amazon Crossing, Elizabeth DeNoma, even speaks Swedish fluently and had a firm eye on remaking the book into English. With her understanding of the Swedish sentiment, nothing of the original intent has been lost. Elizabeth found Tara Chace, who made the excellent translation from Swedish to English. To finalize the English book, another woman with a Swedish connection entered the scene: editor Jane Fransson managed to help us sharpen the focus and provide context for English speakers.

The teams at Bokfabriken, at Nordin Agency, and in the foreign publishing houses did the rest, almost without my knowing how it happened. Susanne Krutrök helped me with the PR pieces. Henrik Karlsson edited and commented on what must have been one thousand pages of names and organizations countless times and made sure that my story was intelligible in under half as many pages. As Stephen King put it: "To write is human, to edit is divine." Under Gunnar Wall's eager guidance, I have managed to resist the urge to present unconfirmed information and learned that the facts are enough. He also taught me so many new things about the Palme assassination along the way.

I never met Stieg Larsson, but through people who were close to him, I have done my best to take the measure of the man. Eva Gabrielsson has been the most important to my understanding Stieg as a person and what kept him going. Gerry Gable told me about his humor and their mutual work to fight right-wing extremism and their research into the man in Cyprus. Through Daniel Poohl, I was able to find out more about the time just before Stieg passed away, and I gained access to his important archive. A number of other people who knew Stieg contributed their time, materials, and anecdotes. In particular, I would like to mention Anna-Lena Lodenius, Sven Ove Hansson, Håkan Hermansson, and Graeme Atkinson. Unfortunately Lesley Wooler passed away as this book was being written, but he provided important information about his undercover work in Northern Cyprus, which served as the basis for Stieg's memo to the police.

Some people have risked life and limb for what was in the beginning just my project, but which became ours, especially Lída Komárková, Fredrik Haraldson, and Staffan Boije af Gennäs. Lída is the bravest person I've met. Fredrik served as my consigliere through many difficult moments. And Staffan also completed an edit of the manuscript with fresh eyes.

South Africa is a completely different world than safe Sweden, and I had help from a number of people there. Boris Ersson told me about the potentially lethal situations in which he met South African agents in 1994 and gave me tips before my own trip to South Africa. Mari Sandström and I met many times and talked about how she met her source in 1987 and about what his story might mean. Simon Stanford came to South Africa with me and, among other things, helped me feel safer. Hennie van Vuuren and Andrew Feinstein gave me insight into South Africa's role in international arms trading. Rolf Ekéus and Paul van Zyl contributed their thoughts and contacts. Craig Williamson sent reading hints that led me forward. Evelyn Groenink answered my questions about the dealings and murders of powerful men—read her new book, *Incorruptible*. Birgitta Karlström Dorph told me about her important work in South Africa under apartheid.

The Swedish right-wing extremists are a chapter unto themselves. My meetings with Joel Haukka provided me with amazing insights into the 1980s world of intelligence agents and right-wing extremists. Lars Borgnäs and Anders Leopold contributed with answers about some of the people in the book. Daniel Lagerkvist gave me a vast quantity of important documents.

Nicholas Schmidle has been part of this project for more than four years and traveled to Sweden twice and once to South Africa. Without Robert Aschberg, I might never have received the key to the archive. Without Jonas Elgh, Ola Billger, and Björn Hygstedt, there would not have been any articles in *Svenska Dagbladet*.

Finally, I could not have rowed this transatlantic liner ashore without family and friends. Arne Valen, Björn Albrektson, Fredrik Söder, Maria Sandell, Calle Stocklassa, Fredrik Wolffelt, and Hasse Pihl. Rut & Lucia. Zuzka & Zuzka. Everyone at Genera who let me play hooky from work. Other friends, family, and relatives who put up with me when I seized every opportunity to talk about the Palme assassination. And finally everyone I've failed to mention from this eight-year-long project. Thank you!

About the Author

Jan Stocklassa is a Swedish writer and journalist focusing on large-scale conspiracies in international politics. In his books, Stocklassa uses a narrative nonfiction style to unveil previously unknown facts about important events in recent history.

His breakthrough came with the critically acclaimed bestseller *Stieg Larsson's Archive: The Key to the Palme Murder*, a book published in 2018 that has been sold in more than fifty countries and translated into twenty-six languages. Following its publication, Swedish police began actively pursuing the leads presented in the book regarding the assassination of Swedish Prime Minister Olof Palme.

His professional career includes being a Swedish diplomat, launching the *Metro* newspaper in Prague, and collaborating as a journalist with major media houses in Sweden and abroad, as well as coproducing the movie and TV series *Stieg Larsson: The Man Who Played with Fire*.

About the Translator

Photo © 2006 Libby Lewis

Tara Chace has translated more than forty novels from Swedish, Danish, and Norwegian. Her most recent translations include Christina Rickardsson's *Never Stop Walking*, Bobbie Peers's William Wenton books, Jo Nesbø's Doctor Proctor's Fart Powder series, and Martin Jensen's The King's Hounds trilogy. An avid reader and language learner, Chace earned her PhD in Scandinavian languages and literature from the University of Washington in 2003. She enjoys translating books for adults and children. She lives in Seattle with her family.